To Sharon and my mother
and to the memory of my father

iv

WILLIAM RANDOLPH HEARST

His Role in
American Progressivism

Roy Everett Littlefield, III

UNIVERSITY
PRESS OF
AMERICA

Library of Congress Catalog Card Number: 80-5729

Picture Credit:
Mr. William Randolph Hearst, Jr., p. 391

Acknowledgements

I am deeply indebted to a great number of
people for their assistance while preparing this
book, which began as a seminar paper and later
developed into a dissertation. I wish first to
acknowledge the indispensable aid and criticism
given by Dr. Thomas Henderson, whom it was my
good fortune to study under at The Catholic
University of America. Others at Catholic gave
wisdom and good advice that I greatly appreciate:
Dr. Thomas West and Dr. Maxwell Bloomfield. In
addition to the detailed knowledge all three have
extended, they portray an unfailing personal
concern for students, a quiet wisdom, and a con-
tagious enthusiasm for scholarly research. Dr.
West's keen sense of literary style is evident
throughout this work. I am beholden to Mr.
William Randolph Hearst, Jr. who gave most
generous co-operation, aided me in research,
allowed me complete access to the Journal-
American morgue, and reminisced openly about
his father. I would like to thank Dr. Maury
Bromson and Mr. W. A. Swanberg, who have shared
with me their information and insights. It is
a pleasure also to record the friendly assistance
of Mr. Edmund Henshaw, Clerk of the United States
House of Representatives; Mr. George Perros,
Archivist in Charge of Legislative Records at
the National Archives; and Dr. F. Warren Roberts
and Mrs. Charlotte Carl-Mitchell, Archivists at
the University of Texas. The staffs of several
institutions were most courteous and helpful:
Library of Congress; Enoch Pratt Library;
United States Senate Library; United States
National Archives; Columbia University Library;
University of Texas Library; and The Catholic
University of America Library. I am grateful to
my mother who typed several drafts of the manu-
script with endless patience; and I thank Kyle
Mahoney who meticulously typed the final version.
My debt to my wife, Sharon, is immeasurable and
inexpressible. The criticism and counsel of a
number of friends and fellow students have con-
tributed in a less tangible, yet equally vital,

manner. All these persons helped me avoid many
more errors than the ones I have assuredly committed to print.

TABLE OF CONTENTS

Introduction

As an expanding nation embarked on a new century and a new era William Randolph Hearst, next to Theodore Roosevelt, was the most spectacular figure in American politics. A newspaper tycoon, muckraker, United States Congressman, and a political candidate on the city, state, and national level, he evoked more violent feelings and more extremes of judgement than any other American in public life.[1]

While a student at Harvard, Hearst had come to realize the impact that public communication in general, and Joseph Pulitzer's style of journalistic sensationalism in particular, could have on a modern literate society. The newspaper could educate, influence, direct, and control public opinion. It was important to Hearst that the newspaper allowed for personal impulse and an ability to reach millions of Americans daily.

After his arrival in New York City in 1895 to take control of the _Journal_, Hearst appointed himself leader of a social and political movement which his newspapers helped to create. In his finest moments, he was a champion of the underprivileged and the discontented. He aimed to be in the tradition of Thomas Jefferson, Andrew Jackson, and Abraham Lincoln, the greatest of American statesmen, he thought, because they had led a popular politics that restored the rights and powers of the "plain citizen."[2] He attributed their success in large part to the use of the weapons of their personal wealth in the fight against the classes who looked upon special privilege as their right.[3] The history of the country moved in cycles, this serious student of history believed, and the nation was again ready for a radical movement.[4]

Hearstism encompassed a wide range of social and political discontent.[5] Unlike most reformers of the day, Hearst appealed to the working class and the recent immigrant groups for his strength.[6] He directed his own crusades, campaigns, and efforts through his lieutenants and his newspapers, rarely working with businessmen or professional reformers. As he saw mayors, governors, and presidents fail, he decided that he could do better and he entered politics.[7] By 1904 he had come to think that he would have to be elected President of the United States in order to enact his own progressive platform. Whatever historians think of his vanity and his self-serving schemes, he was consistent in his liberal reform programs, and did stir many notable social and political advances. But he became a pariah to many middle class reformers and failed to win the continued support of most respectable progressives, and his unwillingness to combine forces with other reformers limited his success.

This book is not a biography of William Randolph Hearst; it attempts to place him in the context of the progressive politics of the years between 1895 and 1920 when his influence was great. His movement was unique in its abandonment of traditional political action, in the nearly fanatical trust with which its worker and immigrant forces looked up to a single individual to deal with social and political ills. Louis Filler has said that he was, more than any other individual, the absolute expression of all the blind need and ignorance and resentment which troubled the working and lower classes.[8] As a leader in the movement intended to correct social and economic inequities, he fared better than his enemies have believed. This book re-examines both the theory that the progressive voter was invariably middle class and the criticism of Hearst presented in such well-known works as <u>Citizen Kane</u>[9] and Ferdinand Lundberg's <u>Imperial Hearst</u>.

This work relates three stories simulta-

neously. It looks at yellow journalism, and
not as an underside of American newspaper
publishing, but as an enterprise that furthered
some of the most vigorous and engaging techniques
of modern journalism. In attempting to get at
Hearst's yellow journalism as a public phenomenon,
I avoid elevating his motives but I will some-
times take his most inflated statements without
comment, both as instances of his style and as
ways that yellow journalism explained itself.
This book, moreover, tells about the centrality
of journalism within democratic politics, a
centrality that Hearst techniques illustrate.
My story also is about a strain of progressivism,
compounded of Hearst's techniques, his rhetoric,
and his public positions. My examination of
Hearst is critical but on the whole favorable.
I like his politics and I find his newspapers
interesting and a refreshing departure from the
staid sheets that preceeded him. His excesses
and his inflations of rhetoric are sufficient
commentary on themselves.

Historians have long disagreed about Hearst.
Few contemporaries knew him personally, and few
of those who did know him were able to formulate
definite impressions of his personality. Few
researchers since have examined his personal
papers. All must agree that at the turn of
the century he continually challenged the
imagination of the American people. It could
neither take him nor let him alone.[10]

Footnotes

[1] Lloyd Morris, *Postscript to Yesterday*; *America: The Last Fifty Years* (New York: Random House, 1947), p. 230.

[2] Hearst to former Democratic Representative John Jacob Lentz from Ohio (1897-1901), February 13, 1903, New York *Journal-American* morgue, Balcones Research Center, University of Texas at Austin, hereafter referred to as J.A.M.

[3] Hearst to the Iroquois Club of Chicago, March 17, 1903, J.A.M.

[4] Hearst notes for an article intended to appear in *Hearst's Magazine*, April 1912, J.A.M.

[5] Morris, *loc. cit.*

[6] Since the 1950's scholars, primarily influenced by Robert Wiebe's *The Search For Order* (New York: Glencoe Press, 1973) and Samuel P. Hays' *Conservation and the Gospel of Efficiency* (Cambridge: Harvard University Press, 1959), have stressed the importance of businessmen and professionals in the political reform movements of the early twentieth century.

[7] Hearst interview with Lincoln Steffens. Lincoln Steffens, "Hearst, The Man of Mystery." *American Magazine*, November 1906, p. 15.

[8] Louis Filler, *Crusaders For American Liberalism* (New York: Harcourt, Brace and Company, 1939), pp. 132-133.

[9] Although the central character of the movie *Citizen Kane* was named Charles Foster Kane, its subject was William Randolph Hearst. Pauline Kael, *The Citizen Kane Book* (Boston: Little, Brown and Company, 1971), p.3

[10] Morris, *loc. cit.*

Whatever is right can be achieved through the irresistible power of awakened and informed public opinion. Our object, therefore, is not to inquire whether a thing can be done, but whether it ought to be done, and if it ought to be done, to so exert the forces of publicity that public opinion will compel it to be done.

—William Randolph Hearst

I
The Rise of a Patrician Reformer

Young Hearst, as the only child of million-aire parents, could have had almost all the material objects that he wanted. If he had decided to manage his father's holdings in real estate or mining interests he could have led a comfortable, relatively uncomplicated, luxurious life. Instead, he sought the intangibles: to reform social conditions, to be loved by the American people, and to hold power over the minds of men. He was shy and a loner. He realized that his own wealth would make for mistrust of any reform effort he undertook in the name of the common people, and that his motives could be misunderstood. He would try diligently to overcome these obstacles.

To begin to understand William Randolph Hearst's political values and career requires some knowledge of his parents, George Hearst and Phoebe Apperson Hearst. George Hearst was born in 1820 in sparsely settled Franklin County, Missouri. As a youth he received only two years of formal schooling. In 1846 his father died leaving him thousands of dollars in debt. In 1850, then a muscular man over six feet tall, he headed west in search of gold. He suffered through nine lean years before striking it rich in 1859. A year later he returned to Missouri, where his mother was near death, and soon began courting eighteen-year-old Phoebe Apperson, a school teacher in Stedman, Missouri. Phoebe was the daughter of Randolph and Drusilla Apperson, prosperous slave-owners who owned a handsome farm on the Meramec River. Because her parents strongly opposed the match, George and Phoebe eloped and were wed on June 15, 1862. On April 29, 1863 Phoebe gave birth to their only child-- William Randolph.[1]

Because George Hearst spent great amounts of time at his mines, located more than two hundred miles from his home, Phoebe became very maternal

and possessive, engulfing her son with affection.[2]
George and Phoebe were poles apart in their out-
looks and their marriage was not close.[3] George
Hearst was a rough, uncouth, illiterate, pen-
niless gold hunter who amassed a great fortune
through mining, stock raising, and farming.[4]
Lavish in his expenses for the relief of the
poor, he was a kind hearted man of good sense
and quick perception who developed clearly
defined ideas on public questions. He served
as a Democratic United States Senator from
California and was very popular among Congressional colleagues and politicians in California; and it was said that he never forgot
old friends. From his father Hearst developed
a loyalty to the Democratic party and a respect
for the capabilities of the lower classes.[5]
George was a fine example of a lower class individual reaching great heights. He was a self
made man who believed that the American people
were capable of taking care of themselves. He
opposed government aid to the poor and underprivileged.

According to Cora Older, Hearst's official
biographer, Hearst inherited from his parents a
spirit sensitive to suffering and eager to aid
the unfortunate,[6] but it would seem that his
mother's role was far more important than his
father's. Phoebe, a noted philanthropic worker,
disagreed with her husband's views concerning
society's disadvantaged. She developed early in
life the rule "help the individual help himself."
In numerous public addresses and writings she
encouraged the wealthy and the local, state, and
federal governments to assume responsibility for
the social and political inequities in American
society.[7] Phoebe donated over one million dollars
to the University of California, established
kindergartens in California and Washington, D.C.,
founded the Parent Teachers' Association, and
was a driving force in charitable and educational
work nationwide. Young Hearst was very close to
his mother and she had a major impact on his
activities and policies, especially between his
father's death in 1891 and her own death in 1919.[8]

2

Phoebe believed that education was the answer to all problems, but her son did not prove to be a good student. Hearst's mischievous childhood continued in school. He was shy but had an aggressive urge for sensation and recognition. He could manipulate others to get what he wanted.[9] Hearst had the intellectual capacity to breeze through courses but, except for history and geography classes, was bored with school. His early education was mainly entrusted to private tutors, but in San Francisco he attended intermittently four different grammar schools. His frequent changes indicated his trouble with authority.[10] In August of 1879 he entered St. Paul's School in Concord, New Hampshire. This first long term separation from his mother left him homesick.[11] In the fall of 1881 he left the school by request, because of a schoolboy prank.[12] He returned to San Francisco and with private tutors prepared for college.

In the fall of 1882 Hearst entered Harvard University. During his sophomore year he relieved Eugent Lent, a childhood companion, of his duties as business manager of the _Lampoon_, a struggling humor magazine. Attacking the magazine's financial problems with ingenuity, Hearst began to sell advertisements to shopkeepers in Cambridge. He organized student solicitors to canvass the Boston metropolitan area and wrote letters appealing for money to Harvard graduates and friends. He put the magazine on sound financial footing. He was fortunate to work with an extraordinary _Lampoon_ staff that included George Santayna, poet and philosopher; Ervin Wardman, later editor of the New York _Press_; Hammond Lamont, later editor of the New York _Evening Post_; Grover Fling, who would become writer for the New York _American_; William Baldwin, later Third Assistant Secretary of State under Grover Cleveland: F. T. Cooper, later professor at New York University; and Samuel Winslow, later Republican Congressman from Massachusetts. The _Lampoon_

3

fostered in Hearst a new curiosity for newspapers
and he began to study intently the methods of
Joseph Pulitzer's New York _World_ and Colonel
Charles H. Taylor's Boston _Globe_.[13]   He spent a
summer vacation working for Pulitzer's _World_,
and got a letter of introduction to Taylor and
visited the _Globe_ repeatedly to study it from
city room to pressroom.[14]   Following Cleveland's
successful presidential bid in 1884, Hearst
organized a rally and parade. As the ringleader
of the Cambridge demonstration that lasted
through the night, he was suspended by authori-
ties at Harvard University.[15]   He spent the next
few months in Washington, D.C. A letter to his
father made evident his growing interest in his
father's San Francisco _Examiner_:

> I have a strange fondness for our
> little paper--a tenderness like unto that
> which a mother feels for a puny or deformed
> offspring, and I should hate to see it die
> now after it had battled so long and so
> nobly for existence; in fact, to tell the
> truth, I am possessed of the weakness which
> at some time or other of their lives pervades
> most men: I am convinced that I could run
> a newspaper successfully.
>   Now if you should make over to me the
> _Examiner_--with enough money to carry out my
> schemes--I'll tell you what I would do!
>   In the first place I would change the
> general appearance of the paper and make
> seven wide columns where we now have nine
> narrow ones, then I would have the type
> spaced more, and these two changes would
> give the paper a much cleaner and neater
> appearance.
>   Secondly, it would be well to make the
> paper as far as possible original, to clip
> only when absolutely necessary and to imitate
> only some such leading journal as the New

York _World_ which is undoubtedly the best paper of that class to which the _Examiner_ belongs--that class which appeals to the people and which depends for its success upon enterprise, energy, and a certain startling originality and not upon the wisdom of its political opinions or the lofty style of its editorials. And to accomplish this we must have--as the _World_ has--active, intelligent, and energetic young men; we must have men who come out West in the hopeful buoyancy of youth for the purposes of making their fortunes and not a worthless scum that has been carried there by the eddies of repeated failures.

Thirdly, we must advertise the paper from Oregon to New Mexico and must also increase our number of advertisements if we have to lower our rates to do it, thus we can put on the first page that our circulation is such and our advertisements so and so and constantly increasing.[16]

Hearst returned to Harvard University in the spring of 1885. But his entire academic career was ended by another prank. During the 1885 Christmas season he sent to each of his instructors, elaborately done up as a Christmas gift, a large chamber pot with the recipient's name inscribed in the bottom.[17]

At the age of twenty-three, Hearst took control of his father's San Francisco _Examiner_, over the protests of the elder Hearst. In San Francisco Hearst imitated Pulitzer's methods and stationed reporters in a rented office located in Pulitzer's building in New York. He initially doubled the size of the _Examiner_ to eight pages, reduced the number of columns from nine to seven, demanded better news coverage and writing from his reporters, and featured such novelties as a sports story or game score on the front page. As Pulitzer was doing in New York, Hearst launched in San Francisco a series of newspaper

crusades, campaigns, and spectacular exposures.
He attacked abuses and privilege and called for
a broad based movement to secure "radical democracy."

With adequate funds at his disposal, Hearst
bought the best reporters, editors, and business
executives available.[18] Within months circulation increased from almost thirty thousand to
eighty thousand in a city of three hundred
thousand, and after two years the _Examiner_ was
making a profit; within five years it would be
the second most profitable newspaper in the
nation.[19]

For Hearst, San Francisco was an experiment
in arousing passions by denouncing corruption
and attacking privilege. Although the elder
Hearst had discouraged his son from becoming a
newspaper editor, once his son took control of
the _Examiner_ he carefully monitored William's
actions and he fully supported the newspaper.
To ensure his son's success, George Hearst introduced him to city and state politicians and reformers, with whom he urged his son to co-operate.
Under his father's guiding hand Hearst did work
with local leaders to insure reforms. Hearst and
the _Examiner_ played important roles in the
success of the city Labor party.[20] In 1886
Hearst combined forces with H. C. Kinne representing the Knights of Labor, Frank Roney,
Binnette Haskell, and Peter Roberts representing the plaster unions, and State Senator
Patrick Reddy; together they formed a Labor
League, running a full slate of candidates.[21]
The _Examiner_ endorsed the League.[22] Within six
years the People's party was a major local political force, instrumental in the passage of reform measures limiting the work day, limiting
convict labor contracts, and requiring periodic
inspections of working areas.[23] Hearst took on
the powerful Southern Pacific Railroad and forced
a reduction of high freight and passenger rates,
and exposed its unpaid government loans. He com-

bined forces with Franklin K. Lane, Frederick Stratton, and the Federated Trades of San Francisco to secure election reform in California, including the Australian secret ballot, the Purity of Elections Act providing for a registration system and an honest count, and the replacement of the convention system with the direct primary.[24]

But following his father's death Hearst rarely agreed to fraternize as other reformers. He was most comfortable directing his own efforts. Respectable reformers continued to work for him, and he supported them in his newspapers, only for crusades that he was directing. When he went east to run the New York _Journal_ he expanded the tactics and methods that he had used in San Francisco. He acquainted himself with the city's newspaper business, with its public opinion, and with its class and ethnic discontents. When he made his move to New York he brought several members of the _Examiner_'s staff with him. He also brought his democratic and reformist politics, along with bold headlines, terse writing, readable type, and illustrations, which he quickly supplemented with other methods of popular journalism. And, within a few years, he also lured several key editors and personnel from his New York City rivals.[25]

The city in which Hearst was establishing himself had many newspapers, some with small and special readerships, others of more general circulation. Most of them were fairly staid in journalistic techniques.

The important New York City daily conservative newspapers in 1895 included the _Sun_, the _Tribune_, the _Commercial Advertiser_, the _Evening Mail and Express_, and the _Journal of Commerce_. Perhaps Charles Dana's _Sun_ was the best example of a newspaper dominated by the personality of its editor and publisher. The _Sun_'s daily circulation between 1895 and 1898 was 150,000.[26]

Whitelow Reid, a veteran of the New York press, headed the Tribune. The newspaper was conservative in politics as well as technique. Headlines were small and discreet, advertisements were modest, and much space was alloted to editorial opinion. The change in policy from Greeley's liberalism brought a continual decline of prestige. The newspaper became a mouthpiece for the Republican party. Between 1895 and 1898 the average daily circulation was near 25,000.[27] The oldest newspaper in New York City was the Commercial Advertiser. Declining in prestige, influence, and circulation, however, it lacked sufficient funds to report anything except local news. Robert Alexander edited the Evening Mail and Express, a sheet emphatically Republican and pro-business. The newspaper had a small circulation. William Dodsworth owned and edited the Journal of Commerce, a newspaper aimed at a very select audience. It had a daily average circulation of approximately 7,500.[28]

The politically neutral New York City newspapers in 1895 included the Evening Post, the Times, and the Herald. The Evening Post's editor, Edwin Lawrence Godkin, was recognized for his excellent editorial writing, which was characterized by irony and humor. But in news collecting and news writing, the Post could not compete with other city newspapers. It carried few advertisements and had a small circulation, never over 25,000 daily. In 1895 the Times was under the control of a company headed by Charles R. Miller. In the spring of 1896 Adolph S. Ochs purchased the Times, which was on the verge of extinction and immediately reorganized the staff and proclaimed his desire to present all of the news in a non-partisan concise, attractive form.[29] James Gordon Bennett, Jr. directed the New York Herald. French custom and ideas strongly influenced the newspaper. It emphasized theatrical news, society news, and sporting news, and downplayed the importance of editorials. It became the favorite daily of the wealthy. Its average daily circulation was near 100,000. These newspapers were speaking to their small or general constituencies in a city that was changing in its ethnic and social character.

The change would have a large effect on the nature of journalism. Between 1880 and 1919 over seventeen million immigrants entered New York City through Ellis Island, and many stayed in the city.[30] The composition of the current of immigration changed significantly in 1882.[31] The change was so pronounced that the arbitrary labels of "old immigration" and "new immigration" have been applied to those who predominated before 1882, and after, respectively. By 1920 Jews were the largest single ethnic group, the bulk of them among the 480,000 Russians who lived in New York City.[32] Next in size was the Italian community, its numbers rising from 145,000 in 1900 to 391,000 in 1920.[33] The immigrants immediately found themselves at the bottom of the social scale. They were poor, helpless, and without marketable skills.

Between 1894 and 1898 America suffered a commercial depression. Unemployment figures ran as high as 25 percent for the nation and 35 percent for New York City.[34] Jobs were scarce and working conditions horrid. In the wake of the depression, hostility emerged between the old immigrants and the new immigrants as the new arrivals generally accepted jobs paying substandard wages regardless of the working conditions.[35] Employment opportunities and a lack of funds for traveling inland kept most of the new immigrants in the city. Workers were generally afraid to organize to demand better wages and conditions. In 1890 only 2.7 percent of the wage earners in America were organized. The depression pushed the figure down to 1.7 percent in 1895.[36] Between 1895 and 1900 New York City's wage earning population jumped 36 percent.[37] The average number of strikes for any

9

one year between 1895 and 1900 was two and one-half times more than the average number in the preceeding five years.[38] The depression and a labor force growing in self-consciousness contributed to a movement for social betterment that began in the late 1890's.[39]

Joseph Pulitzer, owner of the New York World, had journalistic techniques suitable for these restless times. The paper featured screaming headlines and profuse illustration. The World disgusted conservative readers, but was extremely popular. Pulitzer appealed to the old immigrants. Between 1883 and 1895 the daily circulation increased from 15,000 to 555,570.[40] By 1896 it averaged a daily circulation of 743,024 and a Sunday circulation of 562,903.[41] Selling over five million copies a week in 1898, it claimed to have the largest newspaper circulation in the world.[42] The World conducted several popular crusades, such as opposing high milk rates,[43] demanding adequate city fire protection for tenement dwellers,[44] advancing a public parks program,[45] exposing substandard construction in tenement housing projects,[46] and supporting trade unions.[47] These actions made Pulitzer seem to be a champion to the lower classes.

If he was to succeed in New York City as he had in San Francisco, Hearst would have to compete with Pulitzer for the city's masses; to do this he purchased the Morning Journal on September 25, 1895 for $180,000. Albert Pulitzer had established the Morning Journal in 1882. From its inception the newspaper was inexpensive and, like the World, directed at the common citizen. In 1895 John R. McClean, successful publisher of the Cincinnati Enquirer, purchased the Morning Journal for one million dollars. Circulation and advertisers continually declined and within months it was on the verge of bankruptcy. McClean therefore unloaded the newspaper on a Hearst agent. On

November 8, Hearst's name first appeared on the
editorial page of the New York Journal. Circulation for the Journal under Hearst made greater
advances than any newspaper has ever enjoyed.
Within a year the average circulation reached
430,410 with an average Sunday circulation of
408,779.[48] For the three days following the
destruction of the Maine, over one million
copies of the Journal were printed daily.[49]
Following Dewey's victory at Manila, circulation exceeded 1,250,000 a day for the duration
of the Spanish American War.

Historians and journalists have been harsh on
Hearst's sensationalism and yellow journalism.
Charles Beard wrote that Hearst's newspapers were
inferior to other yellow newspapers because
Hearst's editors had a disregard for the truth.[50]
The purpose of a Hearst newspaper was to "splash
sensation" that would "paralyze" the public,
charged Ferdinand Lundberg in his biography of
Hearst.[51] "In the strict sense, the Hearst papers
weren't newspapers at all," wrote W. A. Swanberg,
author of Citizen Hearst, "they were printed
entertainment and excitement."[52] Because Hearst
fabricated news stories, Swanberg argues, his
newspapers were as sensational, flamboyant, and
irresponsible as any major newspapers ever published in America. Oswald Garrison Villard,
editor of the Nation magazine, charged that
Hearst, because of his lack of sincerity and
intellectual honesty, did more to degrade the
entire American press than any one else in
history.[53] But Arthur Brisbane, editor of
Hearst's New York Evening Journal and Hearst's
closest adviser and friend for thirty-nine
years, relished the role of yellow journalist:

> I am the yellowist journalist in the
> world. If I am not, I want to be. When
> I took charge of the New York Journal I
> got type to attract the newsboys. They
> had other papers on top of the Journal and
> sold it only when it was asked for. I could

not type large enough, so I had artists
make it. I would put across the front
of the paper in large black printing the
words 'WAR SURE' and this caused the newsboys to put the _Journal_ on top of the pack
and the other papers have been on the bottom ever since.[54]

The bold headlines initially put the _Journal_ on
top of the newsboys' piles, but the people read
it and enjoyed it, and purchased the paper the
following day. Hearst was always proud of yellow
journalism and believed that with the quickening
of the public conscience in regard to political
and social conditions the newspaper could legitimately serve as the greatest and most inexpensive
single source of information and entertainment
in a democratic society.[55] A Hearst newspaper
served both as an educator of the public and
as a barometer of public opinion. Large headlines and numerous illustrations were used to
reach immigrants who were barely literate.

Many have since argued that Hearst was
merely a figurehead and had little control of
what actually went into his newspapers, that
Arthur Brisbane, "Andy" Lawrence, Tom Williams,
Arthur McEwan, or other editors directed the
editorial comment and tone of individual newspapers. But Hearst's editors, Brisbane and
Lawrence for example, were differing types of
men with quite different ideologies. While the
final edition of a newspaper reflected the indi-
viduality of a particular editor, all of Hearst's
newspapers bore the imprint of his personality.

The Hearst technique, common to all his
newspapers, centered on getting the visual attention of the public and making the news easily
available. Hearst advised his publishers that
"the average man in the street . . . wants
everything presented to him briefly as well as
brightly. . . . If you want to obtain and retain
any person's attention you must say something

12

worthwhile and say it quickly."[56] Next to the
news itself, the headlines were the most important part of the newspaper.[57] The large, bold
headlines summarized the contents of the articles: a reader, Hearst explained, "should be
able to read the headlines of a newspaper and
get a reasonably clear and complete idea of the
news of the day."[58] The headlines also served
as an advertisement of the newspaper.[59] Hearst
employed wider columns, larger print, and darker
type. Articles were concise, sentences were
usually short, and one sentence paragraphs were
common. Sentences, paragraphs, and especially
articles had emphatic conclusions rather than
building up to powerful conclusions. The least
important details of a story went at the end so
that a reader need not follow through the
account. Brisbane told reporters:

> There is no need ever to use a word of
> more than three syllables in a newspaper.
> Remember that a newspaper is mostly read
> by very busy people, or by very tired
> people, or by very uneducated people none
> of whom are going to hunt up a dictionary
> to find out what you mean.
> And never forget that if you don't
> hit a newspaper reader between the eyes
> with your first sentence, there is no
> reason to write a second.[60]

Hearst also made great advances in the use of
photographs. He recognized their appeal,[61] and
believed that good pictures were a powerful
device for attracting buyers and forming public
opinion.[62]

In a "modern newspaper," Hearst argued,
there was no room for dullness, excess verbiage,
or elaborate writing.[63] He continually reminded his publishers and editors that the
backbone of his newspapers was the news.[64] The
reputation of the newspaper, he wrote, rested

13

on the accuracy and amount of factual reporting.[65] The editorial pages dispensed both
information and opinion. Hearst, who would
write in his lifetime over eleven hundred editorials which frequently appeared on the front
page,[66] told his editors that accurate information strengthened the effect of an editorial
on public opinion.[67] The compound of fact and
opinion made Hearst a pioneer at muckraking.[68]

While the news was the central feature of a
Hearst newspaper, the Hearst editors developed
the element of human interest for its popularity
and for the effectiveness of a human interest
incident in the presentation of the news. The
newspapers also made use of special features.
A typical Hearst daily contained dramatic,
musical, and literary criticism, practical advice, useful information, humorous matter, fiction, labor stories, sports reporting, and
weather reports. Almost every one of these had
its special writer.

Labor stories appealed to both labor members
and to others not directly affected, for the
stories were timely and informative and there
was room for human interest. The Hearst newspapers presented the news of working conditions
from the vantage point of workingmen and their
families. This made for a clearer and more
realistic picture of the actual conditions that
were producing strikes than reprinting the formal
statements of labor and business leaders, and
it created sympathy for workers and strikers.
The influence that Hearst's newspapers had on
public opinion was frequently a factor in
settling labor disputes.[69]

Hearst also devoted large amounts of
space to stories about sports. First of all
he expanded the range of sports stories. Up
until 1896 newspaper sports coverage was almost
exclusively limited to sporting events that the
upper classes either followed or participated in,
such as horse racing or college football. Hearst
urged his writers to cover sports that had a

broad appeal, such as baseball. He did not hesitate to feature a sports article on the front page, or to place a game score in a special headline across the top of the front page. Believing that the sports writers should present their news and photographs with the same care and excellence as his news writers, he employed specialized sportsmen to write sports stories exclusively.[70]

Hearst especially realized the need for simplicity and clarity in reporting purely informative news stories. Articles dealing with investigations, legislation, and political sessions aimed at showing the significance of acts of representative public bodies not only for the home and business of the reader but also for the community, state, and nation.[71] Hearst looked upon such reporting as equipping a democracy with the information it needed for its success.[72] His coverage of the proceedings of criminal and civil courts gave both fair and accurate publicity. Writers were instructed to take matters that were buried in legal technicalities and verbiage, and to present the story clearly, attractively, and simply, without sacrificing accuracy. Hearst newspapers featured police news and crime stories, and reporters actively aided the police in solving crimes. He continually stressed to his city editors the need to cover local news, and his newspapers featured stories on schools, libraries, museums, parks, and real estate. Hearst wrote his publishers:

> If your local news is not notably superior to your competitor's please take the necessary steps to make it so; and please do not be satisfied with anything less than notable superiority.[73]

Local news provided timely and significant information which attracted attention. It also entertained readers by presenting little glimpses of life in their city. Hearst hoped to stimulate the interest of the public in municipal affairs and in public institutions.[74]

On April 9, 1893 Joseph Pulitzer had begun to feature the comic strip in the daily newspaper. He had pioneered the development of colored presses and on February 16, 1896 first experimented with color in a comic strip. Richard Outcault, a Pulitzer artist who had gained notoriety with "Down Hogan's Ally," had begun a new comic strip relating to the unsavory doings of the citizens of a New York City slum. The World's technical staff soon successfully colored the central character's shirt yellow, which spurred the name "The Yellow Kid." The term "yellow journalism" stemmed from this comic strip character.

To compete with Pulitzer, Hearst's Journal staff formulated new comic attractions. Frederick Burr Opper, whose style was to magnify ludicrous situations, was the Journal's leading artist in the 1890's. In December of 1897, in his "Happy Hooligan" strip, Opper matched Outcault's success with color.[75] Other Opper comic strips included "Her Name Was Maude" and "Alphonse and Gaston."

Labor news, weather reports, expanded sports coverage, obituaries, investigations, reports of scandals, police news, local stories, and comic strips helped to make a bigger and more complete newspaper. These features, along with the excellence of the Hearst writers, begin to explain Hearst's remarkable circulation increase. The one cent price made the paper even more appealing. The newspaper cost three to four cents to produce. Advertisement revenues made the difference.[76] Readers actually enjoyed advertisements, and many read them as intently as the news. C. M. Palmer, who initially handled the Journal's advertisements, held that

16

the increase of advertisements in the newspaper was another example of Hearst's simply
giving the people what they wanted and never
had received in journalism.[77] Palmer noted
that the amount and demand of advertisements
increased as the circulation figures increased.[78]
The Hearst advertisement rates were fixed and
were the most reasonable rates in the country.[79]

The product of all these strategies of
design and reporting was a newspaper that an
educated critic might view as tawdry. But for
Hearst, taste and intelligence lay in typeset
and layout, not in refined sentiments or
language.[80] He observed:

> There is no business in which beauty
> is more important than journalism.
> Taste and beauty in makeup and
> illustration and typography each has its
> appeal to the public.
> In fact, a paper which does not excel
> in these directions has a distinctly cheap
> and ordinary appearance, and makes con-
> ditions difficult for the Circulation
> Manager and the Advertising Department.[81]

Hearst continually urged his writers to keep
up with a progressing public taste. He once
wrote:

> Nothing more irritates the writer of
> this column than the statement of some one
> of his profession that it is necessary to
> write or edit DOWN to the public tastes.
> As a matter of obvious fact, it is
> difficult with the utmost effort to
> write UP to the public tastes.[82]

Perhaps the underlying reason for Hearst's
success was a supreme, if naive, faith in the
American people.[83] Some of his contributions in

17

modernizing the methods of sensationalism resulted in changes of considerable substance. He responded to the needs of minorities and oppressed groups, and they responded to him. His role, he thought, was to speak for as well as to the masses of people who patronized his newspapers.[84] He decided that their need would be his cause.[85] This was a class-oriented journalism of a new intensity, concerned with the conditions of anonymous individuals. The newspapers' success can be explained by several factors, but none more important than Hearst's ability to sell them to lower class immigrants who had been ignored by the English-language press. The political campaigns would show that he had won the trust and the confidence of the most vulnerable members of the urban society.

New York City newspapers had a tremendous impact on the entire nation. The World's news service sold news to the Chicago Tribune; the Sun supplied the San Francisco Chronicle; the Journal supplied the San Francisco Examiner and the Chicago Tribune; and the Herald supplied the San Francisco Chronicle, the Boston Herald, and the Chicago Times-Herald. The Herald, Journal, and World were members of the Associated Press, and their news was available for transmission to other Associated Press members.[86] A survey revealed that between February 1895 and April 1898 , fifty-six out of one hundred eighty-one excerpts quoted nationally in newspapers were released by New York City newspapers.[87]

The outbreak of the Cuban Revolution gave the New York City press the opportunity to expand its influence. Few other American newspapers had sufficient capital to have foreign correspondents in a struggle that was the sustained interest of Americans. The daily press became keenly interested in Cuban affairs in February 1895. The Sun, World, and Journal favored the insurgents' cause from the start.

18

But if Pulitzer's <u>World</u> and Hearst's <u>Journal</u> shared sentiments on the Cuban issue, they were competitors for the public that responded to it.

Footnotes

[1] New York *Journal-American*, August 15, 1951.

[2] W. A. Swanberg, *Citizen Hearst* (New York: Charles Scribner's Sons, 1961), p. 7.

[3] Following William's birth, George became involved with another woman causing a family crisis and resulting in Phoebe focusing her love even more firmly on her son, showering him with love and maternalistic excess. *Ibid.*, pp. 9-10.

[4] New York *Times*, March 1, 1891.

[5] Joseph Lincoln Steffens, *The Autobiography of Lincoln Steffens* (New York: Harcourt, Brace and Company, 1931), p. 541.

[6] Cora B. Older, *William Randolph Hearst: American* (New York: D. Appleton Century Company, 1936), p. 4.

[7] New York *Times*, April 14, 1919.

[8] Interview with William Randolph Hearst, Jr., September 25, 1978. Mr. Hearst is a serious student of history, especially history concerning his father. He discussed in length with his father incidents in his father's life that biographers had dwelled on and thus had many interesting and here-to-fore unpublished insights on his father's actions and intentions.

[9] Oliver Carlson and Ernest Bates, *Hearst, Lord of San Simeon* (New York: The Viking Press, 1937), p. 42.

[10] *Ibid.*, p. 39.

[11] Older, *op. cit.*, pp. 44-45.

[12] Swanberg, *op. cit.*, p.22.

[13]John Kennedy Winkler, _William Randolph Hearst: An American Phenomenon_ (New York: Simon and Schuster, 1928), p. 59.

[14]Swanberg, _op. cit._, pp. 26-27.

[15]Carlson and Bates, _op. cit._, p. 42.

[16]Reprinted in New York _Journal-American_, March 4, 1947.

[17]Carlson and Bates, _op. cit._, p. 43.

[18]Sidney Kobre, _The Yellow Press and The Guilded Age_ (Tallahassee: Florida State University Press, 1964), p. 53.

[19]New York _Journal-American_, August 15, 1951.

[20]Peter R. Varcados, "Labor and Politics in San Francisco, 1880-1892" (Ph.D. Dissertation, University of California, Berkeley, 1968), p. 251.

[21]San Francisco _Examiner_, September 26, 1886.

[22]San Francisco _Examiner_, October 18, 24, 31, 1886.

[23]Varcados, _loc. cit._

[24]Eric Falk Peterson, "Prelude to Progressivism, California Election Reform, 1870-1909" (Ph.D. Dissertation, University of California, Los Angeles, 1969), Introduction.

[25]New York _Journal_, November 26, 1896.

[26]Joseph E. Wisan, _The Cuban Crisis as Reflected in the New York Press, 1895-1898_ (New York: Columbia University Press, 1934), p. 27.

22

[27]Ibid., p. 28.

[28]Rowell's Newspaper Directory (Buffalo: The Mathews-Northup Works, The Complete Press, 1902).

[29]Elmer Holmes Davis, History of The New York Times, 1851-1921 (New York: New York Times, 1921), p. 194.

[30]U. S. Industrial Commission, Report on Immigration, vol. 15 (Washington: Government Printing Office, 1901-1902), p. 449.

[31]Prior to that year almost all newcomers had come from Germany, the United Kingdom, and the Scandinavian countries. Following 1882 the majority of immigrants arrived from Italy, Austria, Hungary, Russia, and other south European nations. Henry Pratt Fairchild, Immigration (New York: Macmillan Company, 1913), p. 135.

[32]New York, Fortieth Census, New York State Compendium, p. 62.

[33]Andrew F. Rolle, The American Italians, Their History and Culture (Belmont, California: Wadsworth Publishing Company, 1972), p. 1.

[34]Alice Kessler Harris, "The Lower Class as a Factor In Reform: New York, The Jews, and the 1890's" (Ph.D. Dissertation, Rutgers University, 1968), p. 13.

[35]Between 1890 and 1900 the white labor force in the United States increased from approximately 19,500,000 to 25,000,000. This growth reflected a 13 percent increase in the number of foreign born workers and about a 50 percent increase in the number of native workers of foreign or mixed parentage. The male labor force increased from about sixteen million to over twenty-one million. The foreign born

accounted for 550,000 of this increase and second generation males for over 1,400,000. The number of female workers increased from less than three million to nearly four million. This increase included over 100,000 foreign born and 380,000 born of foreign parentage. E. P. Hutchinson, Immigrants and Their Children (New York: John Wiley and Sons, Inc., 1956), p. 157. See also Ralph Gabriel, The Course of American Democratic Thought (New York: Ronald Press, 1940), p. 281.

[36]Leo Wolman, The Growth of American Trade Unions, 1880-1923 (Washington: National Bureau of Economic Research, Government Printing Office, 1924), p. 32-33.

[37]New York Board of Labor Standards, Annual Report (1895), p. 302; (1900), p. 438.

[38]U.S. Department of Commerce, Bureau of the Census, Historical Statistics of the United States: Colonial Times to 1957 (Washington: Government Printing Office, 1960), p. 99.

[39]Harris, op. cit., p. 288.

[40]New York World, October 2, 1895.

[41]New York World, January 1, 1897.

[42]New York World, January 1, 1898.

[43]New York World, August 31, 1883; February 24, 1884.

[44]New York World, September 10, 1883.

[45]New York World, December 3, 1883.

[46]New York World, September 8, 1883.

[47]New York World, September 2, 1884.

[48]Rowell's Newspaper Directory, loc. cit.

[49] New York _Journal_, February 20, 1898.

[50] Ferdinand Lundberg, _Imperial Hearst:_ _A_ _Social Biography_ (New York: Equinox Cooperative Press, 1936), p. viii.

[51] _Ibid._, p. 54.

[52] _Wall Street Journal_, April 23, 1979.

[53] Oswald G. Villard, _Some Newspapers and Newspaper Men_ (Freeport, New York: Books for Libraries Press, 1923), pp. 15-16.

[54] "Genessee Valley Hunt Club Speech," _Editor and Publisher_, December 9, 1911, J.A.M.

[55] Steffens, "Hearst, The Man of Mystery," _op. cit._, p. 12.

[56] Hearst to Publishers, October 1928, J.A.M.

[57] Hearst to Editors, June 9, 1936, J.A.M.

[58] Excerpt from a message to the San Antonio Convention of Hearst Executives, February 10, 1929, J.A.M.

[59] "Genessee Valley Hunt Club Speech," _loc. cit._

[60] Oliver Carlson, _Brisbane, A Candid Biography_ (New York: Stackpole Sons, 1937), p. 115.

[61] Hearst to Publishers and Editors, November 17, 1932. J.A.M.

[62] Excerpt from a message to the San Antonio Convention of Hearst Executives, February 10, 1929, J.A.M.

[63] Hearst to Publishers, July 16, 1929, J.A.M.

[64] Hearst to Publishers and Managing Editors, January 17, 1930, J.A.M.

[65] Hearst to Publishers, October 1928, J.A.M.

[66] Hearst wrote 1134 editorials, Editorial Records, J.A.M.

[67] Hearst to Editors, January 1930, J.A.M.

[68] Morris, op. cit., p. 239.

[69] See for examples New York American, November 6, 1902, November 30, 1902, April 23, 1903, July 17, 1908, September 13, 1908.

[70] Hearst to Publishers and Managing Editors, November 17, 1932, J.A.M.

[71] Hearst to Publishers of all morning and evening newspapers, February 3, 1930, J.A.M.

[72] Hearst to Publishers and Managers, January 17, 1930, J.A.M.

[73] Hearst to Publishers of all morning and evening newspapers, January 30, 1930, J.A.M.

[74] Hearst to Publishers, February 3, 1930, J.A.M.

[75] New York Journal, December 12, 1897.

[76] Willard Bleyer, Newspaper Writing and Editing (New York: Houghton Mifflin Company, 1927), p. 305.

[77] Charles Austin Bates, American Journalism (New York: Holmes Publishing Company, 1897), p. 27.

[78] Ibid.

[79] Ibid.

[80]Edwin Emery and Edwin Ford, _Highlights of the American Press_ (Minneapolis: University of Minnesota Press, 1954), p. 309.

[81]_Exchanges_ (October 1927), J.A.M.

[82]"In The News," April 23, 1940, J.A.M.

[83]Interview with William Randolph Hearst, Jr., September 25, 1978.

[84]Hearst to the United Irish Societies of Chicago, August 16, 1913, J.A.M.

[85]Hearst to Willis Abbot, _Journal_ Editorial Editor, November 7, 1896, J.A.M.

[86]Marcus M. Wilkerson, _Public Opinion and the Spanish American War: A Study in War Propaganda_ (Baton Rouge: Louisiana State University Press, 1932), p. 7.

[87]Wisan, _op. cit._, p. 34.

II

Struggle for Circulation Supremacy

As the <u>Journal</u>'s circulation increased, a frenzied competition developed for circulation supremacy between the <u>Journal</u> and the <u>World</u>. The major national events that transpired during the newspapers' struggle were the Presidential election of 1896 and the Spanish American War. The papers' reporting of both events would become weapons in their circulation battle.

The Hearst-Pulitzer struggle first centered on the Sunday editions. Hearst made a concerted effort to lure away the best of Pulitzer's staff, offering them salaries of two and three times what they were making with Pulitzer.[1] He attracted cartoonist T. P. Powers, drama critic Alan Dale, and editor Morrill Goddard. By January 31, 1896 he had hired Pulitzer's entire Sunday <u>World</u> staff except for Pulitzer's personal secretary Emma Jane Hogg. Pulitzer, matching Hearst's offers dollar for dollar, hired the entire staff back. But within a day Hearst, outbidding Pulitzer, hired them all back, this time to stay.

Goddard, while working for Pulitzer, had developed a formula for putting out the nation's most spectacular Sunday newspaper. A Sunday edition of the <u>World</u> featured a news section, an editorial section, double page spreads on pseudo science developments, double page spreads on crime and scandal, an entertainment section with an emphasis on the personalities of female models and actresses, sob sister advice, an examination of a prominent literary or social figure and his achievements, sections on sports and society, and a colored comic supplement.[2] Goddard continued this formula on the <u>Journal</u>, where he continually added sections. Three color supplements were added in 1896. An average Sunday <u>Journal</u> ran fifty-two pages in 1896 and eighty pages in 1897. The five cent newspapers steadily rose in circulation from just over 54,000 in November 1895 to over 350,000 in October 1896.[3] By 1898 the average Sunday _Journal_ sold over 600,000 copies.

By February 1896, the _Journal_'s daily circulation had risen to nearly 300,000.[4] To match Hearst, Pulitzer reduced the price of the _World_ to one cent in February 1896.[5] It appeared as if Pulitzer panicked by the Hearst challenge and the results were disastrous. While the _World_'s circulation did rise slightly, advertisers were scared away. As the _World_'s profits began to drop, Pulitzer admitted that he had made a mistake.[6] The _Journal_ continued to gain on the _World_. The _Journal_'s average daily circulation for the month of October 1896 was 417,821.[7]

The November Presidential election intensified the struggle. Both Hearst and Pulitzer had supported Cleveland in 1892, and both had become dissatisfied with his Cuban policy. Though Hearst's mother held the controlling shares of the Homestake Mine, the largest silver mine in the country, and the free coinage of silver would have made his holdings more valuable, both he and Pulitzer disapproved of the money plank advocated by the Democratic party's Presidential nominee William Jennings Bryan. Since both had been loyal to the Democratic party, each faced a serious decision on his allegiance in 1896.

Considering the silver issue a fraud, Pulitzer decided to withhold support for Bryan and remained nonpartisan throughout the campaign. The _World_ presented the views of both Bryan and the Republican nominee William McKinley, pointing to the shortcomings of both candidates and of both platforms.

Hearst sent the _Journal_'s Editor-in-Chief Willis Abbot to Chicago to cover the Democratic party's national convention. Abbot met Bryan two days before he received the nomination and was immediately impressed with him.[8] Abbot saw in Bryan a sincere man who was convinced of the righteousness of his cause, which included the silver plank but also an understanding of the terrible poverty and injustice that had inspired the Populist movement. Abbot realized that Hearst would oppose the plank for free coinage of silver. He therefore formulated with Bryan a comprehensive telegram to Hearst pointing out the opportunity afforded the Journal of being the leading Democratic newspaper in the East.[9] Journal editorial writer Alfred Henry Lewis immediately returned to New York from the convention to help sway Hearst.[10]

Despite the silver issue, Hearst chose Bryan. He later reflected:

I pondered all the day of Bryan's nomination and all the night upon what I should do. I had everything to lose and nothing to gain by supporting him, and I did not believe in free silver.

But I did believe in Democracy. I came to the conclusion that the man might not be sound, but at least he was sincere, and that the cause he stood for was the people's cause.[11]

Abbot, in charge of the Journal's efforts in the Presidential campaign, was initially instructed to avoid mention of the silver issue in his newspapers. Within a month Hearst realized the absurdity of avoiding the major issue of the campaign so he called a meeting of his editors and announced that his papers were putting party principles above his personal principles. The Journal came out for free silver.[12]

The 1896 election was a unique event for

31

nineteenth century politics.[13] Wealthy conservative eastern Democrats turned to McKinley,[14]
and Republican party coffers were filled with the
largest campaign funds of the century, over
fifteen million dollars, while Bryan raised only
$300,000. Republican propaganda warned the
middle classes that a social upheaval might
occur should the thirty-six year old Nebraskan
be elected, and appealed to both the middle
and working classes on the issue of sound money.
The Republicans had gained control of Congress
in the 1894 elections and were now taking credit
for the current upswing in the nation's economy.
Employers and financiers warned factory workers
that if Bryan was elected they would lose their
jobs as the economy declined. They also warned
farmers that free coinage of silver would cause
banks to panic and fail to renew their mort-
gages.[15]

In April, Hearst newspapers began attacking
McKinley as a puppet who was controlled by the
wealthy and powerful conservative industrialist
Mark Hanna, McKinley's closest advisor in the
campaign. Cartoonist Homer Davenport por-
trayed Hanna as a corpulent plutocrat covered
with dollar signs. He pictured McKinley on
Hanna's knee like a ventriloquist's dummy.
Lewis wrote a series of articles, illustrated
by Davenport's cartoons, condemning Hanna.
Supporters of Bryan who wrote in Hearst's newspapers included Henry George of the Single
Taxers, Edward Bellamy of the Nationalists,
W. D. P. Bliss of the Christian Socialists,
Eugene Debs of the Railway Union, and Samuel
Gompers of the American Federation of Labor.
Hearst was preaching Democratic party prin-
ciples and was urging government ownership of
the railroads and public utilities. In public
character he was a champion of the common people
against the moneyed powers.[16]

While Hearst endorsed Bryan, most other
eastern newspapers endorsed McKinley.[17] Hearst's,

in fact, was the only major newspaper in the East loyal to the Democratic party. While the connection cannot be established, his newspaper's circulation increased at the same time: the newspapers were sent daily to Boston, Philadelphia, and Washington. Between October 13 and October 27 the Journal's net daily average circulation increased by 90,495.[18] As the owner of the largest Democratic newspaper in the nation, he was thrust into the Democratic party elite and the Bryanite leadership, and the Journal office building became the Eastern headquarters for the Bryan campaign.

On June 29 the Chairman of the Democratic National Committee wrote to Hearst that his support was making the election of Bryan a possibility.[19] President Cleveland wired Hearst that Democrats nationwide were indebted to him for all that he did for the Democratic party in the campaign.[20] As the election approached local party leaders were daring to think that Hearst had indeed turned the public to Bryan. John Sheehan, a Manhattan Democratic party county leader, congratulated Hearst for his efforts in lining up the workingmen in New York County behind Bryan.[21] New York Committee Chairman Elliot Danforth, observing that when Bryan had been nominated he did not have even the slightest prospects of a national victory, asserted that the Hearst press had caused popular sentiment in favor of the Democratic nominee to grow in strength daily. Danforth predicted victory.[22] On November 3 Bryan and National Democratic Chairman James Jones sent telegrams of praise, thanks, and victorious predictions to Hearst.[23] A letter from Dr. E. M. M'Glyn perhaps represents the perception that Bryan's supporters had of Hearst. M'Glyn congratulated the publisher for spurring the masses to become involved in the election process, and added:

> The movement of the New Democracy logically
> indicates an irresistible tendency to

33

destroy . . . monopoly. It is an uprising
of the honest masses against oppressive
criminal corporations, monometalists, and
trusts, against a plutocracy, a government by wealth . . . /it/ is more a crusade
than a political campaign.[24]

The campaign evoked interests and passions
as never before in a national election.[25] This
manifested itself in the tremendous vote. Bryan
polled 6,492,559 votes, more than any previous
victor and nearly a million votes more than
Cleveland had polled in 1892, yet McKinley won
with a 609,687 vote plurality. McKinley swept
the eastern states, Bryan did not carry a single
state north of the Potomac or east of the
Mississippi above the Ohio.[26]

The Journal sold 1,506,634 copies on election day, "an achievement not only unparalleled
in the history of the world, but hitherto un-
dreamed of /in/ modern journalism."[27] The
Journal was now the world's largest selling newspaper; moreover Hearst had gained the trust of
the Bryan people who would be the leaders of
the Democratic party for the next eight years.

Hearst's analysis of Bryan's defeat offers
insights to his political values. The specific
reason for the defeat, Hearst observed, was
the issue of bimetallism. But he emphasized
Bryan's failure to capture the support he had
sought from labor, or to win the downtrodden
city dwellers, a failure that Hearst connected
with Bryan's having also been the nominee of
the clearly agrarian Populist party. And it
was in large part Cleveland's conservatism, the
publisher argued, that had weakened the party in
1896. Hearst wrote that Eastern workers wanted
a united, progressive, and reformist party.[28]

On November 8, 1896 the Journal celebrated
its first anniversary under Hearst; in a year
he had challenged and surpassed Pulitzer. The

34

paper congratulated itself in an editorial:
"Newspapers are printed for the public and the
Journal is more than content with the public's
judgement of its first year's work."[29] The
Journal, the editor claimed, had established a
reputation for its espousal of democratic causes
and its opposition to the special trusts.[30]

Pulitzer's enterprise suffered the next
year. His income from the World, which had
approached one million dollars annually for
the decade prior to 1895, declined every month
in 1897. Average daily circulation for the
World dropped from 312,000 in 1896 to 289,000
in 1897, the evening edition fell from 360,000
to 341,000, and the Sunday edition went down
from 562,000 to 514,000. As the World lost
readers the Journal gained.[31]

Critics have dismissed Hearst's success as
merely a triumph in a battle of checkbooks, with
Hearst's being fatter than Pulitzer's.[32] It is
true that an enormous amount was spent--Hearst
invested two million dollars of his mother's
money in the Journal.[33] But while Hearst was
more generous with his money, Pulitzer himself
was a millionaire and actually had access to
more money than Hearst did. A close examination
of the Journal and the World reveals that Hearst
surpassed Pulitzer for reasons beyond his securing
the best talent by wages. Reducing the fee of
the daily paper to one cent was effective, as was
the revenue resulting from the increase in the
amount of advertisements. Recognizing that
headlines, illustrations, and other devices
helped but that continued success depended on
the contents of the paper, Hearst employed more
sectional writers than Pulitzer; and this too
contributed to the popularity of the Journal.
And Hearst's appeal to the new immigrants was
of great importance.

Among Pulitzer's special departments was a
section on sports. He drastically altered sports
coverage in the 1880's when he expanded the

<u>World's</u> coverage to include baseball and boxing news,[34] and he appointed the first editor of a sports department in America, H. G. Cuckmore.[35] He did not, however, alter the actual writing style of the sports articles that appeared in his papers. The result was a sports section not altogether good, but better than none. Hearst, who had a higher opinion of the intelligence of the masses, decided to create a sports department featuring stories written by experts for a wide knowledgeable readership.[36] The <u>Journal</u> presented league and divisional team standings, individual statistics, and feature stories. Pulitzer realized that the Hearst method was appealing to more readers than his own method and urged his sports writers to alter their layout and approach.[37] This is an example of yellow journalism becoming the norm.

Throughout his journalistic career Hearst had allowed his writers to sign their own articles, realizing that readers would come to identify with certain writers.[38] Hearst was an innovator of the concept. Arthur Brisbane, who was still a Pulitzer employee in January 1897, very much wanted his own column with a byline but Pulitzer would not allow it. After a continuing conflict between the two men, which culminated in Brisbane defiantly signing his name to a <u>World</u> editorial, Pulitzer suspended him.[39] Brisbane immediately left Pulitzer and went to work for the <u>Journal</u> where he began a thirty-nine year association with Hearst.[40]

Brisbane was the son of a prominent nineteenth century Socialist and absorbed most of his father's views.[41] Brisbane and Hearst shared a belief that the city, state, and federal governments had to assume responsibility for the nation's social and political inequities and that the government on all levels should own and control the basic means of production, distribution, and exchange, with the avowed aim of operating for use rather than profit, and of assuring to each member of society an equitable share of goods, services, and personal liberty.

With the relative freedom that Hearst allowed
him, Brisbane became one of the nation's most
popular columnists. Until Brisbane joined his
staff Hearst had conducted many pragmatic crusades to correct inequities in society. With
the arrival of Brisbane the Hearst newspapers
began to develop a more systematic, almost
ideological approach to social and political
issues.

Perhaps the most revealing cause of the
World's decline and the Journal's advance was
in the difference between the two newspapers in
their attitudes toward the new immigrants. By
1900 the new immigrants in New York City out-
numbered the immigrants of older stocks. Hearst
attempted to appeal to the newcomers. The
Hungarian immigrant Pulitzer, who was consistently sympathetic to the old immigrants and
particularly friendly to the Germans, never
accepted the newer nationalities and attacked
them in the World. In this he shared feelings
among the older immigrant groups, who reacted
not from prejudice alone but from fear of competition for work. Pulitzer had little respect
for the Italians. A World headline read,
"Italians Find a Number of New and Cheap
Residences, Live Happily and Contentedly in the
Midst of Filth and Foul Odors."[42] A Pulitzer
editorial stated that "the modern 'Greek' is a
treacherous, drunken creature . . . to call a
man a 'Greek' is equivalent to branding him a
liar and a cheater."[43] Slavs, Pulitzer wrote,
had worked as scabs in the Pennsylvania coal
mines, where they were living like hogs.[44]
"The world may sympathize with the Chinese so
long as they remain at home and attend to their
own business," Pulitzer announced, "we do not
want them here . . ."[45] But by the late 1880's,
as the new immigrants began to outnumber the old,
Pulitzer refrained from such pointed attacks on
the new immigrants and simply avoided the issue.

Hearst's Journal was cordial to the new

immigrants. The majority in a democracy, Hearst said, always has to consider the rights of minorities; and he added:

> If Democracy is to legislate for the majority alone, and to the disadvantage of injury of minorities, it proves thereby that it is not freer from fault than aristocracies or other forms of class government.[46]

It is a notable statement from a publisher whom many would later judge to be champion of a majoritarian mobocracy. He later wrote:

> It has always been the experience of this free country that the people who have been politically persecuted in foreign lands have become, when received here, some of our most devoted and valuable citizens. Perhaps their experience in other countries had made them appreciate the benefits of this more liberal land and perhaps, too, it was the very progressiveness of these persecuted peoples which made them unpopular abroad and useful and welcome here.

Whereas Pulitzer was negative toward the new-comers, Hearst viewed them as a positive good for the country. He continued:

> At any rate, we have built up our nation to be the greatest in the world out of those people who have had the imagination and courage and the devotion to ideals to make them dissatisfied with reactionary conditions abroad and eager to become a part of our more progressive and more liberal and more liberty loving citizens.
> The country has been a blessing to them and they have been a boon to us . . .[47]

This attitude offered acceptance to the new

immigrants in a frequently hostile world. The new ethnic group, as they learned how to read English, turned to the hospitable pages of the Journal, and it very largely molded their ideas concerning public events.[48] Hearst occasionally published newspapers and columns in German, Italian, and Yiddish, and often had kind things to say about each of the ethnic groups. This was an important source of their sympathy to Hearst's political endeavors.

Hearst also appealed to the lower classes' baser instincts, and his sensationalistic journalism had its most spectacular hour in the times that led to the Spanish American War. Presidents Cleveland and McKinley, along with most business and financial leaders, opposed intervention in Cuban affairs for as long as possible. The principle cause of American intervention was the public demand for it, and much of the responsibility for the public sentiment lies with the press, especially the Journal and the World.

From the inception of the Rebellion in February 1895, the New York City press became intensely interested in the Cuban situation. The Times, Sun, Tribune, Mail and Express, and Commercial Advertiser all initially favored the insurgents' cause. But all of these newspapers wanted the United States to avoid involvement. The Evening Post and Journal of Commerce strongly opposed American intervention, condemned supporters of the rebels, and denounced American newspapers that took up the Cuban cause. But from the start Hearst and Pulitzer advocated every means possible to aid the rebels.

In mid-April, Spain declared martial law and sent fresh troops and supplies to Cuba. Spanish troops at once began to build and fortify tiny forts throughout the island.[49] Spanish officials immediately began to censor the news that was being sent back to America so little dependence could be placed on the accuracy of the reports that did reach the states.

In July a yellow fever epidemic hit Cuba.
For a three-month period the Spanish War Department attributed all hospital deaths to yellow
fever. The danger posed to the United States
was obvious and terrifying. Hearst quickly
capitalized on the epidemic, arguing that Spanish
rule was incapable of combatting it.[50]

In the spring of 1895 Cuban revolutionists
established a provisional government. A conference of delegates assembled at Timaguaya on
September 16, 1895 adopted a constitution and
elected Salvador Cisneros President and Maso
Vice President of the provisional government.
The Journal pledged its support to the new
leaders. An editorial declared that the acts of
the insurgents were "animated by the same fearless spirit that inspired the counsel of the
patriot fathers who sat in Philadelphia on the
fourth of July, 1776."[51]

The Allianca incident in late March 1895
crystallized anti-Spanish sentiment. On March
8, this United States Merchant ship, carrying
wine, bananas, rubber, mustard seeds, and coca,
was attacked by the Spanish gunboat Conde de
Venadito, in the windward passage of Cape Maisi.
The American ship had never entered the three-
mile limit off the Cuban coast. It was, the
Journal said, an instance of the arrogance of
the Spanish military and an insult to the
United States.[52]

In 1895 American officials exercised patience and tried to maintain friendly relations
with Spanish officials. On June 12, President
Cleveland issued a proclamation of neutrality
between the two nations. The Journal denounced
the President's actions, charging that Spanish
rule was reactionary and inept. McClean argued
that the Cuban rebels were fighting for the
basic freedoms and rights that were spelled out

in the American constitution. An editorial
asserted that America was as useful to Spain
as if she was her ally.[53]

Spanish officers began an active campaign
to destroy property. There were continuous
reports of the destruction of sugar plantations,
villages, and railroad property.[54] Journal
correspondent Richard Harding Davis wrote of
the horrors of this wholesale devastation of the
island.[55] The Journal stated that the destruction of the sugar plantation would wipe out
Spanish revenues from the island, after which
Spain would simply lose interest in Cuba and
leave the island to ruin.

In October 1895 the Journal began printing
stories of atrocities of Spanish forces under
Commander Campos. Tales of inhuman stabbings,[56]
needless shootings,[57] and even the bayonetting
of hospital patients,[58] filled the columns
daily. The Journal reported many more instances
of Spanish cruelty than any other New York
newspaper, and was arguing that the United
States had to be the protector of personal
liberties and democratic rule in the Americas.

In January 1896 Spanish officials announced
the appointment of Valeriano Weyler as the new
Captain-General in Cuba. Weyler, with a long
military record, was known for his disciplinarian
tactics.[59] Within a week of assuming command
he formulated a strict definition of treason and
made it punishable by death, ordered the registration of inhabitants, forbade travel, and con-
ferred upon military commanders extraordinary
judicial powers. The Times described this
policy as "martial law with a vengeance."[60]
With Weyler in command, reports of Spanish
atrocities increased.[61]

In 1896 Hearst himself, developing McClean's
arguments, began to urge Congress to intervene
on behalf of the insurgents. He pleaded,

"Recognition of Cuba as a nation by the United States should be prompt and full. It should not wait but come at once."[62] Congressional debate began on the question. In the midst of its denunciations, the _Journal_ did devote some attention to what it saw as the needs of Spain. The United States, it argued, would be doing Spain a service by cutting off her ties with Cuba and thereby freeing her to develop her domestic resources.[63] Hearst was defining a new obligation for United States foreign policy as an active enforcer of democratic principles.

By November the _Journal_ was preparing its readers for a war with Spain that might follow recognition.[64] An "armed conflict with Spain would be short, sharp, and decisive, and it would put the United States in a position to assume a protectorate over Cuba, and that would insure the freedom of that unhappy island."[65]

The platform on which William Jennings Bryan ran in 1896 included a plank sympathetic to the insurgents' cause. The _Journal_ declared that McKinley was controlled by Hawaiian sugar trusts[66] and stood to benefit by a Spanish devastation of the sugar plantations in Cuba.[67] The day before the election the _Journal_ asserted that either candidate could bring an improvement over the inaction of the Cleveland administration.[68] Upon McKinley's election it stated that there was no surer road open for popularity for the new President than the abandonment of the cold-blooded indifference to Cuba to which Cleveland had committed America.[69]

The _World_ and the _Journal_ were spending money lavishly, and pursuing hidden information so energetically as to be, in effect, making news as well as reporting it. The year 1897 marked the beginning of what the _Journal_ referred to as the "New Journalism"--a policy of aggressive reporting of unusual incidents that other papers would have overlooked, some freak ones presented in a popular format that was to

42

become "Ripley's Believe It Or Not," and some
genuinely revealing such as personal correspondence between city officials showing
corruption in Tammany Hall. Poking fun at
its competitors for their lack of initiative, [70]
the Journal adopted the slogan "While others talk
the Journal acts," and occasionally boasted of
the growth in circulation that its vigorous
reporting was bringing it. [71] A decade later
Hearst wrote that the "New Journalism" had
been instrumental in the evolution of journalism
because it was more sensitive to public opinion
than the British Parliament. He added, "The
journalism that talked was a great advance to no
journalism at all. But the future belonged to
the journalism that acted." [72] Nowhere would the
New Journalism be better demonstrated than in
its treatment of the Cuban situation.

Richard Harding Davis and Frederick
Remington were Hearst's highest paid correspondents in Cuba. Davis wrote feature stories
that were usually first-page material. Remington
was an artist assigned to send sketches of
Cuban atrocities to the Journal for publication.
The famous telegram from Hearst, "you furnish
the pictures and I'll furnish the war," [73] supposedly sent in response to the artist's insistence that all was quiet in Cuba and that
war was unlikely, was probably never written.
The telegram is sufficiently disturbing that
only the most confidential denial--in circumstances in which the denial would never become
public or otherwise be to Hearst's advantage--
would be usable as strong evidence of its not
having existed; but Hearst questioned years
later by his son, was to make just such a
denial. [74] There is no copy of any such telegram
in the Journal morgue. All references to the
actual quote are from James Creelman's book, [75]
which uses it as an example of Hearst's greatness
in liberating an oppressed people. It should be
noted that at the time that Hearst supposedly
sent the telegram, Creelman was on the World's

payroll and had been expelled from Cuba by Spanish officials for his gross exaggerations.

Yet the tone of the telegram, real or fictional, does represent how Hearst felt. He wrote:

> Whatever is right can be achieved through the irresistible power of awakened and informed public opinion. Our object, therefore, is not to inquire whether a thing can be done, but whether it ought to be done, and if it ought to be done, to so exert the forces of publicity that public opinion will compel it to be done.[76]

The Journal was aggressive. Hearst was the first newspaper publisher to station in Cuba his own dispatch boat; he sent the Vamoose in December 1896. He was thus assured of getting news from Cuba despite Weyler's strict censorship.[77]

Military reports during the rainy season of 1897 were scant, but by September the Journal was describing insurgent advances. Spain once again responded to the rebellion by sending in large number of reinforcements.[78] The Journal began a seven-month campaign exploiting the horrors of General Weyler's concentration policy. Articles of cruelty, disease and inadequate hospital services, with appropriate illustrations, reached the American streets. The Journal also opened up an attack on McKinley for following a course of inaction similar to Cleveland's.[79]

On August 17, 1897 Hearst began his most famous campaign of the period, ending in the escape from a Spanish prison a beautiful Cuban girl, Evangelina Cosio y Cisneros. Hearst devoted approximately three hundred seventy-eight columns to her. He called her the "Cuban Joan of Arc" and the "Flower of Cuba." Evangelina was the eighteen year old daughter of a Cuban revolutionist who had been arrested in June 1895 and imprisoned at Cienfuegos.[80] He was later

44

sentenced to life imprisonment at the Isle of Pines, south of Cuba.[81] Evangelina accompanied her father. She had a confrontation with Spanish military commander Colonel Berriz and was charged with "rebellion" and sent to Recojidas prison in Havana.[82] Abbot would later write of Hearst's involvement:

> If ever for a moment he doubted he was battling a powerful state to save the life and liberty of a sorely persecuted girl martyr, he gave no sign of it. It was the one dominating, all compelling issue of the moment for him . . . Hearst felt himself in the role of Sir Galahad rescuing a helpless maiden.[83]

This was s key to know how his mind worked. While many _Journal_ employees viewed the affair as a false bit of cheap sensationalism, Hearst was serious in his efforts and his sentimental concern.

The initial articles were written by _Journal_ correspondent George Eugene Bryson, who accepted Evangelina's word as fact. Through the _Journal_'s publicity, the affair became well known. Hearst sent telegrams in the girl's behalf to prominent people throughout the world, including President McKinley's wife.[84] He published replies of support from leading American women such as President McKinley's mother, Mrs. Jefferson Davis, Mrs. Mark Hanna, Julia Ward Howe, Clara Barton, W. C. Whitney, Eugenia Washington, grandniece of George Washington, Mrs. Ulysses S. Grant, the wife of Secretary of State Sherman, and Letitia Tyler Semple, daughter of ex-President Tyler.[85]

In early September Maria Christina, Queen Regent of Spain, ordered Weyler to move Evangelina to a convent until her trial. Weyler refused[86] and Pope Leo XIII made a public appeal for clemency.[87]

On October 10, 1897 the _Journal_ featured a
three-page story announcing that Evangelina had
been rescued three days earlier by Hearst employees. _Journal_ correspondent Karl Decker had
rented a house adjacent to the prison. At night,
after drugging the guards and other prisoners, he
used a ladder to reach the prison roof and then
sawed through the cell bars. Evangelina was
then disguised as a boy and with a forged pass-
port she escaped from Cuba on the Ward liner
Senica.

Hearst got full glory from the exploit. He
published congratulatory comments from the likes
of Mrs. Grant, Mrs. Carlisle, Governor Bradley's
wife, Senator Mason's wife,[88] Clara Barton,[89]
Senator Jones, Senator Turner,[90] Senator Elkins,
Senator Thurston, Governor Mount of Indiana,
Secretary Sherman, and Mrs. Sherman.[91] The
Bishop of London congratulated Hearst for
"magnificent journalism."[92] The Washington
Post, Chicago _Times-Herald_, Dallas _News_,
Baltimore _Post_, Brooklyn _Times_, Chicago _Inter-
Ocean_, Chicago _Chronicle,_ Chicago _Tribune_, and
Columbus _Journal_ all sent statements of praise
to Hearst. On October 17, the Sunday _Journal_
began a three-month novelized version of its
role in the affair. Hearst brought about a
large reception for Evangelina at Madison Square
Garden[93] and arranged for her and Decker to
meet McKinley.[94]

A brief interlude of friendship between
Spanish and American officials took place
during the closing months of 1897. Then
a series of events brought the two nations to
the point of war.

The first was the anti-autonomy riot of
January 12. Spanish officials demolished three
newspaper offices favorable to autonomy. The
incident lasted only a matter of hours but made
evident the fact that Spain would never grant
Cuba the right of self-government.[95] The

Journal's headline the following day read, "NEXT TO WAR WITH SPAIN." It reported severe rioting and predicted American intervention within forty-eight hours. The United States Senate immediately adopted a resolution to provide protection for Americans in Cuba,[96] but Republican opposition blocked all proposed similar resolutions in the House.[97]

Following House debate McKinley decided to send the _Maine_ to Havana. The decision was easy, for de Lome, the Spanish Minister to the United States, had stated that the United States should have never discontinued naval visits to Cuba.[98] The _Maine_ began maneuvers on February 5.

On February 8 and 9 three resolutions and one constitutional amendment, calling for protection of Americans and American property in Cuba, were introduced in Congress. The proposed legislation was overshadowed by the most significant diplomatic incident of pre-war negotiations. On February 9 the _Journal_ published a letter written in December by de Lome to Don Jose Canalejas, a high ranking Spanish politician and editor of the Madrid _Heraldo_. A rebel sympathizer, Gustavo Escoto, who worked in Canalejas' office, read the letter, stole it, and sent it to his political ally Estrada Palma in New York City. Palma translated the letter and took it, in person, to the _Journal_ office and handed it to Sam Chamberlain.[99] De Lome wrote that McKinley was weak and catered "to the rabble," a low politician who desired both to leave himself freedom of choice and to stand well with the jingos of his party.[100] The letter indicated insincerity in Spain's dealings with the United States. De Lome acknowledged authorship of the letter.[101] For five days the _Journal_ featured front-page stories and editorials on the letter. The paper demanded de Lome's dismissal.[102] McKinley requested the removal of de Lome, who resigned on February 17.

The excitement surrounding the de Lome letter had scarcely begun to diminish when, at 9:40 a.m. on February 15, a series of explosions in the forward section of the _Maine_ demolished the ship. Two hundred sixty-six Americans were killed. In the immediate wake of the explosion McKinley urged America to wait for an official investigation before laying blame on Spain. The _Journal_, however, inflamed public opinion by immediately blaming Spain.

For the next week the _Journal_ reported a daily average of eight and one-half pages on stories related to the _Maine_. Hearst sent three yachts and a group of special correspondents to Havana to conduct a private investigation of the explosion. He offered a $50,000 reward for the conviction of those responsible,[103] and began a fund to erect a monument in honor of the _Maine_'s victims.[104] Ex-President Cleveland turned down an offer from Hearst to serve as honorary chairman of the fund.[105] Throughout the crisis, the _Journal_'s circulation was rising dramatically. The average daily circulation for the week of January 9 was 416,885, and it reached 1,025,644 on February 17 and 1,036,140 on February 18.[106]

Official investigations strongly suggested that the explosion had been from inside the _Maine_ and came from no outside force. But the possibility that Spain had been responsible for the explosion made war inevitable.[107] By March Hearst was announcing a plan to organize his own army.[108]

On March 17 Vermont Republican Senator Redfield Proctor addressed the Senate chamber, telling of his recent visit to Cuba and his investigation of Cuban affairs. He described wretched conditions and Spanish misrule in Cuba. The military situation, he said, was such that neither side could achieve victory in the foreseeable future; and all attempts at autonomy would fail. He concluded by advising the Senate against annexation and asserted that Cuba was

capable of governing itself.[109] According to a
Tribune poll, the address was bringing the
more conservative part of the public closer to
interventionism.[110] The _Journal_ observed that
Proctor had confirmed every news story about
Cuba to appear in its pages.[111]

McKinley moved slowly toward Cuban intervention. In late March the House Republicans
expressed disapproval of his actions as negotiations with Spain broke down. Overwhelming
pressure at home and the absence of hope for a
negotiated settlement abroad brought the President
to submit the Cuban problem to Congress. Hearst
urged his readers to petition their Congressmen.[112]

By April all of the New York City newspapers were printing calls to war issued by
prominent public figures, ministers, college
presidents, and members of Congress. Spanish
officials offered the rebels an armistice, but
they rejected the offer on April 11. The New
York newspapers all supported the rebels'
decision. On April 11 McKinley delivered his
message calling for intervention "to save
humanity" and to protect the lives and interests
of Americans in Cuba. By April 16 both Houses
of Congress had passed resolutions for intervention.[113] A single resolution went to the
President on April 17 and the President signed
it within seventy-two hours. On April 21
Spanish officials cut off ties with the United
States. Congress officially declared on April
25 that America had been at war with Spain
since April 21. On May 9 and 10 the _Journal_'s
ears asked its readers, "How do you like the
Journal's war?" and offered a $1,000 prize to
the person who could suggest the most original
way for the nation to launch its war effort.[114]

On June 10 Hearst wrote to McKinley and
offered to equip, arm, and mount at his own
expense a regiment of cavalry to fight in Cuba.
He added:

> While making this offer I request that you
> accept my personal services as a member of
> this regiment suggested. I am conscious of
> a lack of special qualifications to direct
> even in a minor capacity such a body of
> men, and do not, therefore, request any
> position than that of a man in the ranks.[115]

McKinley declined the offer with thanks. Hearst
wrote to McKinley offering to arm and donate to
the United States Navy his steam yacht,
Buccaneer, and requested permission to command
the crew.[116] On June 4 Secretary of the Navy
Charles Allen accepted the yacht under the stipu-
lations that it be manned by Navy personnel and
commanded by a Navy officer. Hearst donated the
yacht. He then made plans to purchase a big
English steamer and then sink it in the Suez
Canal to obstruct the passage of any Spanish
warships in case the Spanish fleet actually
started for Manila.

As the _World_ and the _Journal_ attempted to
match and outdo each other, each suspected the
other of stealing news. To trap Pulitzer, the
Journal published a dispatch from Cuba on the
death of Colonel Reflipe W. Thenuz.[117] When the
World released a full length story on the battle
at Aguadores detailing the heroics of Thenuz
and his subsequent death,[118] the _Journal_ revealed that Reflipe W. Thenuz was a ficticious
name that when rearranged spelled "We pilfer the
news."[119] The _Journal_ reported on the incident
for over a month, and featured stories, cartoons,
and poems on it, along with letters from newspaper editors across the country that condemned
the _World_ for stealing the _Journal_'s news.

In his appetite for Cuba, Hearst chartered
a steamship, the _Sylvia_, from the Baltimore
Fruit Company, hired a crew, and embarked for
the island. Secretary of War Russel Alger
cleared him, believing that he intended to pub-
lish a newspaper for American soldiers in Cuba.

The _Sylvia_ arrived in Santiago on June 18. Once
in Cuba Hearst himself became an enthusiastic
war correspondent.[120] He also got a bit of
action. In a naval battle at Santiago on July
4, the _Infanta Maria Theresa_ had been defeated
and grounded. When Hearst saw Spanish soldiers
waving white handkerchiefs he jumped overboard
and swam to where they were stranded. He took
twenty-nine prisoners aboard the _Sylvia_, then
transported them to a naval ship, the _St. Louis_.
Hearst received an official receipt for the
prisoners.[121] He remained forever proud of that
receipt.[122]

The _Journal_ claimed an average daily circulation of a million and a quarter for the months
of June and July. This was a larger daily average than any newspaper had ever attained.[123] To
its war news the _Journal_ added a labor column
while expanding its sports coverage, advertising,
and illustrating, and Brisbane wrote an increasing number of articles and editorials committing
the _Journal_ to social reform. Then, when Spanish
disasters at Santiago and the Philippines
brought quick peace, circulation dropped off.

Hearst's part in bringing about the Spanish
American War and his actions once war had been
declared are critical to an understanding of
his social movement. The war was a result of
a popular crusade that the press had called
into being.[124] The political elite and the
leading business interests of America all
favored an early restoration of peace in Cuba
and all sought to avert war. Industrial and
banking circles feared that a costly war would
strengthen the position of the silverites. Most
of the northern and eastern states initially
opposed intervention. Cleveland extended pro-
clamations of neutrality. McKinley continued
Cleveland's policy of inaction until he was influenced by party and public pressure. Cuba
afforded Hearst the opportunity to prove the
effectiveness of yellow journalism and a chance

to test his formula that whatever was right, or
what Hearst thought was desirable, could be
achieved through the irresistible power of a
wakened and informed public opinion.

After the war Pulitzer in conversation with
the World's writers, made a cautious admission
that matters had gotten out of hand during the
Cuban conflict and had to be corrected.[125] He
had already sent out an order for his editors
to forget about the circulation struggle and
stop trying to outdo the Journal.[126] At a
staff meeting on November 28, 1898 Bradford
Merrill remarked that the strenuous competition
with the Journal had produced articles containing
exaggeration and falsities, and writers, he
said, were now to tone down articles and base
all articles on factual information. Don
Seitz, who served many years as Business Manager
of the World, added:

> There is and has been for two years, as you
> know, a fierce competition . . . This has
> developed a tendency to rush things. It
> has not been to the advantage of any news-
> paper so doing. The World feels that it is
> time for the staff to learn definitely and
> finally that it must be a normal news-
> paper.[127]

Hearst, on the other hand, was proud of his
methods and their accomplishments. He wrote to
Brisbane, linking the newspaper's ability to
rouse the public to a desire to lead a domestic
social reform movement:

> All must be congratulated on this
> tremendous job. Truly, the victory in
> Cuba was brought about by a broad based
> public demand. It must be remembered as
> we embark on a movement to upgrade social
> conditions that through efforts of exposure
> and exploitation public opinion will compel
> anything to be done that is right. The war
> with Spain was our war but the credit goes
> to the nation. Let us always remember the

>power of an informed public mind.
>   We will work with the Democratic party
>for social advances. But if the Democratic
>party should ever stumble, let us remember
>the power of publicity in forcing action.
>The journalism of action is the journalism
>of the future.[128]

And Hearst would remain proud. He never understood why historians judged his actions so
negatively. He had worked to uphold the Monroe
Doctrine in the expelling of the last of the Old
World powers that still held land in the New
World, and he had marshalled a public opinion
that the same methods could call to social movements.[129] The war itself, it should be observed,
was in some measure a progressive's war.
Cleveland, McKinley, and Hanna, spokesmen for reaction, were against American entry in the conflict. William Howard Taft ultimately decided
that McKinley could not have avoided the "foolish
war with Spain," and was entirely unsympathetic
to Hearst's and Pulitzer's clamor for war.[130]
But Oliver Wendell Holmes, Francis A. Walker,
Edward Bellamy, John Hay, William James, and
Theodore Roosevelt were for it.[131] War was
justified, these spokesmen for reform believed,
when it was a necessary episode in the evolu-
tionary struggle for survival. The splendid
little war theory, put forth by Hay and
Roosevelt, necessitated the war to prevent a
society otherwise so literally sordid and selfish
in its ideals from turning into absolute putres-
cence.[132] Bryan, motivated by a religious con-
ception of brotherhood, supported the war. The
United States took up arms, he believed, when
it was compelled to choose between war and
"servile acquiescence in cruelties which would
have been a disgrace to barbarism,"[133] The
religious press came to stress the righteousness of the cause: the Churchman, for example,
proclaimed it the duty of America to guide the
futures of the weaker peoples of the world.[134]
Woodrow Wilson approved the nations's imperial-

istic actions, explaining that American statesmen had come to a turning point in the progress
of the nation, as they turned from developing
their own resources to making conquest of the
markets of the world.[135] The Wall Street
Journal, Journal of Commerce, and American
Banker converted to the imperial cause by the
summer of 1898, speaking mainly of the commercial advantages of the new basis.

The young journalist from the West had
invaded New York City and successfully challenged Pulitzer at his own game in his home
territory. Pulitzer was old, tired, and
disillusioned. The war effort was in a sense
his last hurrah. It was a showing he was not
proud of. Hearst was young, energetic, and
idealistic. For him the Cuban effort was a
beginning, a chance to prove himself to New
York City and to the nation. Sensationalism,
he believed, had its place in modern journalism.
Exposure, exploitation, and suggested solutions
could educate and direct the public mind. Hearst
confided to Brisbane:

> The average reader called the government
> to war in Cuba. It is now our job to con-
> vince the average reader to call the govern-
> ment to war again--to fight for improved
> social conditions. As this will improve
> the conditions of those that we are ap-
> pealing to, our jobs should be easier
> and our victory more complete.[136]

Footnotes

[1] Lundberg, op. cit., p. 50.

[2] Frank Luther Mott, American Journalism (New York: Macmillan Company, 1962), p. 524.

[3] New York Journal, November 6, 1898.

[4] Ibid.

[5] "Memoranda of Talks with Mr. Pulitzer," Pulitzer Papers, Library of Congress.

[6] Donald C. Seitz, Joseph Pulitzer, His Life and Letters (New York: Simon and Schuster, 1924), p. 214.

[7] New York Journal, November 6, 1898.

[8] Willis Abbot, Watching The World Go By (Boston: Little, Brown and Company, 1933), p. 157.

[9] Ibid., p. 168.

[10] Lewis to Bryan, July 29, 1896, Bryan Papers, Library of Congress.

[11] Hearst Speech, September 11, 1908, New York American, September 12, 1908.

[12] Abbot, op. cit., p. 169.

[13] Louis W. Koenig, Bryan (New York: G. P. Putnam's Sons, 1975), p. 222.

[14] Cook County Democratic Central Committee to Fellow Democrats, October 28, 1896, Bryan Papers, Library of Congress.

[15] James F. Rhodes, The McKinley and Roosevelt Administrations, 1897-1909 (New York: Macmillan Company, 1922), p. 11.

[16]Lundberg, op. cit., pp. 83-84.

[17]New York American, September 12, 1908.

[18]New York Journal, October 27, 1896.

[19]William Harrity to Hearst, June 29, 1896, J.A.M.

[20]Cleveland to Hearst, October 19, 1896, J.A.M.

[21]Sheehan to Hearst, October 11, 1896, J.A.M.

[22]Danforth to Daniel J. Campbell, Democratic Campaign Committee, Chicago, October 27, 1896, J.A.M.

[23]Bryan to Hearst, November 3, 1896, J.A.M.; Jones to Hearst, November 3, 1896, J.A.M.

[24]M'Glyn to Hearst, November 3, 1896, J.A.M.

[25]Lincoln Steffens to Joseph Steffens, November 9, 1896, Ella Winter and Granville Hicks, editors, The Letters of Lincoln Steffens (New York: Harcourt, Brace and Company, 1938), pp. 125-127; Koenig, op. cit., p. 254; Swanberg, op. cit., p. 90; Abbot, op. cit., p. 143; New York Journal, November 5, 1896.

[26]New York Journal, November 4, 1896.

[27]New York Journal, November 5, 1896.

[28]Ibid.

[29]New York Journal, November 8, 1896.

[30]Ibid.

[31]W. A. Swanberg, Pulitzer (New York: Charles Scribner's Sons, 1967), p. 231.

[32]Lundberg, op. cit., pp. 49-57.

[33]Interview with William Randolph Hearst, Jr., September 25, 1978.

[34]Alfred M. Lee, The Daily Newspaper in America: The Evolution of a Social Instrument (New York: Macmillan Company, 1937), p. 629.

[35]New York World, May 27, 1883.

[36]Hearst to Abbot, November 10, 1896, J.A.M.

[37]Pulitzer Memorandum, October 20, 1898, Pulitzer Papers, Library of Congress.

[38]Hearst to Abbot, February 23, 1897, J.A.M.

[39]Pulitzer to Norris, November 27, 1897, Pulitzer Papers, Library of Congress.

[40]Abbot, op. cit., p. 140.

[41]New York Times, December 26, 1936.

[42]New York World, March 25, 1885.

[43]New York World, February 15, 1885.

[44]New York World, April 18, 1884.

[45]New York World, September 3, 1884.

[46]Hearst to the Editor of the Jewish Advocate, March 4, 1940, J.A.M.

[47]Hearst to Morris Margulies, September 10, 1933, J.A.M.

[48]Thomas Jesse Jones, "The Sociology of a New York City Block" (Ph.D. Dissertation, Columbia University, 1904), p. 30.

[49]Richard Harding Davis, Cuba in War Time

(New York: R. H. Russell, 1897), p. 11.

[50]New York _Journal_, November 13, 1895.

[51]New York _Journal_, October 11, 1895.

[52]New York _Journal_, March 13, 1895.

[53]New York _Journal_, May 8, 1895.

[54]New York _Journal_, December 22, 1895.

[55]Davis, _op_. _cit_., p. 20.

[56]New York _Journal_, October 15, 1895.

[57]New York _Journal_, October 23, 1895.

[58]_Ibid_.

[59]New York _World_, January 18, 1896.

[60]New York _Times_, February 18, 1896.

[61]Davis, _op_. _cit_., p. 103.

[62]New York _Journal_, January 31, 1896.

[63]New York _Journal_, June 29, 1896.

[64]New York _Journal_, November 27, 1896.

[65]New York _Journal_, November 17, 1896.

[66]New York _Journal_, October 16, 1896.

[67]New York _Journal_, October 26, 1896.

[68]New York _Journal_, November 4, 1896.

[69]New York _Journal_, November 6, 1896.

[70]New York _Journal_, October 11, 1897.

[71]New York _Journal_, March 24, 1897.

[72]New York _American_, May 29, 1908.

[73]James Creelman, _On The Great Highway_ (Boston: Lathrop Publishing Company, 1902), p. 178.

[74]Interview with William Randolph Hearst, Jr., September 25, 1978.

[75]See, for examples, Lundberg, _op. cit._, pp. 68-69; Carlson and Bates, _op. cit._, p. 97; Swanberg, _Citizen Hearst_, _op. cit._, pp. 107-108.

[76]Unpublished memo from Hearst to his editors. Hearst later gave it to his son who possesses the original. William Randolph Hearst, Jr. gave a copy of it to the author on September 25, 1978.

[77]New York _Journal_, December 6, 1896.

[78]New York _Journal_, September 8, 1897.

[79]New York _Journal_, March 10, 1897.

[80]New York _Journal_, July 14, 1897.

[81]Evangelina Cisneros and Karl Decker, _Evangelina Cisneros_ (New York: Continental Publishing Company, 1897), p. 136.

[82]_Ibid._, p. 188.

[83]Abbot, _op. cit._, p. 216.

[84]Hearst to Mrs. McKinley, August 22, 1897, McKinley papers, Library of Congress.

[85]New York _Journal_, August 25, 1897.

[86]New York _Journal_, September 5, 1897.

[87] New York _Journal_, September 2, 1897.

[88] New York _Journal_, October 11, 1897.

[89] New York _Journal_, October 13, 1897.

[90] New York _Journal_, October 11, 1897.

[91] New York _Journal_, October 13, 1897.

[92] _Ibid_.

[93] New York _Journal_, October 16, 1897.

[94] New York _Journal_, October 24, 1897.

[95] Washington _Post_, January 13, 1898.

[96] U. S., Congress, Senate, 55th Congress, January 13, 1898, _Congressional Record_, p. 582.

[97] New York _Journal_, January 20, 1898.

[98] John Layser Offner, "President McKinley and the Origins of the Spanish American War" (Ph.D. Dissertation, Penn State University, 1957), p. 191.

[99] Abbot, _op. cit._, pp. 217-218.

[100] New York _Journal_, February 9, 1898.

[101] Washington _Evening Star_, February 10, 1898.

[102] New York _Journal_, February 9, 1898.

[103] New York _Journal_, February 17, 1898.

[104] New York _Journal_, February 19, 1898.

[105] Cleveland to Hearst, February 28, 1898, Cleveland Papers, Library of Congress.

[106] New York _Journal_, February 19, 1898.

[107] New York _Journal_, March 7, 1898.

[108] New York _Journal_, March 20, 1898.

[109] U. S. Congress, Senate, 55th Congress, March 16, 1898, _Congressional Record_, pp. 2916-2919.

[110] New York _Tribune_, March 18, 1898.

[111] New York _Journal_, March 18, 1898.

[112] New York _Journal_, March 30, 1898.

[113] New York _Journal_, April 17, 1898.

[114] New York _Journal_, May 9, 10, 1898.

[115] New York _Journal_, June 10, 1898.

[116] Hearst to McKinley, June 1, 1898. J.A.M.

[117] New York _Journal_, June 8, 1898.

[118] New York _World_, June 9, 1898.

[119] New York _Journal_, June 10, 1898.

[120] Creelman, _op. cit._, pp. 210-212.

[121] New York _Journal_, July 6, 1898.

[122] Interview with William Randolph Hearst, Jr., September 25, 1978.

[123] New York _Journal_, July 20, 1898.

[124] New York _Journal_, September 25, 1898.

[125] Swanberg, _Pulitzer_, _op. cit._, p. 254.

[126]Pulitzer to Seitz, September 10, 1898. Pulitzer Papers, Library of Congress.

[127]"World Memorandum," November 28, 1898, Pulitzer Papers, Library of Congress.

[128]Hearst to Brisbane, December 5, 1898, J.A.M.

[129]Interview with William Randolph Hearst, Jr., September 25, 1978.

[130]Taft to Helen H. Taft, July 5, 1898, Taft Papers, Library of Congress.

[131]George Frederickson, The Inner Civil War (New York: Harper and Row, 1965), pp. 208-238.

[132]Ibid., p. 228.

[133]Koenig, op. cit., p. 276.

[134]Foster R. Dulles, America's Rise to World Power, 1898-1954 (New York: Harper Brothers, 1955), pp. 32-39.

[135]Woodrow Wilson, A History of the American People, volume 5, p. 296, J.A.M.

[136]Hearst to Brisbane, December 19, 1898, J.A.M.

III

The Beginnings of a National Social Movement

At the turn of the century political leaders
of both major parties opposed social welfare programs run by the federal government because
they believed that it merely shifted the burden
from one part of the population to another and
contributed in no way to the general well being.[1]
Hearst saw beyond the residue of nineteenth
century individualism and its conservative impli-
cations and recognized that the American struggle
for existence was a chaotic and wasteful scramble
of special interests.[2] "Our problems," he wrote,
"are . . . the encroachments of private interest
upon public right, the aggressions of the more
capable few upon the substance of the less capable many."[3] He believed that business and
professional leaders had adopted a callous view
of the troubles of the poor.[4] With Hearst super-
vising the morning editions and Brisbane editing
the evening newspaper, the _Journal_ undertook
crusades unparalleled in journalistic history.
Corrupt New York became a battlefield for Hearst.

In 1899, through daily exposures, Hearst
obtained a court injunction preventing the
Board of Aldermen from giving forty miles of
street to the Nassau Railroad Company. Thomas
L. Johnson, later to become a reform mayor of
Cleveland, was president of the company which
lost ten million dollars by the injunction.
He wrote Hearst:

> You may be surprised to hear, far from
> denouncing the _Journal_ I believe you have
> acted in the interests of the people. I
> am a railroad man, it is true, but this is
> not a railroad question. . . . The stand
> you have taken in sustaining an injunction
> is a great stand. I believe that the
> people will appreciate your efforts in
> their behalf. As a businessman I must say
> that I think newspapers are often inclined
> to meddle too much in business questions,

but I say that you deserve credit in
obtaining this injunction.[5]

In December 1896 Hearst discovered that
the Consumer's Fuel, Gas, Heat, and Power
Company had secured from the Board of Estimates,
the city's franchise-granting body, a measure
permitting it to lay fuel-gas mains under every
street and public place in New York City, a
privilege worth tens of millions of dollars.[6]
Hearst retained Clarence Shearn, a twenty-six
year old attorney, graduate of New York Law
School, member of the law firm of Einstein,
Townsend, Guiterman, and Shearn, who was making
a name for himself as a reformer willing to
battle everything in Manhattan from Tammany
Hall to beef trusts,[7] to fight against the
franchise grab. Shearn brought suit in Hearst's
name under the New York State taxpayer's act,
a measure authorizing a suit in the name of any
taxpayer against government officials to prevent waste of public funds. Judge R. Q.
Pryor enjoined the Mayor from signing the
franchise.[8] On April 6, 1899 Hearst published a plan for the construction of a municipal gas plant in New York City.[9] Mayor Robert
Van Wyck and all borough presidents endorsed the
proposal,[10] but it was never carried out. On
May 9, 1899 all gas companies, responding to
Hearst's pressure and publicity, reduced their
rates to sixty-five cents, and the Amsterdam
Light and Gas Company dropped its rates to
fifty cents.[11]

The Hearst victory was not complete. Within a year the Consolidated Gas Company, now
controlling the Amsterdam Gas Company, and
Russell Sage's Standard Gas Company formed the
Trust Gas Company and raised the price of gas to
one dollar and five cents, the legal limit.
Shearn brought the Gas Trust to court. The
cases were before the courts for five years.
During these proceedings Hearst added to his
legal staff.[12] Frustrated by legal channels,

Hearst turned to the political process. In December 1904 he presented to Governor Frank W. Higgins facts concerning the city's lighting contract and requested a legislative investigation.[13]

A year later he presented to the legislature a petition signed by one hundred and fifty thousand New York City residents demanding an investigation of the gas company; the legislature approved funds to create the Stevens Investigating Committee.[14] Charles Evans Hughes, its chief counsel, found that the Consolidated Gas Company owned every gas and lighting company in the city and was making a 17 percent profit on the sale of gasoline.[15] The Stevens Committee reported in favor of an eighty-cent gas rate, but the measure was defeated in the Senate.[16] Shearn conducted a lengthy hearing before the State Gas Commission, producing evidence that prompted several senators to change their stands.[17] Within months the legislature passed the Eighty-Cent Gas Law.[18] Federal Judge Lacombe issued an injunction restraining the enforcement of the act. On May 24, 1906 Hearst responded by having Shearn bring a test case against the Consolidated Gas Company before the state Supreme Court.[19] Within a month the court enjoined the company from cutting off the supply of gas to consumers refusing to pay more than the eighty-cent rate.[20] In January 1909 the Supreme Court sustained the Eighty-Cent Gas Law.[21]

Throughout this gas controversy, Hearst maintained a large legal staff that was available to those who could not afford to take the company to court. In the wake of the Eighty-Cent Gas Law, he significantly expanded the size of this remarkable, private version of a consumer's advocate agency. Between 1906 and 1908 he maintained a "Gas Bureau" in Shearn's office. These lawyers, Shearn wrote Hearst, were re-

sponsible for securing more than one thousand
injunctions and more than two thousand separate
writs of mandamus compelling the company to
supply gas at the legal eighty-cent rate.[22]
Following the Supreme Court's 1909 ruling,
Hearst created another department of his "Bureau"
and aided over twenty thousand consumers to re-
cover their rebates. He maintained the department for years and was responsible for refunding
$10,267,281 to the people.[23]

The actions of Hearst's staff were, of
course, publicized in his newspapers, but the
staff did accomplish much in aiding consumers.
Lincoln Steffens, after examining Hearst's confidential letters and directives issued during
the gas fight, wrote, "There is no news in these
instructions. They are so flattering to Hearst
that if I published them, the public would say I
wanted to get a job on his papers."[24]

In 1899 Hearst conducted a campaign against
the Ramapo Water Company, a paper corporation
without water supplies. The Board of Estimates
were considering a 40-year, 200 million dollar
contract with the company. Hearst purchased
shares in the company and engaged attorneys
Einstein and Townsend to present a stockholder's
suit before the state's Attorney General. They
charged that Silas P. Dutcher, president of the
Ramapo Water Company, had for five years failed
to file an annual report with the Secretary of
State as required by law, thus forfeiting company contracts.[25] Hearst then petitioned the
state Supreme Court to dissolve the company. But
the court was unable to act because the company's
secretary left town with all relevant records.
Once again frustrated by the courts, he formed
a Vigilance Committee headed by former Secretary
of the Navy William C. Whitney and Abraham S.
Hewett, former Congressman and Mayor of New
York City. The committee organized mass meetings
of public protest. Hearst continued his battle,

66

engaging State Senator Slater to introduce in
the state legislature a bill providing that
New York City had the right to own its own water
supply. With the passage of the bill, Hearst
had successfully protected the city's right to
municipal ownership. He had not, however, insured municipal ownership.[26]

Many _Journal_ articles and editorials in
1899 were about women's rights, an indication
that Hearst was becoming concerned with national
as well as local social issues. Hearst campaigned for the abolition of capital punishment
for women[27] and urged improved prison conditions.
A series of editorials, stories, and illustrations in the _Journal_ showing that the women's
prison on Raymond Street was a firetrap led to
the construction of a new prison.[28] Hearst
employed several women leaders including Susan
Anthony, Hellen Keller, and Belva Lockwood, the
first woman lawyer to practice before the United
States Supreme Court, Presidential candidate of
the Equal Rights party in 1884 and 1888, and
author of the Congressional enactment of 1903
granting suffrage to women in Oklahoma, Arizona,
and New Mexico. Isabel Ross, in her study of
newspaper women, claims that Hearst did more
than any other newspaper publisher to help the
cause of women in newspaper work and in advancing their writings.[29] Hearst's political
effort began in 1899 and continued for decades.
He advocated women's suffrage, an eight-hour
work day, and periodic factory inspections to
correct inadequate conditions.[30] Concerning
inadequate factory conditions for women he
wrote in 1913:

> The girls can never recover the hours
> stolen from their youth, the vitality stolen
> from their lives.
> Society can never recover the future
> energy and value taken from it when these
> girls are turned out prematurely worn and
> useless as mothers. TRULY WOMEN ARE

SWINDLED AND MISTREATED BY MEN BEYOND
LIMITS OF CREDULITY . . . If women could
fight and unite, as the fishermen and engineers, and other MEN do, they would not be
swindled as they are.[31]

In the summer of 1899 Hearst exposed the
Swift and Company beef trust, which had un-
loaded one hundred and ninety thousand pounds
of condemned beef on American troops in Puerto
Rico.[32] He was able to use the words of Governor
Theodore Roosevelt who had created a sensation
when he told the Senate War Investigating Committee the condition of the meat sent to
American troops in Cuba. Roosevelt testified:

> I could have eaten my hat stewed with onions
> and potatoes just as well. . . . I ordered
> the entire lot thrown overboard. . . . We
> used everything we could find in the way of
> food in preference to 'embalmed beef'--
> captured Spanish cavalry horses, ponies
> bought from Cubans, abandoned mules which
> had been shot. Our men took them in,
> skinned and cured them.[33]

Hearst and the committee turned their efforts
to General Charles P. Egan, Commissary-General
of Subsistence, responsible for the original
contract between the army and Swift and Company.
The committee found him guilty of knowingly
contracting condemned beef and the army relieved him from active service.[34] The investigation caused the country to become beef-
conscious. In September Hearst began to reveal
that the Beef Trust was forcing prices up. In
1901 he employed Ella Reeves Bloor to investigate
New York slaughterhouses and the rebate practices
of packers. Her revealing articles forced a
court injunction stopping the packers' criminal
terrorization of competitors.[35] Hearst-initiated
suits were before the courts until 1905, when
more than three hundred witnesses were sub-
poenaed to appear before the Illinois Grand

Jury. Four corporations were indicted and twenty men, including Ogden Armour, Charles Armour and Edward Swift were convicted of conspiracy, and sentenced to a year's imprisonment.[36] The Hearst suits were instrumental in the great pure foods campaigns.[37]

Using yellow journalism as a powerful tool for reform, Hearst was emerging as the leading newspaper muckraker in the nation. The progressive mind, according to Richard Hofstadter, was characteristically a journalistic mind and journalism's chief contribution at the turn of the century was that of reporting social needs and responsibilities.[38] Hearst's muckraking had thus far gone through three phases: exposé, exposé followed by reform by others, and exposé followed by Hearst action. The battles over gas, water, women, and beef had their own justification, but they were becoming part of a program and strategy of reform that emerged from Hearst's mind. there were no noticeable changes in either the layout of the newspaper or the intensity of the exposés or fights, but it was no longer enough to simply correct a particular grievance or inequity. Instead, in addition to acting to correct the wrong, the Hearst press would make a political issue in each instance, urging elected officials to draft and enact laws to prevent similar wrongs elsewhere.[39]

Believing that the Populists had created a sound and progressive platform, Hearst's views concerning their movement were quite different from those of other progressive urban newspaper publishers. The Populists could never succeed on a national scale, he realized, because no candidate representing a farmers' movement could attract industrial urban voters. "The sanctity of the agrarian myth," he wrote Abbot, "compelled urbanites to think of farmers as conservatives, regardless of the political propaganda they espoused."[40] It was an opinion

69

that recent historians would support; in 1966, historian Norman Pollack argued that the Populists actually formulated a radical indictment of the capitalist system.[41]

The Populists did have some political success in 1892, when their presidential candidate James B. Weaver received over a million votes and twenty-two Electoral College votes. They also elected five United States Senators, ten United States Congressmen, and three governors, and controlled state politics in Kansas. They showed signs of promise, but 1892 was their best year. Between 1892 and 1896 they tried in vain to broaden their appeal to urban laborers, but Democratic and Republican politicians began to steal Populist candidates and issues, combined forces against Populist candidates in some instances, and through fusion with the Populists in other areas, corrupted or stole their organizations.

In 1896 the Populists faced a dilemna. The Democratic nominee, William Jennings Bryan, had a Populist streak and advocated "free silver" and thus, was attractive to the Populists. Reluctantly they nominated Bryan on their own ticket but tried to assert their independence of the Democrats by nominating their own Vice-Presidential candidate, Tom Watson from Georgia. The Populist ticket polled 220,000 votes; the Democrats had eviscerated the political movement.

The Populists had been wrong, Hearst wrote, in nominating Bryan to head the national ticket. Compromise was necessary for political success, but they had sold out to a moderate candidate. Hearst believed that most of their planks should be enacted into law, especially those advocating government ownership of communications and of the railroads, a government controlled postal savings system, a graduated income tax, the popular election of United States Senators, the eight-

hour work day, government control of excess
lands held by the railroads and corporations,
and the initiative and referendum.[42] "A new
movement," Hearst wrote, "concerned with the
same problems but originating with the urban
industrial workers would receive the support of
the disheartened farmers."[43]

In the summer of 1900 Hearst took on the
Ice Trust in New York City. As the summer
heat descended on the city, the New York,
Knickerbocker, Consumers', Montauk, Standard,
Continental, Hygeia, Crystal Lake Union, Yonkers,
City, and Ridgewood companies consolidated,
forming the American Ice Company, which sud-
denly doubled the price of ice. Hearst and
his attorneys Einstein and Townsend applied
to the New York State Attorney General for
dissolution of the Ice Trust on the grounds
that it was jeopardizing the health and life
of the community.[44] Hearst revealed that Mayor
Robert A. Van Wyck and his brother, Augustus,
each controlled four hundred thousand dollars
worth of stock in the trust. He published reports showing that J. Sargeant Cram, President
of the Dock Board, Commissioner Murphy, Tammany
leader Carroll, and Judges McMahon and Newberger
divided among themselves $1,500,000 worth of
stock.[45] The World and the Tribune followed
the Journal's lead and each began investigating
the trust. On June 4 the comptroller cancelled
all city contracts with the American Ice Company
because city officials had stock in it.[46] As
a result, ice prices were lowered by one-third.
Legal proceedings continued until 1908 when
Shearn, acting as Hearst's counsel, placed
Charles W. Morse, the company's president, in
jail for tampering with company books.[47]

Hundreds of urban daily newspapers wrote
editorials praising the actions of Hearst and
the Journal.[48] Hearst was portrayed as a popular national figure, a force for reform, a
champion of the plain people. A representative

71

editorial, appearing in the Concord (New Hampshire) Patriot on May 23, 1900 directly confronted the issue of yellow journalism as a means to social improvement. It read:

> If that kind of journalism which accomplishes great results in behalf of suffering humanity by exposing the inequities of its oppressors is 'yellow' journalism, then its promoters need not be annoyed by the characterization. And if all the so-called yellow journals should exert their influence as the New York Journal is doing under the great editorship of William R. Hearst, they would have few detractors and would require no apologists. The telling blows that the Journal has dealt the American Ice Company, the wickedest trust ever formed to such the lifeblood of the poor, constitute the greatest service ever rendered a newspaper to the public.
> The institutions by Mr. Hearst of legal proceedings has drawn the conspirators to the verge of desperation. Neither the ice trust nor any monopoly of the same character can long withstand such blows as they are now being dealt by the Journal in behalf of the people. If this great newspaper is 'yellow', we trust that it is a fast color.[49]

The next day the Toledo (Ohio) News, in an editorial similar to the Patriot's, stated that the concessions made by the Ice Trust were "the direct result of the warfare conducted by that much abused 'yellow' Journal of New York, which ever raises its voice in behalf of the plain people. No trust can stand a united people backed by a fearless and incorruptible newspaper such as the New York Journal."[50] Even the Times, a newspaper that would oppose Hearst and his methods for decades, praised the public service rendered by the Journal and declared that

72

Hearst had earned public gratitude.[51]

In June Hearst began to focus his attention on the November presidential election. The renominations of Bryan and McKinley were foregone conclusions. Hearst again supported Bryan, even more conspicuously than he had in 1896.

Prior to the Democratic national convention Governor Benton McMillan of Tennessee resigned as President of the National Association of Democratic Clubs, a loosely knit, ineffective, and nearly bankrupt organization enrolling nearly two millions members.[52] During a May meeting in Washington, D.C., conservative and progressive club leaders unanimously elected Hearst to serve as president.[53] It was hoped, stated Chauncey Black, who had served as the president of the clubs between 1887 and 1889, that Hearst could, by means of financial backing and newspaper publicity, turn the clubs into an effective political weapon in the November presidential election.[54]

This marked Hearst's entrance into organized politics, and it was in a position of national prominence. The Atlantic _Evening Journal_ suggested him as a possible vice-presidential nominee.[55] Initiating a membership drive, Hearst urged his readers to join the Democratic Clubs and printed membership forms in all of his newspapers. Daily he listed new and local club activities. Between May 20 and the first annual national convention of club delegates on October 3 and 4, the _Journal_ reported, over three million individuals became club members and there was a daily average of 500 new clubs.[56] Party leaders were impressed, wrote Democratic Congressman John Gaines from Tennessee, with Hearst's accomplishments in reaching and uniting the plain people in a way unique to the American political experience.[57]

Hearst demonstrated to Bryan and the Demo-

cratic party his support for them by establishing
a newspaper in the Middle West. He appointed
S. S. Carvalho, publisher of the Journal, editor
and publisher of the paper. On July 4, less
than a month after Carvalho's arrival in Chicago
and the day the party delegates convened in
Kansas City for their national convention, the
first edition of the Chicago American reached
the streets. Hearst wired Bryan that every
copy printed had been sold, an indication of
sentiment for the Democrats.[58] Bryan responded by congratulating Hearst on his remarkable accomplishments for the party and added, in
vague and flowery terms characteristically employed by political figures, that any Hearst
publication could be expected to espouse policies
supporting the rights and needs of all Americans
on all matters. Concerning the Chicago American,
Bryan wrote:

> The fact that the paper was established
> not merely to make money, but because of
> your desire to aid the Democratic party in
> its fight in the Central States, and because
> with expressed desires of Democratic leaders
> that you should duplicate in Chicago this
> year and the splendid work done by the
> Journal and the Examiner in '96, ought to
> commend the paper to the friends of Demo-
> cracy.[59]

The next day Bryan described Hearst as a dedicated fighter and leader in a struggle to protect individual rights against organized greed.[60]

Hearst in 1896 had been aware of Bryan's
political deficiencies, yet in 1900 he supported the Nebraskan because Bryan's positions
on issues were closer to his than were any other
candidate's.[61] In 1900 the Journal, as it
had been in 1896, was the only newspaper of
consequence along the North Atlantic seaboard to
support Bryan.[62] Hearst offered his telegraphic
services and political cartoons to smaller newspapers supporting Bryan.[63] He also wrote the
Democratic party's campaign book and engaged
Davenport to supply the illustrations.[64]

In the November election Bryan made a poorer showing than he had made four years earlier. He lost his home state of Nebraska, along with Kansas, South Dakota, Utah, and Wyoming--silver states that he had carried in 1896. McKinley's re-election meant that a conservative candidate had once again triumphed over a reform Democrat. Bryan failed, according to the Journal, because of the silver plank and because of his insistence on cutting ties completely with the Philippines.[65] Hearst added that Bryan's defeat was insured by Democrats who opposed him on temporary issues.[66] In the wake of Bryan's second consecutive defeat, the leadership of the Democratic party and the direction the party would take were very much in doubt.

The Journal, which had become the largest selling newspaper in the world and was increasing its circulation by over 7,000 a month, urged party leaders to adopt a progressive program.[67] Hearst believed that the time was right within the party for progressives to make a commitment to secure social legislation providing among other things for factory regulations and inspections, and limitations on child labor, women labor, and the hours of a work day.[68] The Journal, he told his swelling readership, was part of the "New Democracy," a growing social movement.[69] He made his New Democracy sound like an American tradition: it represented a return to the progressive ideals of Jefferson, Jackson, and Lincoln, he said, and was intended to enhance the self-regard of the working classes. Hearst, trafficking in the clichés to which he was continually given, noted that capitalism if properly checked by government controls could be beneficial in society. Being as ingenious and showy as ever, he published on November 8 what he titled the official national and official domestic policies of the New Democracy. Calling for a program of American expansion as opposed

75

to imperial exploitation, he urged the excavation and fortification of a Nicaraguan Canal, the annexation of Hawaii, the maintenance of a large navy and no more than a small standing army, the establishment of strategic bases in the West Indies, and the development of great national universities at West Point and Annapolis. Under internal policy he called for the direct election of United States Senators, the destruction of criminal and oppressive trusts, currency reform, improved school systems, governmental ownership of public franchises, and a graduated income tax.[70]

On November 9 the _Journal_ featured an open letter warning conservative Democrats that their party would be reorganized on progressive principles. It stated that in Bryan's defeat the progressive element of society received an impulse to organize for a peaceful revolution in which Hearst would play a major part.[71] Following his election to Congress, but before he assumed office, Hearst would write President Roosevelt:

> The core of the movement I will represent is composed of the masses of unrepresented and underprivileged peoples who have never before been institutionalized, are barely literate, and are relatively new and unfamiliar with the American political process.[72]

Speaking to supporters at a political rally in 1905, Hearst stated that his progressive program would operate within established institutions to change the status quo by orderly steps rather than by revolutionary means.[73]

While Hearst was travelling in Europe, an ominous attack on McKinley and his conservatism appeared in the _Journal_. It was in response to the assassination of Governor-elect William Goebel of Kentucky, and read in part:

76

The bullet that pierced Goebel's breast
Can not be found in all the west.
Good reason, it is speeding here.
To stretch McKinley on his bier.[74]

The poem was written by Ambrose Bierce without Hearst's knowledge.[75] The published personal attacks increased in number. A little over a year after Bierce's poem had been printed, a Brisbane editorial appeared that said, in reference to the President, "If bad institutions and bad men can be got rid of only by killing, then killing must be done."[76] The first editions reached the streets before Hearst read the editorial, stopped the presses, and removed the incitement to murder.[77] He then sent James Creelman to the White House with an olive branch. Creelman later wrote:

> Mr. Hearst offered to exclude from his papers anything that the President might find personally offensive. Also he pledged the President hearty support in all things as to which Mr. Hearst did not differ with him politically. The President seemed deeply touched by his wholly voluntary offer and sent a message of sincere thanks. These facts are given as an explanation of the actual terms upon which Mr. Hearst and Mr. McKinley were living when Czolgosz fired the fatal shot.[78]

Hearst's newspapers continued to increase in circulation and influence. For the month of November 1901 he sold over twenty-four million newspapers.[79] Lincoln Steffens, in a magazine article published in 1906, would describe Hearst as reaching more Americans at the turn of the century and doing more to protect and help the masses than any other reformer in the nation.[80] The publisher was riding a crest of national popularity when, on September 6, 1901 President McKinley was fatally shot by an anarchist, Leon Czolgosz. While the assassin testified under oath that he had never read a Hearst newspaper,[81] rival newspaper publishers reported that a copy of the _Journal_ had been in his pocket when he fired the fatal shot.[82] Roosevelt, who was serving as Vice-President, would continue to blame the shooting on the methods of yellow journalism. In his first message as President to Congress he referred to Czolgosz as one "inflamed by the teachings of professed anarchists, and probably also by the reckless utterances of those who, on the stump and in the public press, appeal to the dark and evil spirits of malice and greed, envy and sullen hatred."[83] It was obvious that Roosevelt had Hearst in mind.

For the first time since he had become a newspaper publisher Hearst was the target of widespread attacks. Conservative newspapers pointed to the dangers of arousing the masses.[84] The Grand Army of the Republic, meeting in Cleveland on September 14, passed a resolution, "That every member . . . exclude from his household 'The New York _Journal_,' a teacher of anarchism and a vile sheet, unfit for perusal by anyone who is a respecter of morality and good government."[85] There was an attempt at a general boycott of Hearst's newspapers and Hearst was hung in effigy nationwide. Hearst responded in his characteristically bellicose tone:

> From coast to coast this newspaper has been attacked and is being attacked with savage verocity by the incompetent, the fakers of journalism . . .
> One of Hearst papers' offenses is that they have fought for the people, and against privilege and class pride and class greed and class stupidity and class heartlessness with more daring weapons, with more force and talent and enthusiasm than any other newspaper in the country. . . .

78

> Note the thrift of the parasitic
> press . . . It would draw profits from the
> terrible deed of the wretch who shot down
> the President . . . [86]

But the publisher was sensitive enough to the
attacks that he renamed the _Journal_ the
American and decorated it with American flags.

Despite this cosmetic change, damage had
been done to the Hearst reputation; Hearst
needed to initiate some dramatic action or lead
another progressive campaign of national importance to restore the popularity and trust he had
enjoyed with the lower classes and the more
radical intellectuals. The anthracite coal
strike afforded him an opportunity.

Footnotes

[1]Frederickson, op. cit., p. 208.

[2]Hearst to Independent League Watchers, November 6, 1906, J.A.M.

[3]Hearst to the Chicago Iroquois Club, March 17, 1903, J.A.M.

[4]Abbot, op. cit., pp. 150-151.

[5]Older, op. cit., p. 205.

[6]Ibid., pp. 205-206.

[7]New York Times, February 13, 1953.

[8]New York Journal, May 10, 1899.

[9]New York Evening Journal, April 6, 1899.

[10]New York Evening Journal, April 8, 1899.

[11]New York Evening Journal, May 10, 1899; New York World, May 10, 1899.

[12]Hearst to Shearn, November 20, 1904, J.A.M.

[13]New York American, December 23, 1904.

[14]New York American, May 25, 1906.

[15]Older, op. cit., p. 208.

[16]New York American, February 24, 1906.

[17]New York Evening Journal, February 24, 1906.

[18]New York American, May 25, 1906.

[19]Ibid.

[20] New York _American_, June 16, 1906.

[21] Older, _op. cit._, p. 210.

[22] Shearn to Hearst, January 4, 1909, J.A.M.

[23] Older, _loc. cit._

[24] Ibid.

[25] Older, _op. cit._, p. 213.

[26] Ibid., pp. 213-214.

[27] New York _Evening Journal_, March 20, 1897.

[28] New York _Journal_, January 26, 1900.

[29] Isabel Ross, _Ladies of the Press_ (New York: Harper and Row Publishers, Inc., 1936), p. 24.

[30] New York _Evening Journal_, March 20, 1897.

[31] New York _Evening Journal_, January 23, 1913.

[32] New York _Journal_, March 25, 1899.

[33] Ibid.

[34] Older, _op. cit._, p. 215.

[35] Filler, _op. cit._, p. 136.

[36] Older, _op. cit._, p. 216.

[37] Filler, _loc. cit._

[38] Richard Hofstadter, _The Age of Reform From Bryan to F.D.R._ (New York: Alfred A. Knopf, Inc., 1955), p. 105.

[39] Hearst to Brisbane, June 10, 1900, J.A.M.

[40]Hearst to Abbot, November 7, 1896, J.A.M.

[41]Norman Pollack, The Populist Response to Industrial America (Cambridge: Harvard University Press, 1962), p. 9.

[42]Hearst to Abbot, November 11, 1896, J.A.M.

[43]Ibid.

[44]New York Journal, June 4, 1900.

[45]Older, op. cit., p. 226.

[46]New York Journal, June 5, 1900.

[47]Filler, loc. cit.

[48]New York Journal, June 4, 1900.

[49]New York Journal, May 24, 1900.

[50]New York Journal, May 25, 1900.

[51]Older, op. cit., p. 228.

[52]New York Journal, May 21, 1900.

[53]New York Journal, May 20, 1900.

[54]New York Evening Journal, May 21, 1900.

[55]Reprinted in New York Journal, June 5, 1900.

[56]New York Journal, October 4, 1900.

[57]Gaines (1897-1909) to Hearst, October 3, 1900, J.A.M.

[58]Hearst to Bryan, June 4, 1900, Bryan Papers, Library of Congress.

[59]Bryan to Hearst, July 4, 1900, J.A.M.

[60]Bryan to Hearst, July 5, 1900, J.A.M.

[61]Hearst to Bryan, July 6, 1900, Bryan Papers, Library of Congress.

[62]Walter S. Hutchins to Bryan, July 25, 1900, Bryan Papers, Library of Congress.

[63]H. L. Chaffee to Bryan, July 25, 1900, Bryan Papers, Library of Congress.

[64]Max F. Ihmsen to Bryan, July 24, 1900, Bryan Papers, Library of Congress.

[65]New York _Journal_, November 7, 1900.

[66]New York _Journal_, November 8, 1900.

[67]New York _Journal_, November 7, 1900.

[68]Hearst to Brisbane, November 6, 1900, J.A.M.

[69]New York _Journal_, November 8, 1900.

[70]_Ibid_.

[71]New York _Journal_, November 9, 1900.

[72]Hearst to Roosevelt, January 8, 1903, J.A.M.

[73]Hearst Political Speech at Staten Island, November 3, 1905, J.A.M.

[74]New York _Journal_, February 4, 1900.

[75]Interview with William Randolph Hearst, Jr., September 25, 1978.

[76]New York _Journal_, April 10, 1901.

[77]Interview with William Randolph Hearst, Jr., September 25, 1978.

[78] For Creelman's full account see: James Creelman, "The Real Mr. Hearst," _Pearson's_, September 1906, pp. 252-265.

[79] New York _Evening Journal_, December 4, 1902.

[80] Steffens, "Hearst, The Man of Mystery," _op. cit._, p. 13.

[81] Swanberg, _Citizen Hearst_, _op. cit._, pp. 193-194.

[82] New York _Tribune_, September 16, 1901.

[83] New York _Tribune_, December 4, 1901.

[84] Lundberg, _op. cit._, p. 94.

[85] Carlson and Bates, _op. cit._, p. 113.

[86] New York _Journal_, September 19, 1901.

IV

Stands with Organized Labor

When Hearst entered New York City in 1895
the attitude of organized labor officials had
been to avoid involvement in politics. The
American Federation of Labor had evolved
primarily for the protection of skilled labor,
for the preservation of the autonomy of national
craft unions, and for the attainment of immediate
economic advantages. Union leaders, especially
A. F. of L. President Samuel Gompers, had
historically preferred the development of
economic power as opposed to political power.[1]
At the 1895 A. F. of L. Convention, the delegates
adopted a plank that declared, "Party politics,
whether they be Democratic, Republican, Socialistic, Populistic, Prohibition, or any other,
shall have no place in the American Federation
of Labor."[2] The A. F. of L. had drawn a distinct
line between political action in the interest of
labor and party political action.[3] Leaders believed that political action would inevitably
lead to the formation of an independent labor
party.

In 1902 there was no single labor organization or labor position. The A. F. of L., with
over two million members, was the largest assem-
blage.[4] Gompers, President of the A. F. of L.
since its inception in 1886, influenced more than
any other individual the direction of the labor
movement. He concerned himself with specific
legislation on wages, work hours, and injunctions,
but was more concerned with organization, settling internal labor disputes, and continuity.
Labor had few friends and fewer levers of negotiating power. The strike was its greatest
threat and strength.

Hearst supported organized labor throughout his publishing career. He usually featured
strike related stories on the front pages of
his newspapers. _Journal_ and _Examiner_ editorials

consistently supported strikers in their demands for improved working conditions and salaries. During the anthracite coal strike in
1902 Hearst made every effort possible to arouse
strikers and those affected by the strike to
pressure labor and political leaders to force
negotiations and a settlement. "The strike,"
Hearst wrote Brisbane, "gives us an opportunity
to offset the widespread attacks /resulting from
the McKinley assassination/ and to again lead
a fight for labor unions and the needs of the
poor."[5]

The 1902 strike showed the many facets of
Hearst's relationship to organized labor. The
quality of testimony demonstrated that Hearst,
who used his press as a weapon to force negotiations, had the attention of politicians.
Henry T. Gage, Governor of California, wrote:

> I am very glad that William Randolph Hearst
> has taken up the subject /the anthracite
> coal strike/ through the medium of his
> papers . . . and I trust that something
> beneficial may be evolved from his . . .
> efforts.[6]

Hearst became a national spokesman for the labor
movement. Taking a public stand against the
coal operators, he urged President Roosevelt to
intervene in the strikers' behalf. Frank
Stebbins, Mayor of Iowa City, wrote Hearst:

> I am glad to see the American taking this
> step against the operators. . . . In my
> opinion the general public is entitled to
> some consideration, and in the present coal
> famine conditions the rights of the public
> are well-nigh paramount.[7]

The general strike in the anthracite coal
regions of Pennsylvania was one of the most
devastating strikes in American industrial
history. The miners had early succumbed to

monopolistic conditions,[8] living in company-owned housing,[9] and working long hours for meager wages.[10] The workers felt the power of the company on all sides. Early attempts by miners to organize were short lived. The United Mine Workers of America, organized in 1890, was the first union to achieve some success in the Pennsylvania anthracite region. In the fall of 1899, U. M. W. President John Mitchell went to the coal fields to help local chapters recruit miners. By January 1, 1900, ninety-two locals were established with a total membership of 8,893.[11]

The anthracite coal strike began in October of 1900. A temporary settlement quieted differences until April 1, 1902. The miners sought union recognition, a 20 percent wage increase, an eight-hour work day, and a uniform pay scale. The operators refused to negotiate on these demands. Consequently, one hundred forty thousand miners walked off their jobs in May 1902.[12]

The _American_ appealed for negotiations and a settlement. Throughout September, October, and November, it attacked the coal barons' monopoly and criticized the inaction of the Republican administration. During this period approximately two-thirds of the front page was devoted to the strike. As a rule, page two was exclusively devoted to the strike, national news was put on page three, and strike related stories on page six. Daily it ran fifteen to twenty articles in support of the miners. The Sunday editions averaged over thirty articles related to the strike. Hearst urged Roosevelt to enforce the Sherman Anti-Trust laws against the coal monopoly. He claimed to possess documentary evidence of the unlawful character of the coal combination.[13]

As the struggle dragged on for months, Roosevelt became increasingly concerned. "What is the reason," he asked Attorney General

Philander C. Knox, "we cannot proceed against
the coal operators as being engaged in a trust?
I ask it because it is a question continually
asked of me."[14] Knox responded that the President had no power or duty in the matter unless,
as in the decision in the "sugar trust" case,[15]
it could be shown there existed a corporate
pool for transportation.[16]

Hearst petitioned Roosevelt and Knox to
institute anti-trust proceedings against the
major coal companies, and coal hauling railroads.[17] These railroad companies, claimed
Hearst, controlled the only practical means of
transporting coal from the anthracite coal
fields to the inhabitants of various states of
the United States, and were thus violating
Chapter 647 of the Sherman Anti-Trust Act.[18]
He charged:

> . . . the railroad companies engaged in
> mining and transporting coal are practi-
> cally in a combination to control the out-
> put and fix the price which the public
> pays for this necessary article of con-
> sumption. There is substantially no com-
> petition existing between these companies.
> The only limitation to their demands is
> the indisposition on the part of the public
> to buy their product at an exorbitant
> price.[19]

Hearst presented documented evidence to
Attorney General Knox that these companies controlled 96.52 percent of the anthracite coal
sold in the United States in 1900. He charged
that while none of the companies, except the
Delaware, Lackawanna and Western, were permitted
by their charters to operate coal mines or to own
stock in coal mining companies, all of them
except the Delaware, Lackawanna and Western
Company and the New York, Ontario, and Western
Railroad Company, which owned their own coal
mines, owned and controlled both the mining and

and the selling businesses. His suit detailed
the relationships between each of the railroads and its subsidiaries in the coal mining
industry. Although he is accused of sloppiness
in reporting, this was an example of Hearst's
commitment to accuracy in the pursuit of a
working class benefit. In his petition Hearst
wrote:

> For example: Said Reading Company owns and
> operates coal mines through a subsidiary
> company called the Philadelphia and Reading
> Coal and Iron Company, the entire stock of
> which is owned by said railroad company . . .
> Said Central Railroad Company of New Jersey
> owns and operates coal mines, through a sub-
> sidiary company called the Lehigh and
> Wilkes-Barre Coal Company, the entire capi-
> tal stock of which is owned by said rail-
> road company, said companies having practi-
> cally the same officers and directors . . .
> Similarly, the Lehigh Valley Railroad Com-
> pany owns and operates coal mines by means
> of a subsidiary or holding company called
> the Lehigh Valley Coal Company; the Erie
> Railroad Company, by means of the Penn-
> sylvania Coal Company and Hillside Coal
> and Iron Company; the Delaware and Hudson
> Company, by means of Union Coal Company, and
> the Pennsylvania Railroad Company, by means
> of the Scranton Coal Company.
> That in and prior to March 1901 of the
> entire area of said anthracite coal field
> 92.32 percent thereof, was owned by said
> railroad companies and said subsidiary
> or holding companies.[20]

Hearst charged that these railroad companies had formed a monopoly and acted in concert
and combination to systematically eliminate competition in the sale of anthracite coal, constituting restraint upon commerce among the
states. In February 1899, anticipating an attempt
of the independent coal operators in the Wyoming

field to organize and construct a railroad to
procure a lower rate of transportation, company directors gained control of the Temple
Iron Company.[21] Within days the capital stock
of the company increased in value from
$240,000 to $2,866,000, and by the month's
end the company purchased the coal mines in
the Wyoming field owned by the most influential
independent mine operators who were supporting
the plan to organize a rail line.[22] J.
Pierpont Morgan, who held a majority of the
capital stock of the Reading Railroad Company
and Erie Railroad Company purchased, in January
1901, the entire capital stock of the Pennsylvania Coal Company, the most powerful
independent operator of coal mines and the chief
support of the movement to establish an independent transportation route. He had thus
eliminated competition in the sale of coal within New York and in the transportation of coal
between Pennsylvania and New York.[23]

Hearst alleged that the president's of the
respective railroad companies met regularly
at the office of the Central Railroad of New
Jersey at 143 Liberty Street, New York City,
to fix a uniform price for anthracite coal, to
control the output of anthracite coal, and to
adopt measures calculated to make effective a
combination between their companies. In March
1901, these representatives agreed, contrary to
law, to maintain a uniform price for coal mined
in the state of Pennsylvania. Within a month
there was a marked increase in the price of coal.

The charges Hearst made in his petition to
Knox were based on committee reports of the
United States House of Representatives, the
Senate of the United States, and the Senate of
the State of New York, and on the report of
Carroll D. Wright, United States Commissioner of
Labor, to the President of the United States in
June 1902, relative to the coal strike. Accord-
ing to a letter Roosevelt wrote to William Allen

92

White, Hearst privately contacted the President and offered to turn over all of the evidence in his possession, and promised that he would apply no newspaper pressure if the President took an active role in bringing about a settlement.[24] Roosevelt disclaimed any right or duty to intervene in the coal strike on any legal grounds or in any official capacity.[25] It was not the responsibility of the federal government, he said, to interfere in any way in employer-employee relations.[26]

Knox prepared a lenghty report in which he grouped the presidential advisers' alternatives under four heads: to engage military power to restrain interference; to employ some form of equitable remedy to compel operations; to use eminent domain to condemn the mines and to then operate them for public benefit; or to institute a suit against the coal operators or against the members of the United Mine Workers' organization as a combination in restraint of trade. Quoting constitutional provisions, court decisions, and legislative enactments, Knox informed Roosevelt that he could not constitutionally act on any of these proposals, that he could only act on legitimate restraint of trade suits like the one Hearst had submitted.[27]

On October 5 the _American_ urged Congress, which represented the Americans affected by the strike, to initiate action to secure a settlement.[28] Congressmen sympathizing with Hearst's efforts were helpless in the Republican-controlled Congress. Congressman Charles Bartlett from Georgia wrote:

> The _American_ is engaged in a work for the good of the people, and it should receive the endorsement and encouragement of everybody.
> It is doing the only thing that can possibly bring relief to the people at present, and if its efforts fail I know of nothing that can be done until Congress meets.

Indeed, I am not sure Congress can
devise any means for helping the situation.
I do not wish to say anything about the
legal aspect of the cause, for that is to
be decided by the courts; but I regard the
American's fight as one in which the American
people are greatly interested and concerned.[29]

Congressman J. N. Williamson of Oregon could not
see Congress doing anything in the matter. He
wrote to Hearst:

The coal operators are too arrogant, and
something must be done to bring them to
terms. In my opinion the American's proceedings are the only way to awaken them
to a sense of the situation.[30]

Hearst directed efforts to bring the strike
to an end. His newspapers proposed arbitration.
He established a mediation committee composed of
Cardinal Gibbons, John Wannamaker, former Vice
President Stevenson, former Associate Justice
Robert Pryor, and John Dewitt Warner. Hundreds
of Democrats and Republicans sent Hearst telegrams congratulating him on taking a public
stand to force a negotiated settlement. Republican Governor Wells of Utah wrote that
Hearst's plan for a mediation committee was the
most promising proposal thus far.[31] Oklahoma
Governor William Grimes said that Hearst's
actions appealed to the seventy million Americans
who were being robbed and insulted by a handful
of coal barons.[32] L. B. Thomas, Mayor of
Bloomington, Illinois, asserted:

I endorse the action of the American, and I
am sure that the best majority of American
people will take the same view. The position of the local barons has been dicta-
torial and so uncompromising that it has
aroused the anger of the whole nation.[33]

Hearst's voluntary arbitration committee was ineffective but its example helped Roosevelt finally to accept the idea of arbitration.[34] Roosevelt, wanting a commission whose personnel would insure popular support, asked ex-President Cleveland to head a commission which was to make "a full and careful investigation of the present conditions and of the causes that have let to these conditions, including the question whether there has been violence and if so, to what extent; and what, if any, steps should be taken to prevent the recurrence of these conditions."[35] Cleveland reluctantly agreed to assume the service, stating that he considered it his duty to accept.[36] Others requested to serve on the commission were Marvin Hughett, president of the Chicago and Northwestern Railroad Company, Judge William R. Day of the United States Sixth Circuit Court at Cincinnati; John Kernan, noted New York lawyer; and Edgar E. Clark, grand chief of the Order of Railway Conductors.[37] All except Hughett agreed to serve,[38] but the commission never convened.

Hearst decided to take the coal barons to court. On September 10 he sent Shearn to Albany to petition New York Attorney General J. C. Davies to begin anti-trust proceedings against the coal trusts. In early October he secured a trial date. Again Hearst was widely praised for his actions. Mayor A. L. McLeod, from Selma, Alabama, wrote:

> I endorse the _American_'s course. This is the time to test the law, and if it is not effective, then pass one that is. The coal operators are a good set to test it on.[39]

Congressman James Hemenway from Indiana expressed a similar view:

> I sincerely hope that the provisions

95

of the Sherman Anti-Trust Law will reach
this conspiracy. I regard it as a conspiracy for the reason that a few men have
been able to cause untold suffering and
misery.

I further hope that the members of
the anthracite Coal Trust will be pro-
secuted and brought to justice. I believe this is the most effective way of
dealing a blow at the great Coal Trust.

The _American_ deserves great credit
for the stand it has taken on behalf of
the coal miners. If the Sherman Anti-
Trust law is enforced to the letter, the
coal operators will be brought to time.[40]

Hearst enlisted many of the most prominent citizens of New York--church, business,
university and civic leaders--to go to
Harrisburg, Pennsylvania, to petition Governor
William A. Stone to intervene in the strike
to force a settlement. The petition urged the
Governor to convene the state legislature in
extraordinary session to enact legislation to
alleviate hardships resulting from the strike
and to bring it to a quick end.[41]

Hearst employed the methods of yellow
journalism in an effort to create enthusiasm
among his readers and to instill in them a sense
of responsibility, power, and involvement.[42]
In early October a petition addressed to
President Roosevelt appeared daily on the front
page of all Hearst newspapers. Readers were
urged to cut it out, sign it, and send it to
the President. It read:

We, your petitioners, pray that without
delay you will order the Department of
Justice to further the _American_'s suit,
which demands not only the disruption of
the coal trust, but the indictment as
criminals of the Presidents of the con-
federated coal mining railroad companies

96

which have defied and insulted you, and
in their immeasured arrogance ignore what
you have well described as the urgency and
terrible nature of the catastrophe impending over a large portion of the
people in the shape of a winter fuel famine.
Enforce the Sherman Anti-Trust Act
against these public enemies, Mr. President.
Order their immediate indictment as criminals.[43]

Hearst's attempt to force the courts, the
Congress, and the President to assume responsibility and to act in the coal famine became the
major campaign issue for three governors, fourteen United States Congressmen, and over sixty
candidates for lesser offices.[44] On October 1,
the Washington _Post_ observed that Republican
leaders in the states along the northeastern
seaboard were becoming alarmed at the effect
the coal shortage could have on the November
elections.[45] Republican Senator Henry Cabot
Lodge of Massachusetts wrote to Roosevelt, "We
don't care whether you are to blame or not.
Coal is going up and the party in power must be
punished. . . . By the first week in November,
if the strike does not stop and the coal begins
to go down we shall have an overturn."[46] Lodge
opposed government intervention in the strike,[47]
but nevertheless he asked the President, "Is
there anything we can appear to do?"[48]
Roosevelt told the senator:

There is literally nothing, so far as
I have been able to find out, which the
national government has any power to do in
the matter. Nor can I even imagine any re-
medial measure of immediate benefit that
could be taken in Congress. . . . I am at
wit's end how to proceed.[49]

Roosevelt did not act until he believed
that it was politically necessary. Intense
public pressure compelled the President to inter-

97

vene in the negotiations in behalf of the public whose welfare had been jeopardized and whose interest transcended that of either of the contending parties.[50] On October 1 Roosevelt sent telegrams to Mitchell and the presidents of the leading anthracite coal companies requesting them to meet with him in Washington on October 3. This, the first instance in which the chief executive intervened directly between the forces of capital and labor to avert a national calamity, met with general approval in New York City. Mayor Seth Low was pleased that Roosevelt was attempting to use the influence attached to his position.[51] The conservative New York _Tribune_ conceded that the President's decision to act would "excite great interest and general approval throughout the country."[52]

The conference was held on October 3 at the temporary White House on Jackson Place.[53] During the conference the operators pointed to the lawlessness and crime then existing in the coal region, and John Mitchell presented a detailed explanation of the mine workers' proposal to have the President appoint a tribunal to decide the questions at issue. Neither side would concede any issue and the conference dissolved. Roosevelt wrote Hanna:

> Well, I have tried and failed. I feel downhearted over the result because of the great misery ahead for the mass of our people, and because the attitude of the operators will beyond a doubt double the burden on us who stand between them and socialistic action. But I am glad I tried anyhow. I should have hated to feel that I had failed to make any effort. . . .[54]

On October 3 Secretary of War Elihu Root drafted a proposal envisioning the immediate resumption of mining and the appointment of a presidential commission which would consider the questions at issue between the operators and

98

their workers.   Root wrote to J. P. Morgan:

> I think such a proposal to the operators
> would relieve them from injurious effect
> /of/ a very widespread impression that
> they are unwilling to arbitrate differ-
> ences with their workmen in a practical
> way, but at the same time it would avoid
> the objection to dealing with the Mine
> Workers Union. On the other hand, if
> Mitchell should refuse to favor such a plan,
> it would put him in the position of not
> really fighting for arbitration but rather
> for control of his own union over the
> anthracite field.[55]

On October 9 Morgan agreed that "the real issue
as it had been developed was not a question of
whether there should be arbitration of the
merits, but a question of arbitrating with the
United Mine Workers of America."[56] Both the
operators and the strikers approved Root's proposal.[57] On October 16 Roosevelt appointed the
seven-member commission.[58] The miners reported
to work on October 23 and the commission met on
October 24.[59]

The commission conducted hearings until
March 18, 1903; the full report was released to
the public on March 21.[60] In its findings the
commission held that the life of the mine
workers was not so bad as pictured by the
representatives of labor but that the rates of
wages to these workers were lower than those
paid in occupations requiring equal skill and
training. While dismissing union recognition
as not within the scope of its jurisdiction,
the commission strongly endorsed the principles
of trade unionism and collective bargaining.

The commission's report was generally interpreted as a victory for the miners even though
there was no outright recognition of their union.
The American, World, Sun, and Evening Post called

99

it a sweeping victory for the United Mine Workers.[61] "As to the specific awards of the commission in regard to wages, hours, and other matters which gave occasion for the strike," said the _Journal of Commerce_, "these are altogether favorable to the miners."[62] The _Times_ held that the report distinctly put the operators in the wrong,[63] and the _American Federationist_ declared that it justified the hopes and predictions of labor's friends and sympathizers.[64] The mine workers' publication termed it a good decision.[65] The report on the whole was fair and just, wrote John Mitchell, and would insure for labor members a greater measure of justice than was ever accorded them.[66]

Hearst and his _American_ claimed credit for the settlement, but Roosevelt's actions cannot specifically or explicitly be connected with Hearst-generated pressure. Yet Hearst did arouse public opinion to such a pitch, Lodge wrote Roosevelt, that a break would have to come from the "acuteness of the strain."[67] Mitchell observed that the _American_ was directing "terrific" public pressure entirely upon the operators.[68] The New York _World_ labelled the terms of settlement "practically a surrender to public opinion and to the exigencies of the situation."[69]

Hearst's efforts were unique both to the labor movement and to the nation's political experience. He had become labor's most powerful spokesman and was the first newspaper publisher to support striking union members on a national scale. He was also showing, over the objections of Gompers and many labor leaders, that labor would get more effective power in social matters by becoming more involved in the political process. Hearst would later write:

> I think we should congratulate Mr.
> Gompers and the labor leaders for having
> seen the light and for having at last come

to realize that the labor cause is best advanced through a liberal, humanitarian, political movement which represents the interests of all the plain people.

Years ago the Hearst papers began to promote the best interests of labor.

They supported the labor union movement, organized labor unions in their own establishments, and encouraged them in other industries.

They helped as much as any other influence to unify this great movement and to secure for labor its due rights and advantages as far as these things could be secured through economic and social movements.

But Hearst /‾papers‾/ realized at that time that the economic or social movements could only go a certain distance and to secure full recognition and consideration the producing classes, would have to organize politically as well as economically.

We urged this political organization in many editorials, but the realization of this political power was thwarted at the time by the opposition of Mr. Gompers and the labor leaders.[70]

Hearst realized that Gompers was cautiously conservative, but he believed that the rank and file laborers were radically liberal. He confided to Brisbane that Gompers was not the epitome of the labor movement and that the American should continue to make its appeal to them.[71] Gompers maintained that the labor movement should remain independent from political activity or alliances.[72]

In September 1902 Gompers began expressing appreciation to Hearst newspapers for their continued efforts in behalf or organized labor. A friendly correspondence had developed between Gompers and Brisbane since Brisbane went to work for Hearst. These letters are generally short

and almost exclusively on a personal level.
There are few instances when either writer
shared his views on the labor movement. Following a Hearst monetary donation to organized
labor which he requested should remain anonymous,
Gompers wrote:

> Of course I am bound to respect Mr.
> Hearst's request that his name be not
> mentioned as the donor of the money but
> I feel that inasmuch as so much influence
> is sought to be wielded against him and
> his newspaper enterprises, that in justice
> to him and as offset to the unkind ex-
> pressions it would not be amiss to have it
> known that the donation comes from him.[73]

Gompers wrote that Hearst's financial aid and
publicity were invaluable to the miners.[74] He
added that both the destitute families of the
striking miners[75] and the nation's underprivileged affected by the strike were indebted
to the publisher for the monetary drives he had
organized on their behalf.[76] To Mitchell the
labor leader wrote that Hearst had played a
major role in keeping the strikers united. This
was accomplished because of "public opinion and
the spirit of the people which really demanded
justice for the miners."[77] Gompers seriously
considered a Hearst offer to join the
American's staff.[78] He declined the offer,
choosing to remain President of the A. F. of L.

Gompers wrote that the labor movement was
a part of a general social awareness spurred by
yellow journalism but insisted that labor stay
clear of politics.[79] In response to a labor
organizer who requested permission for his local
union chapter to endorse a Congressionsl candidate in the November elections, as the American
was urging, Gompers wrote:

> I beg to refer you to Article III,
> Section 8 of the Constitution of the

102

A. F. of L. which reads as follows:
'Party politics . . . shall have no place
in the conventions of the American Federation of Labor.' While this provision of
the Constitution decrees the course for
the conventions of the American Federation of Labor, it is also a declaration of
policies and principles, and hence, applies
to all affiliated organizations.[80]

Hearst wrote that he had shown union members the advantages of political involvement.
He noted:

> The President settled the strike be-
> cause public opinion demanded it. That
> shows he has the power to act when he sees
> fit. Elected officials more sympathetic
> to the cause of the laborers would be to
> their obvious advantage. If labor leaders
> could be made to see that their member-
> ship could be used as a political weapon
> or of the advantages of aligning their
> movement to a political party, they would
> realize that such action would be self-
> serving.[81]

The strike left an indelible impression on the
American public. Roosevelt believed that the
labor movement had entered a new phase.[82] Urban
sensational newspapers were reaching the rank and
file laborers and were producing a "growing intelligence" among them.[83] The Rochester (New
York) _Herald_ stated:

> In taking up the gage of battle in the
> interests of the people we have no doubt
> that Mr. Hearst will be accused of sensa-
> tional methods.
> Be that as it may, when sworn officers
> of the law refuse or neglect to take the
> initiative in such matters which so vitally
> concern interests of the people it is
> fortunate that a newspaper has behind it a

man with the ability, the energy, and the
means to step into the breach and do battle
for a just cause.[84]

The strike was thus crucial, Hearst wrote, "in
understanding changing attitudes of politicians
toward organized labor." He added,

> Politicians will have a much more difficult
> task appeasing the conservative labor
> leaders. The rank and file laborer would
> do himself more good to join the new Demo-
> cracy than to passively allow the labor
> movement to continue on its present course.[85]

John Mitchell sent numerous telegrams and
letters to Hearst, thanking him both for his
monetary contributions to the striking families
and for all the monetary drives he organized
in their behalf, and supporting his newspaper
methods in informing the nation of the plight
of the miners and in forcing a favorable settlement.[86] Every District President whose local
had gone on strike wrote to Hearst expressing
appreciation for his efforts. A representative
letter read:

> We the undersigned take this oppor-
> tunity and means to convey to you an
> expression of our thanks for the favorable
> attitude maintained toward us by you
> through your papers . . . during the five
> month struggle for justice.
> Fairness has characterized the pre-
> sentation of the strike issues in the
> editorials and the news columns of your
> newspapers, and this has acted as an
> important asset to us an is fully apprecia-
> ted.[87]

Hearst and the American urged the labor
movement to align itself with the Democratic
party in the 1902 Congressional elections. A
November 6 Hearst editorial, entitled "Labor-

Democracy's Natural Ally," publicly urged the union of the labor movement with the progressive wing of the Democratic party. He wrote:

> The Democratic party must associate itself intimately and sincerely with the working people of this country. . . .
> If the Democrats would succeed they must establish with the leaders of labor the relationship which the Republicans have established with the leaders of the Trusts. . . .
> The Democratic party must join with the laboring citizenship of the nation—the backbone of the nation. The Democratic party must give to the man who works the encouragement, support, and the legal protection which the Republican party gives to the Trusts. . . .
> The Democratic party must find its strength and combat the trusts through united and compact organization of the people. . . .
> In the great LABOR unions the Democrats must find the foundation of popular organization and a weapon which shall enable the people to combat the Trusts and control them.
> All recent political events prove that the great political force residing in a combination of TRUSTS AND REPUBLICANISM can be met successfully by a combination of LABOR AND DEMOCRACY.[88]

Hearst's actions during the strike resulted in positive national publicity. As he taught union members the importance and advantages of political awareness and political activity, so too did he realize the need of a new breed of politicians sympathetic to these views. In 1896 and 1900 he balanced personal convictions with self promotion. In 1902, although he did benefit from an increasing newspaper circulation during the coal strike, he was concerned with

bringing about social advancement for the underprivileged. He confided to Brisbane:

> The strike has taught many lessons to us
> all. It has taught me that we must enter
> the political process to force that process
> to change, to acquire a conscience for the
> social evils in America and a willingness
> to correct them. [89]

Footnotes

[1] Marc Karson, _American Labor Unions and Politics, 1900-1918_ (Boston: Beacon Press, 1958), p. 20.

[2] American Federation of Labor, _Proceedings_, 1895, p. 79.

[3] _Annual Report of the A. F. of L. Convention_, Cincinnati, 1896.

[4] Gompers to George Olney, October 13, 1902, A. F. of L. Papers, Library of Congress.

[5] Hearst to Brisbane, September 1, 1902, J.A.M.

[6] Gage to Brisbane, October 12, 1902, J.A.M.

[7] Stebbins to Hearst, October 12, 1900, J.A.M.

[8] S. Perlman and P. Taft, _History of Labor in the United States_ (New York: Macmillan Company, 1922), p. 31.

[9] John Mitchell, _Organized Labor_ (Philadelphia: American Book and Bible House, 1903), p. 357.

[10] _Ibid._

[11] _Ibid._, p. 365.

[12] United Mine Workers of America, _Minutes of Joint Conference of Districts_ 1,7,9, (1902), pp. 25-28.

[13] New York _American_, October 6, 1902.

[14] Roosevelt to Knox, August 21, 1902, Roosevelt Papers, Library of Congress.

[15]United States v. E. C. Knight Co., 156 U. S. 1 (1895). The government brought suit for the dissolution of the American Sugar Refining Company which had secured control of 90 percent of the manufacture of all refined sugar in the country. The Supreme Court, drawing a sharp distinction between manufacturing and commerce, held that the Sherman Anti-Trust Act did not apply because the law was directed only against combinations directly involved in interstate commerce and could not affect companies engaged in production.

[16]Roosevelt to W. Murray Crane, October 22, 1902, Roosevelt Papers, Library of Congress.

[17]Hearst to Roosevelt, October 4, 1902, Roosevelt Papers, Library of Congress.

[18]Hearst to Knox, October 4, 1902, Roosevelt Papers, Library of Congress.

[19]Hearst to Roosevelt, October 4, 1902, Roosevelt Papers, Library of Congress.

[20]Petition of William Randolph Hearst to Honorable Philander C. Knox, October 4, 1902, Roosevelt Papers, Library of Congress.

[21]The Temple Iron Company, organized under the laws of the state of Pennsylvania in 1873, operated an iron furnace in Reading, Pennsylvania and was not engaged in the business of coal mining. The names of the directors and the railroad companies of which they are officers and their percent of stock in the Temple Iron Company were as follows:
George F. Baer,
        Reading......................42.25 percent
Eben B. Thomas,
        Central R. R. of N. J. ......17.30 percent
F. D. Underwood,
        Erie........................ 2.59 percent

William Truesdale,
   Delaware, Lackawanna, and Western..... 6.55 per
Alfred Walter,   cent
   Lehigh Valley R. R. Co. ....16.87 per
R. M. Olyphant,   cent
   Delaware and Hudson Co. .... 2.29 per
Thomas P. Fowler,   cent
   N. Y., Ontario and Western............ .28 per
Irving A. Stearns,   cent
   Delaware, Susquehanna, and Schuykill.. 1.38 per
   _____ cent

                                        89.51 per
                                              cent

[22]Petition of William Randolph Hearst to
Honorable Philander C. Knox, October 4, 1902,
Roosevelt Papers, Library of Congress.

   [23]Ibid.

   [24]Roosevelt to White, October 6, 1902,
White Papers, Library of Congress.

   [25]"Roosevelt's Remarks at the Opening of
the Washington Conference," October 3, 1902,
Roosevelt Papers, Library of Congress.

   [26]"Roosevelt's Address at the National
Convention of Employers and Employees,"
September 25, 1902, Roosevelt Papers, Library
of Congress.

   [27]Knox to Roosevelt, October 10, 1902,
Roosevelt Papers, Library of Congress.

   [28]New York American, October 5, 1902.

   [29]Bartlett to Hearst, October 12, 1902,
J.A.M.

   [30]Williamson to Hearst, October 12, 1902,
J.A.M.

[31]Wells to Hearst, October 13, 1902, J.A.M.

[32]Grimes to Hearst, October 13, 1902, J.A.M.

[33]Thomas to Hearst, October 12, 1902, J.A.M.

[34]Roosevelt to Joseph B. Bishop, October 5, 1902, Roosevelt Papers, Library of Congress.

[35]Roosevelt to Cleveland, October 10, 1902, Roosevelt Papers, Library of Congress.

[36]Cleveland to Roosevelt, October 12, 1902, Roosevelt Papers, Library of Congress.

[37]Telegrams sent October 11, 1902, Roosevelt Papers, Library of Congress.

[38]Day to Roosevelt, October 14, 1902, Roosevelt Papers, Library of Congress; Kernan to Roosevelt, October 12, 1902, Roosevelt Papers, Library of Congress; Clark to Roosevelt, October 15, 1902, Roosevelt Papers, Library of Congress; Hughett to Roosevelt, October 14, 1902, Roosevelt Papers, Library of Congress.

[39]McLeod to Hearst, October 12, 1902, J.A.M.

[40]Hemenway to Hearst, October 12, 1902, J.A.M.

[41]New York _American_, October 6, 1902.

[42]Hearst to Brisbane, October 1, 1902, J.A.M.

[43]New York _American_, October 15, 1902.

[44]Telegrams to Hearst, J.A.M.

[45]Washington _Post_, October 1, 1902.

110

[46]Lodge to Roosevelt, September 22, 1902, Roosevelt Papers, Library of Congress.

[47]Lodge to Roosevelt, September 25, 1902, Roosevelt Papers, Library of Congress.

[48]Lodge to Roosevelt, September 27, 1902, Roosevelt Papers, Library of Congress.

[49]Roosevelt to Lodge, September 27, 1902, Roosevelt Papers, Library of Congress.

[50]A. M. Schlesinger, _Political and Social History of the United States_ (New York: Macmillan Company, 1925), p. 448.

[51]Low to Roosevelt, October 2, 1902, Roosevelt Papers, Library of Congress.

[52]New York _Tribune_, October 2, 1902.

[53]Those in attendance were President George Baer of the Reading; President William Truesdale of the Lackawanna; President Thomas Fowler of the New York, Ontario and Western; Chairman Eben Thomas of Erie; David Wilcox, vice-president and general counsel of the Delaware and Hudson; John Markle, representing the independent operators; John Mitchell representing the United Mine Workers; Thomas D. Nichols, Thomas Duffy, and John Fahy, district presidents of the United Mine Workers; Attorney General Knox; Secretary George Cortelyou; and Carroll D. Wright.

[54]Roosevelt to Hanna, October 3, 1902, Roosevelt Papers, Library of Congress.

[55]Root to Morgan, October 9, 1902, Root Papers, Library of Congress.

[56]Root to Mark Sullivan, June 6, 1927, Root Papers, Library of Congress.

[57]New York _American_, October 19, 1902.

[58]White House Press Release, October 16, 1902, Roosevelt Papers, Library of Congress. The members were: Brigadier General John M. Wilson; Mr. E. W. Parker, chief statistician of the Coal Division of the United States Geological Survey and an editor of the Engineering and Mining Journal of New York; Judge George Gray; Mr. E. E. Clark, Chief of the Order of Railway Conductors; Mr. Thomas H. Watkins, "as a man practically acquainted with the mining and selling of coal"; Bishop John L. Spaulding; and Carroll D. Wright, to serve as recorder of the commission.

[59]New York American, October 25, 1902.

[60]There is a typewritten copy of the report in the Roosevelt Papers, Library of Congress.

[61]New York American, World, Sun, Evening Post, March 24, 1903.

[62]New York Journal of Commerce, March 23, 1903.

[63]New York Times, March 24, 1903.

[64]"'Baerism' Dealt a Crushing Blow," American Federationist, May 1903, p. 370. J.A.M.

[65]United Mine Workers Journal, March 26, 1903, J.A.M.

[66]John Mitchell, "The Ascent of Labor," Collier's Weekly, April 11, 1903, p. 12, J.A.M.

[67]Lodge to Roosevelt, October 11, 1902, Roosevelt Papers, Library of Congress.

[68]Mitchell to H. N. Taylor, October 11, 1902, A. F. of L. Papers, Library of Congress.

[69]New York World, October 15, 1902.

[70]Hearst to Brisbane, August 28, 1924, J.A.M.

[71]Hearst to Brisbane, October 7, 1902, J.A.M.

[72]Gompers to Alice H. Sotheral, October 16, 1902, A. F. of L. Papers, Library of Congress.

[73]Gompers to Brisbane, September 15, 1902, A. F. of L. Papers, Library of Congress.

[74]Gompers to Brisbane, September 23, 1902, A. F. of L. Papers, Library of Congress.

[75]Gompers to Hearst, October 15, 1902, A. F. of L. Papers, Library of Congress.

[76]Gompers to Brisbane, September 27, 1902, A. F. of L. Papers, Library of Congress.

[77]Gompers to Mitchell, October 15, 1902, A. F. of L. Papers, Library of Congress.

[78]Gompers to Brisbane, October 20, 1902, A. F. of L. Papers, Library of Congress.

[79]Gompers to Mitchell, October 24, 1902, A. F. of L. Papers, Library of Congress.

[80]Gompers to Fred Ingalls, November 4, 1902, A. F. of L. Papers, Library of Congress.

[81]Hearst to Brisbane, October 16, 1902, J.A.M.

[82]Theodore Roosevelt, An Autobiography, (New York: Charles Scribner's Sons, 1926), p. 461.

[83]"A Great Battle Splendidly Fought," American Federationist, November 1902, p. 807, J.A.M.

[84]New York American, November 30, 1902.

[85]Hearst to Brisbane, October 15, 1902, J.A.M.

[86]Mitchell to Hearst, October 22, 1902, J.A.M.

[87]Thomas Duffy (President, District #7, U.M.W.A.), Thomas D. Nichols (President, District #1, U.M.W.A.), and John Fahy (President, District #9, U.M.W.A.), to Hearst, November 15, 1902, J.A.M.

[88]New York _American_, November 6, 1902.

[89]Hearst to Brisbane, October 28, 1902, J.A.M.

V

An Absentee Progressive Congressman

In response to a Hearst request, Tammany
Hall leader Charles Murphy offered Brisbane the
Democratic nomination to the United States
Congress from the Eleventh District.[1] Brisbane
was Hearst's initial choice to be a political
candidate of the "New Democracy."[2] Brisbane
believed that Hearst, who had established his
sixth newspaper, would be a more appealing candidate because of his name recognition and because
of his existing ties to the Democratic party
leadership.[3] Hearst initially set his sights
on New York City's Eleventh District, a Democratic stronghold with no announced Congressional
candidates. The district was a cosmopolitan
area--stretching across Manhattan, including
the slums of the West side, the mansions of
Park Avenue, and the business district of Broad-
way. Hearst later explained his decision to
accept the Tammany nomination:

> My early ambition was to do my best in
> newspapers, and I still propose to do a
> newspaper part. But when I saw Mayors
> and Governors and Presidents fail, I felt
> that I'd like to see if I couldn't do
> better. I'd like to go into office, any
> office almost, to see if I can't do the
> things I want to see done.[4]

Hearst entered politics hoping to champion
the needs of the discontented in what he believed was a tradition common to Thomas
Jefferson, Andrew Jackson, and Abraham Lincoln.
In a letter to former Congressman Jacob Lentz,
he interpreted these leaders as men as the
embodiment of the common will of their times,
and clearly foreshadowed the role he would try
to fill himself:

> The history of the country is really the
> history of a few great men. In these men

115

are crystallized the country's real life and
worth. Theirs is the genius which gives
expression and reality to the convictions
and principles of the people whom they represent . . . All three of these men stood
for the rights of the people, and their
views have been represented in every
great practical movement until these
latter days.[5]

He believed that the masses of plain people in
America were being exploited by political
leaders. Thinking of himself as a great man, he
aimed to aid these people by fighting privilege
with the weapons of his own personal wealth as
Jefferson had. He confided to a friend that
he would fashion his political life in the mold
of Jefferson:

Though a man of considerable wealth, of
excellent family connection, and of unparalleled political position, Jefferson
always taught by precept and example the
superiority of dignity and simplicity over
pomp. Though no man ever suffered more
from printed malice, Jefferson understood
and proclaimed the necessity of a free
press as the guardian of Republican liberty.[6]

In 1902 Hearst was a loyal Democrat and
worked to elect party candidates, even Tammany
nominees. Republican Governor Benjamin Odell,
Jr. was seeking re-election as Governor. The
leading candidates for the Democratic party's
nomination were Bird Coler, New York State
Comptroller, and former three-term Governor
David B. Hill, who had been defeated in 1894
by Levi Morton. Murphy backed Coler because his
election would give Tammany effective control of
New York City affairs. Murphy, Brisbane, and
Hearst worked out a mutual agreement in which
the Hearst newspapers would endorse Coler in
exchange for the Eleventh District Democratic

116

party's Congressional nomination. Confiding to Brisbane, Hearst wrote that he would have supported Coler without the deal.[7] Hearst's papers endorsed Coler and he won the nomination but lost the subsequent election.[8]

On October 6, 1902, a delegation of Tammany leaders called upon Hearst in his private room at the Hoffman House and solemnly informed him that he was their unanimous choice for the district's Congressional nomination.[9] O'Sullivan, serving as Chairman of the Notification Committee, told the editor that he had been nominated to combat a government that catered to the favored few. The state Democrats hoped, O'Sullivan added, that as a Congressman, he would force Congress to consider the welfare of all Americans.[10]

Hearst accepted the nomination and delivered a speech to the Committee. He said in part:

> I believe that of the eighty millions of people in this country, five or six millions are ably represented in Congress, in the law courts, and in the newspapers. It would be immodesty on my part to imagine that I could add much to the comfort or prosperity to the few who are so thoroughly well looked after. My ambition is to forward the interests of the seventy millions or more of typical Americans who are not so well looked after. Their needs seem to offer a wider field for useful effort . . .

He identified the trust issue as the most important one of the day:

> Nothing is so important to these people as the regulation of financial power . . . Congress must deal with the matter through law, and therefore Congress first of all

117

must be made to represent the people and
not the trusts. The people will never be
protected against the trusts by a Senate
in which the trusts occupy many seats and
control a majority . . . Adequate laws must
be passed to punish criminally trust owners
and officers for criminal infractions of
law. The whole complicated system of civi-
lized society . . . was devised to prevent
the powerful and unscrupulous individual
from overriding the rights of his weaker
brethren. The laws must now be applied and
where necessary must be strengthened to
protect the people against the powerful and
unscrupulous criminal combination known as
a trust.[11]

The speech was reprinted several times in both
the _Evening Journal_ and the _American_. It was
more sagacious, and also more specific in
identifying an issue and a remedy, than conventional Tammany Democratic class rhetoric.
Although seeking a seat representing Manhattan's
West Side, Hearst clearly aimed to act as a
national figure in Congress.

Hearst himself ran a low-keyed campaign.
He had great difficulties addressing crowds and
in adjusting to a candidate's life. He could not
deliver an address with either eloquence or
ease and shyed away from public speeches and
crowds. Through editorials, front page news
stories, and personal interviews, Hearst used
his newspapers to reach voters.

Hearst's campaign revolved almost entirely
around issues concerned with the recent coal
strike. He continually told voters that they
needed to elect candidates pledged to involve
the government in the correcting of social and
economic wrongs. The great majority of Americans
were becoming increasingly involved in the
political process and would demand a "politics
of action."[12] Hearst pledged to represent these

118

people and to set an example of the new type
of politician.[13]

Hearst continually labelled Republicans
as comrades of the trusts and stressed that
the Coal trust, the Beef trust, the Ice
trust, and the Railroad trusts had demonstrated a need for intelligent legislation
in regard to combinations.[14] He stated:

> The trusts have received many privileges
> from the Republican party and the Repub-
> lican party has in turn received so
> many favors from the trusts that a bond
> has grown between them, uniting them like
> the Siamese twins, and you cannot stick a
> pin in the trusts without hearing a
> shriek from the Republican party; and you
> cannot stick a pin in the Republican party
> without hearing a roar from the trusts.[15]

He pledged, if elected, to introduce legislation
to control the trusts.[16]

Despite his conspicuous alliance with
Murphy and with Tammany Hall, Hearst attacked
the corrupt policies and practices of machine
politics in general and of Tammany in particular.[17] Tammany Hall leaders endorsed Hearst,
overlooking his attacks on their methods and
policies. They supported him because they
recognized the power of his newspapers, because
he was supporting Coler, and because they knew
that a Congressional seat was a small price to
pay to appease him and to get him out of the
city.

Given a chance to respond to Hearst, the
World observed, local labor leaders endorsed
his candidacy.[18] A representative endorsement read:

> Whereas the organized workingmen of
> the United States have frequently sought

119

in vain for legislative benefits from
Congress and,
　　　　Whereas, their only remedy lies in
getting representatives of the whole people
in that body;　　and,
　　　　Whereas, William Randolph Hearst has
proved his sincere interest in the welfare
of the masses, and would doubtless continue
to champion our cause if elected to Congress,
　　　　Resolved, by the executive and standard
engineers, that we recommend the election
of William Randolph Hearst to Congress from
the 11th New York District.[19]

In the election, Hearst defeated the
Republican candidate, Henry Birell, by a
vote of 26,953 to 10,841, in a district of
228,447 inhabitants, constituting the largest
plurality ever in the district.　Hearst was
responsible for the large plurality, but
Tammany could take credit for the victory.
The district's voters have sent a Democrat
to Congress each election since Orland Porter's
victory in 1882.　Running on a Tammany-
Democratic ticket, Hearst could have won the
election without conducting a campaign.　His
workers, however, conducted a whirlwind campaign, including bands, fireworks, and rallies,
which resulted in the 31 percent plurality.　He
did get the voters to the polls.　It would be
two full decades, when women voters doubled
the number of electors, before another congressional candidate's vote in that district
would equal his 1902 total.　The American's headline called his victory the greatest Democratic
majority in the city's history and the lead
article affirmed that Murphy was the hero of
a glorious day:[20]　both were examples of a
sensationalist's use of his media for self-
serving purposes.　Arkansas Senator James K.
Jones, Chairman of the Democratic National Committee, wrote Hearst:

There is no mistaking the widespread dis-

satisfaction with the people in power, while
our splendid majority in New York City
gladdens the hearts of Democrats all over
the country and fills them with hope for
the future. . . .
No man contributed more than you to
the favorable features of the result.
Your . . . great papers exercised a wide
influence in the country at large, while
your personal activity and management in
organizing and arousing the party, especially in New York City, but also in other
sections, are understood and appreciated,
I am sure, by Democrats everywhere. . . .
I am sure . . . your career of usefulness
in the party has but just begun.[21]

On election night, Hearst sponsored a great
rally and a big fireworks display in Madison
Square Park. A crowd of 40,000 assembled to
watch the election results on a large stere-
opticon screen that Hearst had rented. At
approximately 10:00 p.m., as a photograph of
the Congressman-elect was being flashed on the
screen, a nine inch fireworks bomb exploded pre-
maturely, igniting a string of nearby fireworks
bombs. The results were disastrous; the explosion resulted in eighteen deaths and nearly
one hundred injuries.[22]

Stories of the explosion appeared in the
early editions of all the New York City newspapers except the American. Hearst editors,
fearing that their chief would be held liable,
did not report the incident. When Hearst arrived
at his office, he sent out a directive to print
the story.[23] The story was relegated to an
inside page and no illustrations were used, nor
was Hearst's name mentioned in the article. It
laid the blame of explosions on the fireworks
company and pointed out that a foreman of the
company was being held on $10,000 bail.[24]

Hearst was the single biggest user of fireworks in the city, but fireworks were commonly used.[25] He had been issued a permit to use them in the election night rally, and had frequently used them to entertain his readers. It was the third fireworks-related accident in the city in two weeks.[26] Numerous law suits were lodged against Hearst. Involved in the court proceedings for decades, he was never found guilty of any offense in the matter and was never required to pay any monetary sum in damages.

The disaster dampened the overwhelming victory, but Democrats nationwide did take notice of the Hearst vote.[27] He led the state ticket in the Eleventh District by over 3,500 votes.[28] Mayor Eugene Schmitz, Labor Party mayor of San Francisco, credited Hearst with insuring several Democratic Congressional victories nationwide.[29] In a public address, former Vice President Stevenson reflected on a Hearst victory:

> It means the election of that splendid Democrat William R. Hearst for Congress. His election will be gratifying to Democrats everywhere . . . His great services to our Party in the past have endeared him to all Democratic hearts. By his election, his state will have another able representative in the Congress of the United States. By his election his field of usefulness will be enlarged, and all that he has accomplished in the past will be but the earnest of greater services yet to be rendered to his Party and his country in the future. In honoring him you honor yourselves.[30]

Hearst himself was enthusiastic and optimistic in victory, writing to Brisbane:

> We have won a splendid victory. We are allying ourselves with the workingman,

the real Americans. This is just the beginning of our political actions. Our
social aspirations have a greater chance
than ever to be realized. . . . [31]

It was a single victory in a contest in
which the results were never in doubt, yet it
led Hearst supporters to visions of him in the
White House. Practical politicians thought that
it was ridiculous for this unproven politician
to have such high aspirations, but he was
coming to realize that the more powerful office
he held, the more sweeping social changes he
could institute.[32] The Hearst presidential
boom officially began on November 3, 1902.[33]
The Alpha Club was formed at the Astor House in
New York City. Former Governor James Budd
announced to Hearst supporters, "Hearst is a
name to conjure with."[34] Local labor leaders
were elected officers of the club.[35] The Democratic party had no clear leader or frontrunners
for the 1904 Presidential nomination. Bryan
was the most powerful figure within the party,
but it was unlikely that the delegates would go
with him for three successive elections. He
might, however, support Hearst if the publisher
emerged a serious and popular candidate. Hearst
had been a conspicuous Bryan supporter and
Bryan was writing in 1902, a series of articles
for his newspapers.

Even the conservative Grover Cleveland was
impressed by the Hearst boom. In an interview
concerning the results of the Congressional
elections, Cleveland singled out Hearst's victory as perhaps the most significant. The
former President was not bestowing praise on
Hearst, but he was defining specific differences
between the publisher and other politicians.
Hearst was a fearless and aggressive individual,
Cleveland said, who would usher in a new type
of politics on Capitol Hill: a politician unwilling to compromise, demanding immediate
action, and appealing to the masses of people

123

for justification. He added that Hearst would make his mark in Congress and in society as a power and spokesman for the needs of the poor.[36] Cleveland's former Vice-President Stevenson stated:

> William Randolph Hearst's fidelity to his party in its past struggles has endeared him to all Democratic hearts. He is indeed a name to conjure with whenever Democrats are assembled. He is the champion of the rights of the people. He has at all times the courage of his convictions. In public life, as in private station, he will be found the fearless defender of the weak against the strong arm of power. The interests of all people are safe in his keeping.[37]

Hearst was gaining both respect and prestige within the Democratic party. The Atlanta Daily News declared that while most Eastern Democrats had deserted Bryan and the party in 1896 and 1900, Hearst unselfishly had donated enough money to the party to cover the necessary expenses of the campaigns. He had liberated a nation from the despotic rule of the Spanish Kingdom, the Daily News added, and was now liberating a country from the rule of trusts:

> It is no exaggeration to say that Mr. Hearst has done more in the last six years than any other man in the country. He has become the young David who is going out to slay Goliath and his following of monstrous trusts.[38]

An American editorial stated that the masses of people were flocking to Hearst and Hearstism because of his devotion to Democratic principles. Hearst's newspaper figures were indisputably the highest in the world. In the month of September 1902 the American's circulation was nearly 30,000,000, a gain of 6,000,000 over the

same month of the previous year.[39]   Hearst ad-
hered, the _American_ said, "to the interests of
the whole people as opposed to special interests hostile to the common welfare," and it
added that he believed in the "doctrine that
the manhood and not the money of the Republic
shall rule."   The editorial claimed that "the
American people have recognized a friend and
a champion."[40]

Congressman-elect Hearst continued his
efforts to appeal to the labor unions.   He
afforded heavy and favorable coverage to the
annual A. F. of L. convention, held in mid-
November, in all of his newspapers.   Although
a settlement had been reached in the anthracite
coal strike, Hearst renewed his attacks on the
coal trusts.   For the poor of New York City,
who were the group most affected by the strike,
he imported over 30,000 tons of coal and sold
it at a reduced rate.[41]   He polled fifty-four
Republican Congressmen and reported that fifty
of them supported trust-control legislation.[42]
He challenged Roosevelt to live up to his
reputation for being a trust buster:

> The people of the United States have a
> right to expect ACTION from you against
> the trusts in general and the coal trust
> in particular.   No conspicuous public man
> of your party has so vehemently as your-
> self expressed a desire to protect the
> public from exploitation at the hands of
> combinations of predatory capital.   And
> you have well said that 'words are good
> when backed up by deed and only so'. . . .
> For that non-enforcement of the laws, Mr
> President, your Attorney General is re-
> sponsible to you, and if you shall uphold
> him in his refusal to act against the coal
> trust, you will be responsible to the
> American people.[43]

He wrote that the railroad coal trusts were

violating the Sherman Anti-Trust law because the acquisition by a holding company of stock control of competing carriers constituted an illegal monopoly.[44] Hearst and Shearn initiated legal proceedings against such arrangements[45] and in 1904, the United States Supreme Court ruled that they constituted an illegal monopoly.[46]

Hearst's private correspondences reveal the consistency of his ideas for the advancement of organized labor. In February 1903, he wrote Lentz:

> . . . the chief duty of government is to insure the welfare of the plain people. I believe that the force fighting with Democracy . . . is the force of organized labor. It realizes most practically the national solidarity which Lincoln expressed when he said: The strongest bond of human sympathy outside of the family relation, should be one uniting all working people.
>   The labor organizations are organizations of men struggling for men's rights, American equality, independence and opportunity. They can compete in power with the organizations of capital. No force in this country, save the force of organized manhood, will be able to cope successfully with the power of organized wealth.
>   To succeed the Democratic party must work . . . in cooperation with the organized manhood and independence of this country, the greatest Democratic force of today.[47]

He wrote to his chief counsel that "conservative business leaders were organized and united to protect themselves. They speak of reform, but it is reform to insure the status quo."[48] The workers had to protect themselves, he believed, from the organization and movements of those classes that looked upon social privilege as their right.[49] Democratic Congressman Champ Clark from Missouri stated that Hearst's efforts at organ-

126

izing laborers and initiating legal proceedings against corrupt trusts were effective remedies to combat the movement of business leaders.[50]

On April 28, 1903 Hearst wed Millicent Wilson, a young actress. Only thirty guests attended the simple ceremony.[51] The groom, who turned forty the following day, was twenty years older than his bride. His opponents viewed the match as solely a political move to give the candidate an image of respectability, maturity and stability. Lundberg wrote:

> Hearst's marriage occupied a central position in his political affairs before the World War. Hearst agents could and did point out that he was a respectable married man.[52]

It does not appear, however, that Hearst was seeking respectability by marrying an actress, the daughter of a vaudeville hoofer.

Once married, Hearst sought to alter his public image. He began to crave personal publicity. He became conscious of his appearance and appeared in public only when dressed in the traditional black broadcloth, with a broad brimmed hat and a frock coat, regardless of the temperature.[53] Before his election to Congress, he was always referred to in his newspaper as "W. R. Hearst." Following his election to Congress, he was identified in his newspapers as "William Randolph Hearst." The "William Randolph" was born with his political career as he began to advertise himself, using editorials, news stories, bold headlines, and photographs, like a brand of goods on the market.[54] He hired a private political secretary, Lawrence J. O'Reilly, and began publication of his seventh newspaper, the Los Angeles _Examiner_.

Hearst moved to Washington in November and into a house formerly owned by Elihu Root, in Lafayette Square, directly across Pennsylvania

Avenue from the White House. Scores of Congressmen and Washington correspondents closely followed
the actions of the young publisher-politician.
Few knew him personally, but he was a presidential
aspirant and his name had been in the public eye
nationwide for the preceding six years.[55]

Hearst drew appointments in the 58th Congress
to the Labor Committee and to the Committee on
the Irrigation of Arid Lands. He had desperately
wanted a spot on the Labor Committee, but his request was initially denied by Democratic Minority
Leader John Sharp Williams of Mississippi. He
did not passively accept the decision. He petitioned labor leaders nationwide and they responded in his behalf. Telegrams and petitions
poured in to Williams and House Speaker Cannon
asking that Hearst be named to the Labor Committee. A Williams appointee reluctantly bowed
to the show of strength and Hearst was added to
the committee.[56]

In many regards Hearst was an effective
reform Congressman: in many traditional ways
he failed. He continuously introduced popular
legislation and proceeded to educate the public
and promote such legislation in his newspaper.
He did not, however, work through the proper
channels to insure its passage. Hearst-sponsored
legislation was directed to subcommittees where
it was pigeonholed. He refused to conform to the
normal expectations and rules of the House. He
holds the all-time record for absenteeism for a
Congressman who is neither ill nor disabled. As
a member of the 58th and 59th Congresses, he
voted a total of only twenty-six times. He
answered present to only two of one hundred and
seventy roll calls in the 58th Congress.[57] He
rarely attended floor debates. Seat number 86
was rarely occupied.[58]

Hearst's actions in Congress reflected his
personality. He was most comfortable, and believed that he could achieve the most success,

by working by himself. On his first, and one of
his rare, addresses on the floor, he justified
his lack of effort in House debates:

> The gentlemen from Massachusetts apparently
> criticizes my action, or lack of action on
> the floor of this House. I wish to say in
> reply that I am proceeding here in the way
> that I think most effective to my constit-
> uents. I have heard incompetents speak on
> the floor of this House for hours for the
> mere purpose of getting their remarks in the
> Record; and I have heard the best speakers
> deliver the most admirable addresses on the
> floor of this House without influencing
> legislation in the slightest particular. I
> do not know any way in which a man can be
> less effective for his constituents and less
> useful to them than by emitting chewed wind
> on the floor of this House.[59]

The 58th Congress, with a Republican majority
of thirty-one, was controlled by old-line Republican stalwarts like Boise Penrose, Joe Cannon,
and Marcus Hanna who favored privilege, protection, and the divine right of sound money.
They supported and represented the system that
Hearst attacked in his newspapers. In speaking
of the House leadership, Hearst stated in an
address on the House floor:

> I am proud to have incurred the hostility of
> that class of individual, and I shall make
> it my duty and my pride to continue to incur
> that hostility of that class of individuals
> as long as I am in journalism or in poli-
> tics.[60]

His actions and aloofness alienated him from
House Democratic leaders as well. He was not
even on speaking terms with Williams.[61]

Hearst further antagonized fellow Congressmen by using his newspapers to attack political

opponents. On February 13, 1905, Democratic
Representative John A. Sullivan, who had assailed
the publisher for his absence at the introduction
of his own Railroad bill, rose to vent his anger
at the American's attack upon him:

> I presume my criticism that it might
> have been well for the gentlemen from New
> York to have taken the floor and discussed
> his own bill seemed to him an infraction of
> this monarchial dignity and he thereupon . .
> /had/ my name duly registered for slander in
> the political assassination of his news-
> paper. I trust the gentleman will have the
> decency to avail himself of the privilege
> of this floor after the fashion of a manly
> man, instead of hiding under the cover of
> further cowardly newspaper attacks.
> . . . Totally bereft of the sense of
> proportion, /Hearst/ raises his profaning
> eyes toward the splendid temple of the
> people's highest gift--the Presidency of the
> United States--blissfully unconscious of the
> woeful contrast between qualifications re-
> quisite for that high office and his own
> contemptible mental and moral equipment.62

Hearst, in his turn, levelled vicious charges on
Sullivan. He reported that in 1885 Sullivan, who
was then seventeen, and his father had kicked to
death an intoxicated customer in the father's
Boston saloon. The account was factually correct.
The elder Sullivan had been convicted of man-
slaughter and given a prison sentence while the
son had been placed on probation for one year.63
Hearst admitted to a newspaper reporter that the
entire incident was disagreeable to all involved
and he stated that he believed his conservative
Democratic House opponents had put Sullivan up
to his speech.64

Among Congressional colleagues Hearst was
referred to as the "Apostle of discontent."65

130

Being interested in only a narrow range of legislation, he was active in matters dealing with social problems but neglected all other Congressional duties.

Observers believed that Hearst would be a Bryan spokesman on Capitol Hill. Because of Hearst's unselfish support for Bryan in 1896 and 1900 and because Bryan was writing for the Hearst newspapers, it was easy to identify the two men as members of the same wing of the Democratic party.[66] But they were from different political molds. Bryan was a progressive candidate, definitely to the right of Hearst. Given to emphasis, he analyzed social and economic issues largely in religious terms, with the literalism of the fundamentalist. He was an articulate champion who viewed public problems through humane and moral lenses. All trusts merited condemnation, he contended, because "there could be no good monopoly in private hands until the Almighty sends us angels to preside over the monopoly."[67] Hearst, however, discussed social issues in economic terms. He supported government ownership of public utility companies, and at times called for trust busting as a measure of control. He wrote:

> There are two compelling reasons for careful thought and intelligent legislation in regard to combination.
> One reason is found in the fact that combination is continually increasing in spite of the utmost efforts of its opponents to end it.
> The second reason is found in the fact that combination displays quite as definite advantages as disadvantages, and the necessity for preserving those advantages is as urgent as the necessity for eliminating the disadvantages.

To justify his growing newspaper empire, Hearst

was arguing that combinations could benefit
society:

> The advantages of combination are the
> advantages of better organization, more ef-
> fective operation, and cheaper production.
> The disadvantages of combination arise
> mainly from the misuse of the power of com-
> bination, which has developed into monopoly.
> If, then, combination is inevitable and
> in the main desirable, we must by careful
> thought discriminate between the advantages
> and disadvantages of combination, and by
> intelligent legislation permit the legiti-
> mate development of the advantages of com-
> bination and prevent the misuse of the
> power of monopoly.
> The growth of combination along harmful
> lines of coercion and oppression, or along
> even the legitimate and beneficial lines of
> natural development, is likely eventually to
> result in monopoly.
> As a matter of fact, the ultimate aim
> of combination usually is virtual monopoly,
> and a Trust may be described as a combina-
> tion that has reached the stage of virtual
> monopoly.[68]

Hearst would not compromise on issues and generally refused to combine forces with colleagues.
While Bryan was a party man, Hearst was a one-
man party.

Congressman Hearst attended his first Labor
Committee meeting on January 7, 1904 and immediately attempted to involve labor leaders in the
legislative process. He and Gompers were on
friendly terms and, within a month, Gompers appeared before the Committee to defend House Resolution 4063, the Hearst supported eight-hour work
day bill.[69] Although he had previously appeared
before Congressional committees, this was the
first time he appeared as a representative of the

American Federation of Labor.[70] While Hearst did
not believe that Gompers truly represented the
poorer laborers, he did believe that the labor
leader's appearance before the Committee was a
momentous event for the advancement and recognition of organized labor, and he silently took
credit for it.[71] By 1906 Gompers was a frequent
witness before the Labor Committee and frequently
wrote committee members urging them to attend committee hearings in which pro-labor legislation was
scheduled to be debated.[72]

Hearst attended thirteen of the Labor Committee's twenty-one sessions during the 58th
Congress even though he was not appointed to any
subcommittees. The Committee was most concerned
with the eight-hour work day and convict labor
laws, but no bills relating to either issue were
passed out of committee. A resolution was passed
authorizing that a letter be sent from the Committee to the Secretary of Commerce and Labor
expressing token support for the eight-hour work
day.[73] Hearst rarely spoke in committee meetings
but actively supported and publicized pro-labor
legislation in his newspapers.

Congressman Hearst introduced ten bills and
five resolutions during his first term in office.
His proposed legislation called for the creation
of investigatory circuit courts with jurisdiction
to enforce anti-trust laws; for the Congress and
the President to present to each other detailed
estimates of appropriations before either presented their budgets for the next fiscal year;
for an increase in the powers of Interstate Commerce Commission: for the establishment of a
parcel post system; for governmental regulation
of towing at sea; for increased regulation of
interstate commerce; for government acquisition
and control of the Panama Railroad Company; and
for effective suppressions of trusts.[74] He promoted all of his bills in his newspapers, but
did little with his fellow Congressmen.

Following his unsuccessful bid for the 1904

Democratic party's presidential nomination, Hearst ran for re-election to the House of Representatives. He was developing into a polished and relaxed candidate but did not conduct a whirlwind campaign as he had in 1902. He reluctantly and half-heartedly supported his party's presidential candidate. Running in a safe district he made few public appearances. This and Roosevelt's popularity in the Presidential election explains why his vote was slightly less than he had gotten in 1902.[75] He remained, however, a popular figure with the masses and a vote getter. In his campaign he pledged to continue the actions and methods he had employed in the 58th Congress. In the election he received 59.3 percent of the popular votes, polling 26,255 votes and out-distancing his Republican opponent, Henry Clay, by 11,397. He again ran well ahead of the rest of the Democratic ticket, polling over 1700 votes more than his party's presidential nominee.

Hearst was even less active in the 59th Congress than he had been in the 58th Congress. During his second term he was involved in two major elections in New York City and he established the Boston _American_, his eighth newspaper. He overextended himself and shirked most Congressional duties. The Republicans increased their majority in Congress from thirty-one to fifty and held 243 of the 386 seats in the House. Hearst had virtually no chance of steering his legislation through Congress.

During the 59th Congress, the House Labor Committee dealt with four issues with which Hearst was concerned: the eight-hour work day, convict labor laws, women labor laws, and child labor laws. He directed extensive newspaper attention to all of these,[76] but in the Congressional committee where he had a chance to influence legislation, he attended only four of twenty committee meetings and did not attend a meeting during the final ten months of his term.[77]

The newspaper crusades were effective muckraking efforts. Hearst claimed that child labor, as an example, was the nation's most serious crime, that it was systematically destroying American youth. He argued that it was legalized murder of the child's body and soul and was more disgraceful than any form of slavery.[78] A typical Hearst editorial read:

> This is a nation of combined senti-
> mentalism and greed--ready to cry over a
> sentimental song or a trashy play in which
> a child suffers, ready to take the profits
> of the labor of a child slave.
> The child labor system of this country,
> which will get worse and worse . . . will
> have a dreadful effect upon the future of
> this country. It will give us a race of
> human beings stunted mentally, physically,
> and morally . . .
> For the sake of a few dollars we are
> breeding in this country a dangerous race of
> men and women; A RACE THAT WILL HAVE AGAINST
> CIVILIZATION A MOST DEADLY GRUDGE. We are
> adding to the body politic thousands upon
> thousands THAT WILL HAVE A RIGHT TO LOATHE
> AND DESPISE THE GOVERNMENT WHICH CALLS IT-
> SELF A REPUBLIC. WE CANNOT AFFORD TO NEG-
> LECT THEM BUT WE ARE NEGLECTING THEM.
> If any one man should proceed deliber-
> ately in public to take a little girl of 10
> or 11 years of age and choke her to death
> with his fingers, HOW PROMPTLY HE WOULD BE
> LYNCHED. But hundreds of employers can choke
> thousands of boys and girls SLOWLY and nobody
> interferes. They are organized in the scared
> process of turning child life into cash.
> How long will the process go on with
> the approval or the heartless indifference
> of the American people?[79]

By 1906 Tammany was embracing Hearst's issues,[80] and in 1913 the state legislature passed into law a series of stringent labor reform laws.[81]

Hearst introduced sixteen pieces of legislation in the 59th Congress. His proposals called for the direct elections of United States Senators; for a national system of roads; for stricter penalties for the giving or receiving of rebates in interstate commerce; for the protection of trade and commerce against restraints and monopolies; for the establishment of a parcel post system; for the regulation of railroad freight rates; for federal funds to replace buildings destroyed in a west coast earthquake; for the protection of seamen in coastwise traffic; for an increase in salary of members of the United States Supreme Court; for government control of the telegraph system; for the suppression of all trusts; for strict penalties for those convicted of election fraud and bribery; for government control of all corporations engaged in interstate commerce; and for governmental regulation of railroad transportation. He did publicize these complex and well thought out proposals in his newspapers.[82]

The Hearst Federal Incorporation bill elaborated on the machinery necessary to give the Interstate Commerce Commission the power to fix railroad rates and to create an Interstate Commerce Court. The Commission, increased in numbers and divided into various departments, would deal with excessive charges and monopolistic abuse in various lines of business.[83] The Court, consisting of twelve justices appointed by the President for twelve-year terms with one-third of the terms ending every presidential term, would review and enforce the findings of the Interstate Commerce Commission.

On March 1, 1907 Hearst introduced a bill to secure uniformity of legislation throughout the nation on the subject of incorporation. It was more detailed and inclusive than the 1900 and 1904 Bryanite Democratic plank that had vowed to subject intrastate trusts to control by the state legislature, restrict monopolistic corporations from doing business outside the state of their incorporation, and to prohibit a corpora-

tion from controlling more than a specific per-
centage of a commodity's market. Hearst's bill,
entitled "A Bill to Provide for National Incorporation and Control of Corporations Engaged in Commerce Among Several States," intended to secure
a practical and practicable method of investigating and controlling the issue of great volumes
of capital stock and limiting that issue to cor-
responding property and possessions of actual
and estimable value.[84]

It died in committee, but President Taft's
Federal Incorporation bill, introduced in February
1910, closely resembled Hearst's proposal in
goals and methods. Hearst had proposed the
establishment of a Bureau of Corporations, in
the Department of Commerce and Labor, to regulate
all national corporations which voluntarily
registered. To protect the investing public
against ficticious and worthless stock issues,
Congress made a company's directors liable to the
company stockholders for damages which resulted
from misrepresentation. The making of such
false statements was declared a felony. The
bill prohibited the loan of the corporation's
money to stockholders, directors, or office-
holders, and stringently prohibited the payment
of any dividend except from surplus profits.
Hearst proposed the enactment of a differential
franchise tax. Those corporations not joining
the Bureau would be taxed 5 percent of their
gross receipts while corporations that joined
would be taxed an extremely low figure. The
Taft bill did not include this franchise tax.

While Hearst had virtually no immediate impact on the House, he did have his followers in
Congress. In what was generally referred to as
the "Hearst brigade," Congressmen of unquestioned
honesty allied themselves to him because of the
progressive measures he introduced in the House
and presented in his newspapers. In the 58th Congress the brigade consisted of six men: William
Lamarr (Florida), Dorsey Shackleford (Missouri),
James Robinson (Indiana), John Garner (Texas),
Champ Clark (Missouri), and William Warnock

(Ohio). It expanded in the 59th Congress to
include Ariosto Wiley (Alabama), James Matthew
Griggs (Georgia), Charles Bartlett (Georgia),
Allan Langdon McDermott (New Jersey), and Samuel
Cooper (Texas). These Representatives, with
McDermott being the lone exception, served in the
58th Congress. They joined the "brigade" following the disputed New York City mayoralty
election of November 1905.

Hearst controlled the Congressional actions
of "brigade" members. These members carried out
his will in subcommittees and committees, and on
the House floor. Charles Willis Thompson, a
political observer, wrote of floor debate on
eight-hour work day legislation:

> . . . Without uttering a word except in a
> whisper . . . apparently having nothing to
> do with the debate, for three quarters of an
> hour he /Hearst7 kept the House in turmoil.
> He issued assignments to his followers as if
> he were issuing them to his reporters in
> his newspaper office . . . The old-time
> Democrats looked on silently at the curious
> scene. The members of the 'Hearst brigade'
> would come over to their chief and get their
> assignments. Immediately afterwards the
> man assigned to the work would arise and
> throw a new bomb into the Republican side.
> All this time the chief never changed his
> position . . . [85]

Hearst went to Congress hoping to captain
the nation's discontent, but failed to adjust to
the life of a public officeholder. As a reform-
minded Congressman, Hearst outran his hour. The
railroad measure that he formulated later
strengthened the Interstate Commerce Commission
and created the Interstate Commerce Court. He
sponsored legislation calling for a national
system of roads, for an increase in the salaries
of United States Supreme Court Justices, for the

eight-hour work day, for a constitutional amendment for the direct elections of United States
Senators, and for the creation of a parcel post
system; similar bills would be molded into law.
He also introduced legislation that would have
funneled federal funds into irrigation and conservation, slum improvements, subway improvements, and better health and recreation facilities.

Hearst did not seek re-election to the 60th
Congress. Having been completely frustrated with
the ways of Capitol Hill, he realized that the
conservative opposition was so well organized
that a reform politician had to be elected President of the United States to have an impact on
national legislation. He therefore looked to the
1908 presidential election.[86] He had been elected
to Congress a much publicized publisher who
championed the rights of the underprivileged in
his newspapers. When he left Congress fifty-
three months later, he was the most controversial and least understood politician in the
nation.

Footnotes

[1]Frederic Palmer, "Hearst and Hearstism," Collier's, October 6, 1906, p. 16.

[2]Carlson and Bates, op. cit., p. 115.

[3]Brisbane to Hearst, October 1, 1902, J.A.M.

[4]Hearst Interview, Steffens, "Hearst, Man of Mystery," op. cit., p. 15.

[5]Hearst to Lentz, February 13, 1903, J.A.M.

[6]Hearst to Mr. G. F. Rinehart, April 3, 1903, J.A.M.

[7]Brisbane to Hearst, October 1, 1902, J.A.M.

[8]New York American, November 6, 1902.

[9]Tammany leaders included ex-Senator Thomas O'Sullivan, John Quinn, William Dalton, George Washington Plunkett, Bernard Meyerbery, P. H. Keahon, Robert Nich, George Shannel, Peter Dooling, Frank Run, Cornelius Donovan, John Shrady, Charles O'Neil, and James Frawley.

[10]New York Times, October 7, 1902.

[11]Hearst Acceptance Speech, October 6, 1902, J.A.M.

[12]New York American, November 1, 1902.

[13]New York American, November 2, 1902.

[14]William Randolph Hearst, "Initial Steps in Trust Control" no date, J.A.M., (This was in a folder marked "Not for Publication/Do Not Release").

[15]New York Times, October 28, 1902.

[16]New York American, October 28, 1902.

[17]New York *American*, October 29, 1902.

[18]New York *World,* October 26, 1902.

[19]Electrical Standard Engineers Local No. 20 to Hearst, October 25, 1902, J.A.M.

[20]New York *American*, November 5, 1902.

[21]Jones to Hearst, November 8, 1902, J.A.M.

[22]New York *Times*, November 6, 1902.

[23]Hearst Directive, November 5, 1902, J.A.M.

[24]New York *Evening Journal*, November 5, 1902.

[25]New York *Times*, November 5, 1902.

[26]New York *World*, November 5, 1902.

[27]*Ibid*.

[28]New York *Journal*, November 6, 1902.

[29]New York *Evening Journal*, November 6, 1902.

[30]Stevenson Speech at Madison Square Garden, October 27, 1902, in New York *American*, November 5, 1902.

[31]Hearst to Brisbane, November 5, 1902, J.A.M.

[32]Interview with William Randolph Hearst, Jr., September 25, 1978.

[33]New York *American*, November 4, 1902.

[34]New York *Evening Journal*, November 7, 1902.

[35]New York *American*, November 4, 1902.

[36]Cleveland interview with the Norfolk (Va.) Dispatch, November 17, 1902, J.A.M.

[37]New York American, November 20, 1902.

[38]New York American, November 30, 1902.

[39]New York American, December 4, 1902.

[40]Ibid.

[41]New York American, November 17, 1902.

[42]New York American, December 2, 1902.

[43]Hearst to Roosevelt, January 8, 1903. J.A.M.

[44]Hearst to Roosevelt, October 4, 1902, Roosevelt Papers, Library of Congress.

[45]New York Tribune, January 27, 1903.

[46]Northern Securities Company v. U. S. 193, U. S. 197, 1904.

[47]Hearst to Lentz, February 13, 1903, J.A.M.

[48]Hearst to Shearn, January 9, 1903, J.A.M.

[49]Hearst to The Chicago Iroquois Club, March 17, 1903, J.A.M.

[50]New York American, February 13, 1903.

[51]New York American, April 29, 1903.

[52]Lundberg, op. cit., p. 100.

[53]Palmer, op. cit., p. 18.

[54]Ibid.

[55]Swanberg, Citizen Hearst, op. cit., p. 209.

[56]Charles Willis Thompson, Party Leaders of the Times (New York: G. W. Dillingham Company, 1906), pp. 239-240.

[57]New York Times, October 6, 1906.

[58]U. S., Congress, United States Congressional Directory, Volume XXXIX, p. 208.

[59]U. S., Congress, House, 58th Congress, 3rd session, February 13, 1905, Congressional Record, p. 2482.

[60]Ibid.

[61]Thompson, loc. cit.

[62]New York Times, February 14, 1905.

[63]New York Times, February 15, 1905.

[64]New York Tribune, February 14, 1905.

[65]Thompson, op. cit., p. 234.

[66]Ibid., p. 233.

[67]Koenig, op. cit., p. 297.

[68]Hearst, "Initial Steps in Trust Control," loc cit.

[69]U. S., Congress, House, Labor Committee, 58th Congress, 2nd session, February 7, 1904, Minutes, National Archives.

[70]United States Senate Library, Microfiche Collection of individuals who have testified before Congressional Committees.

[71]Hearst to Brisbane, February 4, 1904.
J.A.M.

[72]Gompers to J. J. Gardner; W. Call; H. P. Goebel; K. Haskins; G. W. Norris; J. T. Hunt; H. T. Rainey; A. O. Stanley; T. B. Davis; R. Bartholdt; J. P. Conner; W. R. Hearst, May 26, 1906, A. F. of L. Papers, Library of Congress.

[73]U. S., Congress, House, Labor Committee, 58th Congress, 2nd session, April 13, 1904, Minutes, National Archives.

[74]U. S. House Journal, Volume 111, 112, 113, (Washington: Government Printing Office, 1905), p. 816.

[75]Roosevelt appealed to the urban immigrant and working groups, and a lot of voters did not bother to split tickets. New York American, November 9, 1904.

[76]Thompson, op. cit., p. 243; New York, Times, February 14, 1905; New York Tribune, October 5, 1905; New York Times, August 1, 1906.

[77]U. S., Congress, House, Labor Committee, 59th Congress, Minutes, National Archives.

[78]New York American, October 7, 1906.

[79]New York American, March 25, 1906.

[80]John D. Buenker, Urban Liberalism and Progressive Reform (New York: Charles Scribner's Sons, 1973), p. 93.

[81]Including those regulating sanitary conditions, the hours of labor for women and children, workmen's compensation, and factory regulation. Thomas M. Henderson, Tammany Hall and the New Immigrants (New York: Arno Press, 1976), pp. 123-124.

[82]See for examples, New York American, April 21, 1903, New York American, March 13,

1904; New York American, January 17, 1905; New
York American, January 19, 1905; New York
American, February 21, 1905; New York American,
May 6, 1906; New York American, October 4, 1906;
New York American, February 6, 1908; New York
American, December 28, 1908; New York American,
December 12, 1916.

[83]William Randolph Hearst, "When Combination Becomes Monopoly What Shall Fix
Prices?" no date, J.A.M. (This was in a folder
marked, "Not for Publication/Do Not Release").

[84]Hearst, "Initial Steps to Trust Control."
loc. cit.

[85]Thompson, op. cit., pp. 242-243.

[86]Interview with William Randolph Hearst
Jr., September 25, 1978.

VI

Hearst for President

In the summer of 1904, William Randolph
Hearst challenged Alton Brooks Parker, from New
York, for the Democratic party's presidential
nomination. He entered the July St. Louis convention with one hundred and four instructed
delegates. Because the Republicans had nominated their accidental incumbent, the increasingly popular Theodore Roosevelt, the Democrats
had to nominate a dynamic individual to challenge him.[1] Instead, an internal and crippling
power struggle ensued between the party's conservative and its progressive elements,[2] a struggle too deep rooted to be resolved at the national
convention.[3]

Although one-term congressmen rarely make
serious bids for the Presidency, Hearst was
President of the National Democratic Clubs, with
an alleged three million members,[4] and the owner
of eight large newspapers, located in New York,
Chicago, Los Angeles, San Francisco and Boston.
He could address millions of Americans daily.
Only the President could rival his ability to
reach so many voters.[5] Max Ihmsen headed
Hearst's presidential bid and by July 1904 had
organized over two hundred active William
Randolph Hearst Clubs nationwide.[6] Ihmsen was
a thirty-four year old newspaperman. At the age
of eighteen, he had joined the staff of the
Pittsburgh Leader and Post as a political cor-
respondent. In 1893 he moved to New York to
assume similar duties with the New York Herald.
Two years later Hearst lured him to the Journal.
In 1904, while on the Hearst payroll, he was a
member of the Democratic National Congressional
Committee and was serving as Secretary of the
National Association of Democratic Clubs. The
clubs endorsed Hearst for President.[7]

Hearst believed he could win in the general
election if he could wrestle the nomination from

the old-line conservative Democrats.[8] In his
newspapers he was promoting well formulated
political proposals, all revolving around a central theme that social inequities in American
society were the responsibility of the local,
state, and federal governments, issues he believed to be popular with the masses of voters.

Hearst succeeded in uniting the conservative wing of the Democratic party against him.
The business, professional, and political elite
distrusted this millionaire who denounced pre-
datory wealth and proposed what they believed to
be socialism. They challenged his intellectual
qualification and accused him of buying votes and
using newspapers for self promotion. A rival
newspaper's editorial read:

> . . . it is not simply that we revolt at
> Hearst's . . . shrieking unfitness mentally
> for the office he sets out to buy . . .
> There has never been a case of a man of such
> slender intellectual equipment, absolutely
> without experience in office, impudently
> flaunting his wealth before the eyes of the
> Republic saying, 'Make me President.' This
> is folly. This is to degrade public life,
> but there is something and more fearful . . .
> It is not a question of politics but of
> character. An agitator we can endure; an
> honest radical we can respect; a fanatic we
> can tolerate; but a low voluptuary trying
> to sting his jaded senses to a fresh thrill
> by turning from private to public corruption
> is a new horror in American politics. To
> set the heels of contempt upon it must be
> the impulse of all honest men.[9]

The images of Hearst presented by his political and publishing rivals were handicaps, and
his wealth and aggressive journalism were obstacles in his quest for the nomination. Opponents raised questions about his sincerity and
motives. The New York Tribune fostered and sus-

148

tained the rumor that he was attempting to buy the nation's hightest office. In one article, entitled "Hearst Offers Cash," the _Tribune_ quoted an unidentified Hearst supporter as saying that Hearst was tempting the Democratic National Committee with a $1,500,00 donation in exchange for the nomination. The party had no cash funds for the upcoming campaign, claimed the unidentified source, so if it refused the offer it would have to appeal to the nation's trusts for operating funds.[10] Following the Indiana Democratic party convention in early May, the _Tribune_ quoted delegate John Kern concerning bribery money:

> We are menaced for the first time in the history of the Republic by the open and unblushing effort of a multi-millionaire to purchase the Presidential nomination. Our state has been overrun with a gang of paid agents and retainers. . . . The Hearst dollar mark is all over them . . .[11]

There were Hearst opponents who believed that Hearst was honest and dedicated to the reform legislation he proposed in Congress and promoted in his newspapers, but opposed him because he was too radical, both because his proposals sounded socialist and because they feared an individual who could use for self-promotion the sensationalist methods of the nation's largest newspaper chain.[12] Democratic United States Senator Edward Carmack, from Tennessee, predicted that a Hearst nomination would ruin the Democratic party because his was a one-man movement and not a party movement and because his aggressiveness would create incurable wounds within the party.[13] Congressman John A. Sullivan labelled him the Nero of modern politics, attempting to incite class conflict to destroy the respectable elements of society.[14]

Led by state Democratic leader David Hill, conservative Democrats in New York state actively worked for a Parker nomination. Conservative

149

Democrats had endured two Bryan campaigns and believed their only chance of victory was with a conservative candidate.[15]

The New York _Times_ endorsed Parker and labelled the growing Hearst support nationwide the "Hearst disease." Hearstism, the conservative newspaper explained, was a natural incident of Democratic convalescence from a prostrating attack of Bryan. A _Times_ editorial contended that it was not possible for the Bryan malady to run its terrible course without leaving the Democratic party in such a state that the disease of the Hearst type could easily gain a foothold.[16] It added that Hearst based his political movement on an appeal to the poor and was sacrificing everything to represent them. A representative of the poor elected to the presidency, the _Times_ emphasized, was a threat to the status quo of American Society.[17]

By early spring, 1904, Hearst and Parker were the only announced candidates for the nomination, and the only candidates with any sort of organization. Hearst's strategy was to hold Bryan's support and to broaden his appeal to organized labor, urbanities, and the lower classes. His appeal to the lower classes in the South was a precarious political decision, but it demonstrated his commitment to progressive policies,[18] and was similar to his attitude toward the new immigrant groups, who were almost as reviled as blacks.

The main obstacle that Hearst encountered in his attempt to secure Bryan's support in the South was concerned with the problem of race. The segregation rampant in the South at the turn of the century could, in large part, be traced to Democratic party leaders. Southern officials had resorted to Negro disenfranchisement. Hearst, we have seen, was not ignorantly majoritarian. Realizing that people could be racist. nativist, and other unsavory things, he favored the advancement of the last man in the procession.[19] In his

150

New York newspapers he many times defended the Negroes despite adverse popular opinions and writings. Following the New York City race riot on August 15, 1900, he blamed the city's police for inciting the riot. The race riots, he wrote in a _Journal_ editorial, demonstrated that there was only one general type of human nature in America, not two types divided by sectional lines. He condemned those who incited the riot and added that if more Negroes lived in the city, they would experience the same problems they experienced in the South.[20] He remained consistent on this issue. On July 15, 1905, a front page article in the _American_ blamed the race riots of the previous day on Irish teenagers.[21] His was the only city newspaper to make such an accusation. Hearst desperately wanted his party's 1904 nomination, but would not sacrifice principles to attain it. He wrote to his New York City editor:

> Ours has been a broad based movement. We are working to better the conditions of the underprivileged. We cannot carry the banner for laborers and immigrants and ignore what is happening in the South.[22]

He tried in vain to convince lower class white southerners that the economic situations of classes were more important than clinging to social racism. He argued that political leaders had kept this class hatred alive so that the lower class whites, believing that they were better than someone else, would not be concerned with social legislation.[23] He told the lower classes that color was not as important as economic positions.[24] He wrote to Brisbane:

> If Southerners could unite by station, regardless of color, all would improve. If classes stay divided by color, then the controlling classes continue to control.[25]

Parker played to southern prejudices. On a

151

campaign swing through the South in 1903 he ignored both the rash of lynchings and the systematic exclusion of Negroes from voting. In an
address entitled "Due Process of Law," given before the Georgia Bar Association, he argued that
if the Fourteenth Amendment was not already part
of the constitution, it was not probable it would
be incorporated. He added that it would never
have been adopted had it been understood that it
gave Congress the power to enforce the restrictions on state powers contained in the amendment.[26] The Nation indignantly declared:

> For him the great bulwark of the suffrage,
> with the penalties laid down for discrimi-
> nation against any class in its exercise,
> simply did not exist.[27]

Hearst failed to muster any support among
southern delegates. In the national convention,
the delegates from Virginia, North Carolina,
Tennessee, Mississippi, Alabama, Georgia, and
Louisiana voted for Parker one hundred and fifty-
eight to zero for Hearst.

The Hearst drive was a remarkable organi-
zational and emotional effort. His most outspoken supporter in the South was Thomas E.
Watson, who shared Hearst's view of the economic
unity of classes. Watson had been elected as a
Populist to Congress in 1890 and 1894. In 1896
he was the choice of the Populist National Convention for Vice-President. In October 1903 he
published the Life and Times of Thomas Jefferson.
"Because he is today working with splendid ability
along the same lines which Mr. Jefferson marked
out a hundred years ago," wrote Watson, "I
dedicate this book to WILLIAM RANDOLPH HEARST."[28]
It was a day in which a Herbert Croly could
write of Hearst as an expression of "the radical
element in the Jeffersonian tradition," to be
feared as "revolutionary in spirit because he
was unfair to capitalists." Croly compared him
to Robespierre, believing his ambition was to

bring about a socialistic millenium."[29] Hearst
offered Watson a large salary to edit one of his
New York City newspapers and to help him in his
fight.[30]

In the spring of 1904 Hearst rented a railroad car and canvassed western and southern
states. His newspapers covered his actions and
promoted his candidacy. Conservative members
underestimated his appeal. In May, former President Cleveland issued a statement explaining that
when conservative leaders "began to experience
alarm over the strength this man Hearst was
seemingly developing," he had decided to join
the Parker supporters, because it "appeared
necessary to concentrate upon some available man
in order to stifle the Hearst movement."[31] Albert
Beveridge wrote to Roosevelt that the liberals,
developing extraordinary strength in urban areas,
were Hearst supporters but would support
Roosevelt against Parker.[32]

As the time for the convention approached,
a Parker or Hearst nomination seemed inevitable.
Much of Hearst's support came from organized
labor, the lower classes, the radical elements
in society, and western party leaders remem-
bering his support of Bryan. Hundreds of newspapers nationwide endorsed him. The Nevada legislature sent him a resolution thanking him for
his continued efforts against the coal trusts.
Both the Tennessee and the Arkansas legislatures
invited him to address their respective chambers.[33] Damaging rumors circulated that he had
spent over $2,000,000 to secure the nomination.
But because money was being funneled into his
Boston paper, he did not have an abundance of
available cash. His campaign expenses totalled
$150,000.[34] That money was spent almost exclu-
sively for printing expenses, fireworks, hall
hire, banners, badges, music, and transportation.[35] He had spent more in each of the two
Bryan campaigns than he did in his own attempt.

153

Considering the obstacles he faced, the
effectiveness of Hearst's campaign suggested the
broad support his personality and program were
generating on the grass-roots level. He carried
the state Democratic conventions in Illinois,
California, Iowa, Kansas, Idaho, Nebraska,
Nevada, Washington, South Dakota, Rhode Island,
Arizona, Wyoming, and New Mexico, and the Democratic convention in the Territory of Hawaii.
He won over parts of the delegations from Maine,
Minnesota, Oregon, Indian Territory, West Virginia, Oklahoma, and Puerto Rico. Florida was
the first state to conduct a popular primary
and he picked up four of ten delegates. He
entered the convention with one hundred and four
instructed delegates and the endorsement of four
hundred fifty newspapers.[36] A political colum-
nist wrote that money could not have bought the
kind of support and enthusiasm that he had been
able to command.[37] Hearst believed that Bryan
would endorse his candidacy and that the endorsement would insure the nomination.[38]

There was great speculation on the course of
action Bryan would take. A formal endorsement
from Bryan would make Hearst a serious candidate; Bryan's dismissal of Hearst's candidacy
would insure his defeat. Most political observers believed that a Bryan endorsement of
Hearst was a foregone conclusion.[39] He supported Hearst on the issues of an eight-hour
work day, a graduated income tax, the direct
elections of United States Senators, and government ownership of the railroads. Although he
privately admitted six weeks before the convention that he would not endorse Hearst,[40]
publicly he remained uncommitted until the candidates were presented to the convention delegates.
He was considering another presidential bid in
1908 and did not want his control of the liberal
wing of the party challenged.

Liberal party members in New York State
openly challenged conservative party leaders in

their support of Parker, who had been Chief Judge
of the New York State Court of Appeals and had
been active in state politics since 1885 when he
managed David Hill's first gubernatorial campaign. Parker was highly respected for his conservative judicial opinions, for his ability in
campaign organization, and for his conservative
stands on social issues. He was a conventional
jurist who interpreted contracts literally in
private suits and narrowed the application of
remedies in equity suits. He tended to uphold
legislative actions. He was a Social Darwinist
at root and most of his opinions simply reflected his laissez-faire convictions.[41] He refused to take a public stand on issues concerning public franchises, employer liability,
direct election of United States Senators, and
the monetary standard. The New York State
Liberal Democrats met it Cooper Union Hall in
June 1904 to protest the fact that all seventy-
eight of the state's delegates were pledged to
him.

Samuel Seabury, a young aristocratic lawyer
committed to the cause of municipal ownership,
headed the convention and supervised the framing
of a platform which called state party leader
David Hill a traitor to the wishes of the party
and people, and advocated public ownership of
natural monopolies and the direct election of
United States Senators.[42] The convention voted
to send a delegation of twenty-five to the
national convention to support Hearst. Seabury,
an outspoken Hearst supporter, headed it. The
party had no success in St. Louis as all of the
state's delegates voted for Parker. The fears of
these liberals were realized when Parker telegrammed the convention and declared for the gold
standard.[43]

Conservative Democrats, fearful of Hearst's
preconvention strength, circulated rumors that
Grover Cleveland would become a candidate if
needed to prevent a Hearst nomination. Cleveland

155

did not discourage these rumors. He urged conservatives to unite behind Parker,[44] and was
seriously considering a bid if there were any
doubts of Parker's winning the nomination.[45]
Acknowledging that Parker was a weak candidate,
he confidentially remarked that both Richard
Olney of Massachusetts and George Gray of
Delaware would be good, but he believed that
since neither had gained any momentum, the
conservatives should unite behind Parker to
insure a conservative nominee.[46]

Hearst's elaborate headquarters were
stationed directly across from the convention
hall. Hearst introduced fireworks, rallies,
and demonstrations to national conventions. His
convention strategy was to get four hundred
delegates to pledge against Parker. He would win
the nomination, the publisher confided to his
American editor, if Parker failed to muster the
necessary two-thirds vote in either the first
or the second ballot.[47]

Fourteen thousand emotion wrought Democrats jammed into the convention hall on July
6.[48] The party's discords reverberated across
the nation for the next seventy-two hours. Hearst
supporters packed the isles, cheering and hissing
at will in attempts to tie up proceedings. They
had limited success in influencing party platform planks. Hearst's views were couched in
general and somewhat redundant terms. He contributed to the winning of a plank demanding the
enlargement of the Interstate Commerce Commission, and to another urging comprehensive
laws to prohibit interstate business to corporations found to be monopolies by "any court of
competent jurisdiction." His planks for the direct election of United States Senators, for
jury trials in labor injunction cases, and for
lower tariffs, were incorporated in the platform.[49] With the inclusion of only these minor
reform provisions, the platform gave neither the

GOP nor big business any reason for unrest. The New York Journal of Commerce congratulated the business interests on the adopted party platforms and claimed that "there was no danger of violent or extreme measures whichever party prevailed."[50]

Hearst was instrumental in preventing John Sharp Williams from including in the platform a militantly racist plank. In his keynote address, Williams had told the delegates:

> The Democrats make no disguise in the fact that they want to retain this country . . . as a home for the White man and a nursery for his civilization . . . /We/ will not hypocritically pretend to sympathize with those who desire . . . the Africanization or Mongolization of any state or community within the bounds of the American Republic.[51]

Hearst refused to allow his delegates even to consider a racist plank and threatened to pull them from the convention proceedings if one was adopted.[52] A Nation editorial attacked Williams, adding that the delegates did not dare to vote openly for the repression and disenfranchisement of the Negroes.[53] The delegates adopted a more moderate statement which condemned the Republicans for rekindling anew the embers of racial and sectional strife.[54]

The gold plank was again a much disputed issue among Democrats. Bryan diligently worked for the incorporation of a plank declaring for the free coinage of silver. David Hill and former New York Lieutenant Governor "Billy" Sheehan led Parker supporters in declaring for a gold standard plank. Eastern delegates wanted to recant the party's pronouncement for free silver which they believed had cost them two successive elections. The Committee on Resolutions, following fifteen hours in continuous session, adopted a plank stating that because two billion dollars of gold had been mined since 1900, the silver issue "was removed from the field of political consideration."[55] Bryan urged the delegates to reject the plank. To appease him, convention Chairman Champ Clark appointed a subcommittee of three--Bryan, Hill, and Williams--to work out a compromise.[56] The result was to omit all mention of money from the platform.[57]

Early Friday evening, July 8, Delphin M. Delmas, a San Francisco attorney, a renowned orator, and political ally of Senator George Hearst, nominated Hearst for President. He reflected on Hearst's efforts and support to the Democratic party, and spoke of his movement to upgrade social conditions in the nation, emphasizing his unpublicized deeds: the hospitals he had established in California, the universities he aided financially, the millions of dollars he spent to feed and shelter the needy in New York City and Chicago during the winter months. The most important question before the delegates, Delmas said, was "whether the government shall be carried on for the benefit of the people, or whether it shall be manipulated for the benefit of the privileged class,"[58] Hearst was a Jeffersonian Democrat, he added, and he quoted the Congressman as telling his constituents in November of 1902:

> I have devoted all my energies and abilities, whatever they may be, to the cause of the plain people, and I shall continue to do so.[59]

In presenting the publisher to the convention, Delmas proclaimed him to be:

> The unconquered antagonist of all schemes by which man, trampling right and justice underfoot, builds his fortune upon oppression and wrong, the foremost living advocate of the equality of men . . . the champion of the rights of toil, the foe of

privilege and monopoly, the friend of all
who are laden . . . [60]

Clarence Darrow, a lawyer of national repute who championed the cause of the underprivileged in various cases including labor
disputes and social issues, seconded the nomination. He said that Hearst had broadened the
Democratic party's appeal to organized labor,
rank and file laborers, urban immigrants and the
nation's underprivileged. The party had to
accept the fact, he added, that Hearst was
initiating an inevitable shift in the party's
class appeal. He pleaded:

> Even at this late hour it would be well
> to remember that the whole Democratic Party
> is not inside these convention walls, much
> less in the seats of the delegates assembled
> here . . . It is not made up alone of pawn-
> shops in the narrow, crooked lane which men
> call Wall Street--shops where human souls
> are placed in pawn for gold. The United
> States is the countless millions who do
> their work and live their lives and earn
> their bread without the aid of schemes or
> tricks . . .
> It may be the hour of reason and judge-
> ment has passed by, that this Democratic
> Convention will be unmindful of the humble
> and the weak; but sometime when the fever
> of commercialism has run its course, when
> humanity and justice shall once more control
> the minds of men, this great party will come
> back from the golden idols and tempting
> flesh pots, and once more battle for the
> rights of man.[61]

In reporting on the demonstrations following the Hearst nomination the _American_'s
headline read, "CHEERS FOR HEARST CAME FROM THE
HEARTS, SAY DELEGATES."[62] The thirty-eight
minute applause was an impressive showing of

159

support and strength.[63]   Delegates from California, Arizona, Iowa, Nevada, Oklahoma, South
Dakota, Kansas, Washington, Rhode Island, Illinois, and Minnesota joined in the demonstration.[64]   Tammany Hall representatives did
not stir for either Hearst or Parker, but
Murphy did smile enigmatically when the Hearst
rally began.[65]

Champ Clark nominated Francis M. Cockrell
of Missouri, who had been a brigadier general
in the Confederate army and had served in the
United States Senate since March 4, 1875.   The
mystery surrounding Bryan was soon ended as he
seconded the Cockrell nomination.   In with-
holding support from Hearst, states Louis
Koenig in his political biography of Bryan, he
was committing a patently self interested act.
He was at a stage in his political career when
he was vulnerable to new rivals who might dis-
place his monopoly of leadership of the party's
liberal wing.[66]   Ihmsen told a New York _Times_
reporter that any endorsement of Hearst would
have put Hearst into a position of influence and
power and his voice would in the future rival
Bryan's.[67]   Moved perhaps by feelings of guilt
for abandoning his former ally, Bryan closed
his speech:

If it is the choice of this convention
that the standard shall be placed in the
hands of the gentleman presented by California, the man who though he has money, pleads
the cause of the poor: the man who is best
beloved, I can safely say, among the
laboring men, of all the candidates proposed; the man who more than any other
represents peace, make Hearst the candidate of this convention, and Nebraska will
be with you.[68]

Bryan may have had legitimate misgivings about
the publisher because of his lack of political
experience, his non-conformist behavior in

160

Congress, his journalistic aggressiveness, and the rumors of purchased delegates. Abbot, a Hearst employee and advisor at the convention, later wrote that "many of his delegates at the St. Louis convention were obtained by purchase and perhaps more by intimidation through his newspapers."[69] Rumors about this abounded at the convention, but this writer found no evidence in the Hearst files to substantiate them.

Martin Littleton, the distinguished New York attorney, in a lackluster address, nominated Judge Parker. He said in part, in a veiled slap at Hearst:

> If you ask me why he has been silent, I tell you it is because he does not claim to be the master of the Democratic Party, but is content to be its servant. If you ask me why he has not outlined a policy for this convention, I tell you that he does not believe that policies should be dictated, but that the sovereignty of the people is in the untrammeled judgement and wisdom of its members . . . [70]

As the nomination speeches were given, conditions were chaotic on the convention floor. Hearst supporters made repeated attempts to tie up the proceedings. Periodically they would yell in unison:

> Boom, Boom, Boom.
> First, First, First.
> California, California.
> Hearst! Hearst! Hearst![71]

Despite these efforts, Parker dominated the first ballot with 658 electoral votes, nine less than a two-thirds majority; Hearst placed second with 200 votes; and Cockrell had only 42 votes. Hearst ran ahead of Parker with the delegates from Iowa, Arizona, California, Colorado, Idaho, Illinois, Kansas, Nebraska, Nevada, New Mexico,

161

Rhode Island, South Dakota, Wyoming, and Hawaii.
The remaining one hundred and nine delegate votes
were scattered among several others who were not
serious candidates.[72] The Idaho delegation began
a rush for the bandwagon, switching their votes
to Parker. In all, twenty-one delegates, including eleven Hearst delegates, switched to
Parker. The delegates then gave Parker a unanimous vote by acclamation.[73]

The Vice-Presidential nomination went to
eighty year old Henry Gassway Davis, a political,
lumber, rail, and mining veteran from West Virginia. Before the Civil War he had been a Whig
and during the war a Unionist, turning Democrat
after the peace. He had been active in efforts,
both legal and vigilante, to prevent the ex-
tension of civil rights to Negroes.[74] Less
than three months before the election, he had
proposed to the West Virginia legislature that
the Negroes should be disenfranchised in that
state.[75]

The following day Parker stunned the convention by threatening to turn down the nomination. He stated in a telegram addressed to the
New York delegation that he supported the gold
standard and advised the delegates to select a
new nominee if they could not accept his position. It read:

> I regard the gold standard as firmly and
> irrevocably established and shall act
> accordingly if the action of the con-
> vention today shall be ratified by the
> people. As the platform is silent on the
> subject my views shall be made known to the
> convention, and if it proves to be un-
> satisfactory to the majority, I request you
> to decline the nomination for me at once,
> so that another may be nominated before
> adjournment.[76]

The telegram caused some premature hope

162

and excitement among Hearst supporters, but Hearst knew he had been defeated. "The gold issue," he confided to his campaign manager, "is the only issue I agree with Parker on."[77] The Hearst effort had caused party regulars to take notice, but did little more.

Sheehan and Thomas Ryan, members of the New York delegation, led the Parker forces in the ensuing convention debate. Conservative delegates assailed Parker for his arrogance.[78] Parker delegates threatened to withdraw their votes.[79] The Missouri delegation considered presenting a resolution to remove Parker from the nomination.[80] Finally, Williams, who had labelled the telegram an arrogant and treacherous attack on the party, realized that the withdrawal of Parker's name would be tantamount to declaring for free silver.[81] He therefore combined forces with southern delegates in drafting a response, which was approved by the delegates, to Parker:

> The platform adopted by the convention is silent on the question of the monetary standard because it is not regarded by us a possible issue in this campaign, and only campaign issues were mentioned in the platform. Therefore, there is nothing in the views expressed by you in the telegram just received which would preclude anyone entertaining them from accepting a nomination on the said platform.[82]

The actual telegram never reached Parker, but its text appeared in all of the daily newspapers.[83] The "gold telegram" insured that there would be no change in platform or candidate.

In view of the results at the Democratic convention, Thomas E. Watson's nomination by the People's Party received serious attention in some circles. The Tribune thought it "a mistake for political prophets to class him as a negligible quantity," since he was "distinctly persona grata with the radical Democrats" and likely to attract the many discontented of that party.[84] But populism was fading from political strength. The fifteen hundred populist papers of 1896 had been reduced to twenty-three in 1904.[85] After the election Watson would admit that his party had commanded "almost nothing to start with in the way of party organization, campaign funds, and newspaper support."[86] He conducted a nationwide campaign, consisting almost entirely of stump speeches. He directed his entire appeal to the Hearst Democrats who had been betrayed by "a Wall Street maneuver" at St. Louis.[87]

Hearst urged his supporters to remain devoted to liberal principles and to do what they believed to be right in the upcoming election.[88] He immediately endorsed Parker's candidacy. On July 9 he instructed all of his editors to support the entire Democratic ticket.[89] The following day editorials endorsing Parker appeared in all of his newspapers.[90] In a July 10 interview with the Chicago Record-Herald he conceded that he was not entirely satisfied with the Democratic party's platform, but added that in the spirit of party loyalty he would support it and Parker.[91] The Hearst newspapers refrained from printing a single word against Parker between the time he was named the party's nominee through the November election. They did not campaign energetically for him, but simply reported the campaign.

Bryan and Hearst both campaigned for Parker, but neither did so with much enthusiasm. Both entertained ambitions for 1908 so their loyalty to the party and their standing as "good Democrats" could not be doubted. But as the campaign developed, both gave less and less support. Thomas Ryan and August Belmont, archtypes of financial conservatism, donated large amounts to Parker, who was praised by

Wall Street titans like James Hill and Jacob Schiff, and was endorsed by conservative newspaper editors like Adolph Ochs and Henry Watterson. Leading conservatives, including David Hill, Dan Lamont, Charles Hamlin, became Parker's leading counselors. Most troublesome to Hearst and Bryan was that a majority of liberal Democrats, so they estimated, preferred the election of Theodore Roosevelt.[92]

In early October Hearst issued and published in his newspaper a lengthy letter to all members of the National Association of Democratic Clubs urging all Democrats to unite. He affirmed that a great majority of Americans were liberal and Democratic. These people, the club President added, did not put money above men nor did they believe that a government established by all the people should be taken out of their hands and turned over to a selfish few to be exploited for their own profit.[93] In the letter he never once mentioned Parker by name or urged members to vote for him.[94]

Hearst privately admitted that he opposed what Parker represented. A Parker supporter wrote the nominee that the National Association of Democratic Clubs were not all aiding in his candidacy; that they would not campaign for him unless they got the word to do so from Hearst.[95] Former President Cleveland wrote to Parker that Hearst's support was crucial to his campaign and that he should somehow appease the liberal editor.[96]

Throughout the campaign the Democratic party was in disarray and members of the progressive wing were not willing to compromise. A convincing Republican victory, they believed, would insure a liberal nominee in 1908.[97] A "Radical Democracy Club" was formed in Brooklyn and pledged its support to Watson. Club members appealed to Bryan and Hearst to refrain from supporting Parker. They were clinging to their principles and urged Hearst and Bryan to do the same.[98] Brisbane summed up the views of these Democrats when he wrote to Bryan:

> I hope sincerely that your work will be done in the future for real radicalism, that you will live in history as a man who made a fight for the principles and questions that are going to last a hundred thousand years . . . The Democratic party seems not to be very closely united here. I am rather inclined to think it is going to lose the election. I called it the Democractic party, because it got hold of that name in the interests of Wall Street. My own hope is that it will get the beating that hypocrisy deserves.[99]

In the ensuing campaign progressives did not flock to Roosevelt, but millions of Americans who were opposed to the malefactors of great wealth accepted and cheered his image. Roosevelt broadened his appeal by appointing qualified individuals from minority groups, Negroes, Catholics, and Jews to government positions. During the campaign, he invited Booker T. Washington to the White House and pushed through Congress a new pension order making age alone a sufficient requirement for voter eligibility.

Parker had been selected as his party's nominee because of his "safe and sane" views and because of his close ties to New York wealth. His association with Wall Street prevented Democrats from claiming that their party was leading the fight against the trusts. Parker conducted an insipid campaign. In the final days of the campaign he created his only excitement when he accused Roosevelt's campaign manager George B. Cortelyou, former Secretary of Commerce, of blackmailing corporations for campaign contributions. There was no evidence behind the accusations and no need for Cortelyou to resort to blackmail. Cortelyou assured Roosevelt that he

would be elected without a promise or pledge of
any kind, expressed or implied, to any corporation or individual.[100]

Parker fell to Roosevelt in the grandest
Republican victory since 1872. The Republican
outdistanced him 7,628,461 to 5,043,223. No
major political party candidate had received
so few votes in twenty years. In the Electoral
College vote Roosevelt led Parker 336 to 140.
The New York _Times_ called the President's
election the greatest personal triumph ever
achieved by a presidential candidate.[101] Parker
did carry New York City by over 80,000 votes.[102]
The election returns gave Watson a vote of
117,183. This vote, which was more than double
that received by the Populist candidate in
1900, was a great disappointment to Populism.
The liberals who defected voted for Eugene V.
Debs, whose vote leaped from around 90,000 to
over 400,000.

The election results corroborated Hearst's
belief that the future success of the Democratic
party lay with the liberal element in society.
In an _American_ editorial printed the morning
after election day, Hearst called for changes
in the composition and orientation of the Democratic party:

> The Democracy has had enough 'conservatism'
> to last it for a generation--forever, let
> us hope. The Democratic party has no right
> to be in any degree 'conservative' in the
> sense meant by these disqualified advisers
> and discredited critics. . . . It is the
> fundamental duty of the Democratic party
> to be radical in assailing wrong.

He clearly identified the despotic enemies of
the people who now controlled the party:

> The oil trust wants the Democracy to be
> 'conservative.' The beef trust wants the
> Democracy to be 'conservative.' All those
> 'business interests,' which are not business

167

interests at all, but piratical interests,
want the Democracy to be 'conservative.'
The aim of the plundering trusts has been
to reduce the Democratic party to a 'conservative' servitude--to make it nationally
. . . a mere attachment to the Republican
party, and its organization cannot be
employed by the people when they seek to
strike at their despoilers and oppressors.
The American masses demonstrated on Tuesday
how much respect and liking they have for
a 'conservative' Democratic party.

It was not enough that the party be wrested away
from these powers; it must become a party with
explicitly radical commitments:

. . . The greatest need of this republic
today is an aggressive and well organized
radical party--a devoted party to intelligent progress. Tuesday's tremendous Republican sweep has made it certain that the
republic's greatest need will be supplied.
Henceforward the Democratic party,
taught by a gigantic defeat the consequences of attempting to republicanize itself, will be radical in its spirit and its
proposals--patriotically and wisely radical.
It will be radical in its demand for the
destruction of the criminal trusts. It will
be radical in its demand that the protection
of the tariff shall be taken away from
industrial combinations which openly rob
the American citizen by charging him higher
prices for the enforcement of the laws
against combinations in restraint of trade.
It will be radical in its demand for an
income tax, in order that wealth shall be
made to bear its rightful share of the cost
of government. It will be radical in
fighting intrenched privilege in the interest of the underprivileged.[103]

A week later he added that a party organized

168

along radical lines was the Democrats's only hope for survival.[104]

The trust issue, wrote Hearst shortly afterwards, was clearly the most important issue to the masses of the people. He pledged to introduce in Congress legislation to regulate the trusts and he wrote that the primary motive of the Democratic party should be to abolish government by trust. In an editorial he wrote:

> Never in the history of this country has arrogant, overpowering, predatory wealth been as menacing as it has been now; through the wide exposures of its methods has it been as thoroughly detested as now. The criminal trust issue is the dominating issue in the minds of the whole American people.[105]

The safe, sound, judicious, and conservative approach of the Democrats proved disastrous. Now Bryan and Hearst could both look to the 1908 nomination. G. Warren Hayes, national Democratic delegate from West Virginia, told reporters that Hearst was the party's only logical choice in 1908.[106] Hearst, no doubt, believed that Bryan had betrayed him in St. Louis, but he remained silent on the matter, realizing the political consequences of alienating the Bryanites.

In 1904 Hearst failed to muster any support with Eastern delegates. He was making a concerted appeal to the urban masses, but was failing to make any significant inroads with urban party regulars. He decided to continue and not abandon his broad appeal. Having gotten only 7 Northeastern votes to Parker's 237, in the convention balloting, he set out to prove himself a viable Eastern urban candidate. A central issue of Hearstism was to clean up corruption in politics. To demonstrate that he was a poli-

169

tician of action and to prove to the nation his
urban appeal, he intensified his attacks on the
methods and policies of Tammany Hall.   In
1904 he was re-elected to the United States
Congress as a Tammany candidate. A year later
he broke with the New York political machine
and, in 1905 and 1906, put New Yorkers through
two spectacular campaigns.

Footnotes

[1]Albert J. Beveridge to Roosevelt, April
28, 1904. Beveridge Papers, Library of Congress;
Beveridge to Roosevelt, August 9, 1904,
Beveridge Papers, Library of Congress.

[2]New York _Tribune_. July 4, 1904.

[3]Beveridge to George Harvey, November 14,
1904, Beveridge Papers, Library of Congress.

[4]A. M. Schlesinger, ed., _History of American
Presidential Elections_, vol. 3 (New York:
Chelsea House Publishers in association with
McGraw-Hill Book Company, 1971), p. 1977.

[5]Beveridge to McClure, September 29,
1905, Beveridge Papers, Library of Congress.

[6]James Allen Myatt, "William Randolph
Hearst and the Progressive Era, 1900-1912"
Ph.D. Dissertation, University of Florida,
1960), p. 6.

[7]Schlesinger, _loc. cit._

[8]Hearst to Lawrence, June 1, 1904, J.A.M.

[9]New York _Evening Post_ March 1, 1904.

[10]New York _Tribune_, March 23, 1904.

[11]New York _Tribune_, May 12, 1904.

[12]Nicholas Butler, President of Columbia
University, to Roosevelt, November 9, 1905,
Roosevelt Papers, Library of Congress.

[13]New York _Tribune_, February 21, 1904.

[14]New York _Times_, February 14, 1905.

[15]New York _Tribune_, February 21, 1904.

[16]New York _Times_, April 1, 1904.

[17]New York _Times_, April 12, 1904.

[18]New York _Times_, April 20, 1904.

[19]Hearst to the Workingmen's Committee, October 22, 1906, J.A.M.

[20]New York _Journal_, August 16, 1900.

[21]New York _American_, July 15, 1905.

[22]Hearst to Cory Noble, February 8, 1904, J.A.M.

[23]Brisbane to Thomas Watson, June 23, 1904, J.A.M.

[24]Atlanta _News_, March 7, 1904, J.A.M.

[25]Hearst to Brisbane, February 10, 1904, J.A.M.

[26]Schlesinger, _op_. _cit_., p. 1976.

[27]_Ibid_.

[28]Thomas E. Watson, _The_ _Life_ _and_ _Times_ _of_ _Thomas_ _Jefferson_ (New York: D. Appleton and Company, 1903), introduction.

[29]C. Vann Woodward, _Tom_ _Watson_ (New York: Oxford University Press, 1963), p. 356.

[30]Brisbane to Watson, June 23, 1904, J.A.M.

[31]Woodward, _loc_. _cit_.

[32]Beveridge to Roosevelt, August 9, 1904, Beveridge Papers, Library of Congress.

[33]_Tammany_ _Times_, December 26, 1903, p.3, J.A.M.

[34]_Pearson's Magazine_, September 1906, J.A.M.

[35]Winkler, _op. cit._, p. 190.

[36]New York _American_, June 30, 1904.

[37]Eltweed Pomeroy, "A Political Forecast," _Arena_, June 1904, pp. 578-581, J.A.M.

[38]Hearst to Ihmsen, June 25, 1904, J.A.M.

[39]New York _American_, June 30, 1904.

[40]Bryan to Thomas Alexander, May 18, 1904, Bryan Papers, Library of Congress.

[41]Schlesinger, _loc. cit._

[42]Walter Chambers, _Samuel Seabury: A Challenge_ (New York: The Century Company, 1932), p. 78.

[43]New York _American_, July 10, 1904.

[44]Grover Cleveland, "Democracy's Opportunity," _Saturday Evening Post_, February 20, 1904, J.A.M.

[45]Richard Olney to Cleveland, May 18, 1904, Cleveland Papers, Library of Congress.

[46]Cleveland to William F. Vilas, June 24, 1906, Cleveland Papers, Library of Congress.

[47]Hearst to Abbot, June 28, 1904, J.A.M.

[48]New York _Times_, July 7, 1904.

[49]New York _American_, July 9, 1904.

[50]New York _Journal of Commerce_, July 9, 1904, J.A.M.

[51]New York _American_, July 7, 1904.

[52]New York _American_, July 8, 1904.

[53]_Nation_ editorial, undated, J.A.M.

[54]New York _American_, July 9, 1904.

[55]Charles A. Bridge, "History of Judge Parker's Famous Gold Telegram," New York _Herald_ Report, July 1908, Alton Parker Papers, Library of Congress.

[56]_Ibid_.

[57]New York _American_, July 9, 1904.

[58]New York _Tribune_, July 10, 1904.

[59]New York _American_, July 9, 1904.

[60]_Ibid_.

[61]_Ibid_.

[62]_Ibid_.

[63]New York _Times_, July 9, 1904.

[64]New York _Evening Journal_, July 9, 1904.

[65]Abbot, _op. cit._, p. 253.

[66]Koenig, _op. cit._, p. 386.

[67]New York _Times_, July 6, 1904.

[68]New York _Evening Journal_, July 9, 1904.

[69]Abbot, _op. cit._, p. 251.

[70]New York _Evening Journal_, July 9, 1904.

[71]New York _American_, July 9, 1904.

[72]The votes were scattered among Richard Olney, George Gray, E. C. Well, John Sharp,

N. M. Towne, Bird S. Coler, and George McClellan.

[73]New York _Times_, July 10, 1904.

[74]New York _American_, July 10, 1904.

[75]Schlesinger, _op. cit._, p. 1982.

[76]Parker to William Sheehan, July 9, 1904, Parker Papers, Library of Congress.

[77]Hearst to Ihmsen, July 9, 1904, J.A.M.

[78]New York _Times_, July 10, 1904.

[79]New York _World_, July 10, 1904.

[80]New York _World_, July 11, 1904.

[81]New York _Times_, July 11, 1904.

[82]Bridge, _loc. cit._

[83]_Ibid._

[84]New York _Tribune_, July 8, 1904.

[85]Woodward, _op. cit._, p. 359.

[86]Atlanta _News_, November 14, 1904, J.A.M.

[87]The _Saturday News_ (Joliet, Illinois), September 17, 1904, J.A.M.

[88]Hearst to Lawrence, July 9, 1904, Milton Blumberg, ed., _Official Reports of the Proceedings of the Democratic National Convention_ (New York: Publisher's Printing Company, 1904), p. 254.

[89]Hearst to all Editors, July 9, 1904, J.A.M.

[90]New York _American_, July 10, 1904.

[91] New York _American_, July 11, 1904.

[92] Koenig, _op. cit._, p. 394.

[93] Hearst to The National Association of Democratic Club Members, October 4, 1904, J.A.M.

[94] Hearst to Brisbane, July 31, 1904, J.A.M.

[95] Josephus Daniels to Parker, September 21, 1904, Parker Papers, Library of Congress.

[96] Cleveland to Parker, July 14, 1904, Parker Papers, Library of Congress.

[97] Koenig, _loc. cit._

[98] Durbin Van Vleck to Bryan, August 25, 1904, Bryan Papers, Library of Congress.

[99] Brisbane to Bryan, August 9, 1904, Bryan Papers, Library of Congress.

[100] Roosevelt to Dr. Lyman Abbott, October 7, 1904, Roosevelt Papers, Library of Congress.

[101] New York _Times_, November 10, 1904.

[102] New York _American_, November 4, 1904.

[103] _Ibid._

[104] New York _American_, November 11, 1904.

[105] New York _American_, November 9, 1904.

[106] New York _American_, July 10, 1904.

VII

A Challenge to Tammany Hall

In 1905 Hearst challenged Tammany Hall for the New York City mayorship with only a loose organization called the Municipal Ownership League. By early 1905 he had become convinced that in New York neither Republican nor Democratic leaders represented or cared about the needs of the masses of plain people in America and that a third party, a radical or liberal party, could be successful on all levels.[1]

Samuel Seabury, who was dissatisfied with city and state Democratic party leaders, played a significant role in Hearst's 1905 attempt. In the spring of 1905 Seabury wrote a two hundred page booklet, entitled "Public Ownership and Operation of Public Utilities in New York," explaining the ideals and goals of the newly formed Municipal Ownership League. He had hit upon an issue close to Hearst's own way of thinking. The two met in late September and agreed to join forces in an attempt to clean up the New York City government.[2] The city's William Randolph Hearst League, which Ihmsen had organized to direct Hearst's presidential candidacy, merged with the Municipal Ownership League and Hearst and Seabury sought a suitable candidate to enter the 1905 mayoralty campaign. The Hearst-Seabury alliance continued through the 1905 city elections and the 1906 state elections.[3]

Hearst urged Seabury to run for mayor on the Municipal Ownership platform; Seabury urged Hearst to enter the campaign; and Brisbane urged a drafting of Judge William Gaynor. Seabury wrote to Hearst that he would accept the nomination but believed he could do more good running for the state Supreme Court on the Municipal Ownership League ticket. The league's ticket had its greatest chance for success, wrote Seabury, with Hearst as its head.[4] In early October Hearst publicly declined the nomination:

> I do not feel that it would be for the best
> interests of the independent movement /for
> me7 to become its leader . . .
> I think that this movement can be best
> brought to success under some other man, and
> I will fight harder than I would for myself,
> and more effectively than I could for my-
> self, for any upright man that will make
> an honest fight against the bosses and the
> forces of corruption . . . [5]

While his public excuses for declining the nomination were concerned with the best interests of
the newly formed league, his private writings
reveal a personal motive. He wrote to his legal
counsel that he was considering a run for City
Hall, but had his sights on the 1906 gubernatorial election and feared that a poor showing
in an unplanned and unorganized challenge to
both Tammany and the Republican party in 1905
could be political suicide. [6]

On October 4, 1905, the Municipal Ownership League delegates convened at the Grand
Central Place. When Hearst appeared on the platform, they gave him a seven minute ovation. [7] In
his keynote address, he began to sound like a
candidate:

> Have we left any government by the people?
> You have your votes and the privilege of
> casting them, but for whom? For Mr.
> Murphy's puppet, or for Mr. Odell's puppet?
> If you want gas that will burn and not really
> poison, you can vote for Mr. Murphys puppet
> and you won't get it . . .
> I do not really believe that the corpo-
> rations are at fault. I do not believe that
> Mr. Murphy or Mr. Odell is at fault--I am
> afraid you are at fault. You are a sleeping
> majority, pledged by pygmies. Wake up!
> Nominate independent men. Men who will lead

you to victory, restore this city to a
government of the people, by the people
. . . [8]

Seabury engineered the nomination of Hearst. The
delegates approved it with a response that seemed
to be genuinely spontaneous.[9] The following day
Hearst declined the nomination.[10]

In the interim Tammany nominated George
McClellan for re-election. McClellan, a forty
year old Princeton alumnus, had been elected to
the 58th Congress from New York City's Twelfth
Congressional District. He had served in Congress until December 21, 1903, when he resigned
to assume the duties as mayor of New York City.
In his speech accepting the nomination in 1905
he attacked the notion of municipal ownership:

> As a Democrat I believe the community is
> best governed which is least governed and
> that if individual effort and private enter-
> prise can accomplish the same result as
> government, government has no right to
> interfere.[11]

He promised, if re-elected, to continue the policies and practices of his current administration.[12]

On October 7 the Republicans nominated
Charles Evans Hughes. Hearst endorsed him, and
when he declined the nomination the publisher
wrote:

> The nomination of Charles E. Hughes gave
> promise for a short time that an unas-
> sailable man could be supported on a non-
> partisan basis. Mr. Hughes' declination
> destroyed that hope.[13]

Delegations representing the city's Italians
and the German Americans called on Hearst and
urged him to accept the Municipal Ownership

179

League's nomination.[14] He reconsidered and on
October 10 accepted it. In a public address he
said:

> The situation in this city is so grave
> and the condition of the public in the face
> of organized bossism is apparently so help-
> less that no man has a right to consider
> anything else, least of all his private
> affairs or personal inclinations. The one
> thing to be considered is the necessity of
> giving to the people an opportunity to vote
> for some man of whom it may at least be
> said that he would, if elected, represent
> those that voted for him and not any boss
> or corporation or selfish private interest.[15]

On October 12 the league delegates assembled at
Carnegie Hall and nominated Hearst. In his
acceptance speech Hearst pledged that his
administration would be honest, efficient, and
progressive.[16]

Following the nomination of Hearst, the
League attempted to fuse with the Republicans
to unite opposition to Tammany.[17] Efforts for
fusion were only partially successful. A
ticket was assembled which included twenty of
thirty-six Republican assembly candidates in
Manhattan and nine of twenty-one Republican
assembly candidates in Brooklyn. The GOP
fused at the lower levels because its only
chance for victory was with the support of the
Hearst press; the Republicans would not fuse on
the Hearst nomination because he was a Democratic Congressman who had presidential aspirations as a Democrat.[18] On October 10 the Republicans settled on William Ivins, a prominent
city reformer. He focused his attacks on
McClellan and Tammany, ignoring, for the most
part, the Hearst candidacy. His key campaign
issues were the city's inadequate water supply,
inadequate schools, and filthy slums.[19]

Hearst used his newspapers to conduct his

campaign. What he said in political rallies appeared daily in German, Yiddish, Italian and English. His newspapers, aided by the wizardry of Homer Davenport, Frederick Burr Opper, T. E. Powers, and Tad Dorgan, successfully utilized political cartoons as political weapons. Hearst directed his attacks exclusively at McClellan and Tammany.

McClellan focussed his attacks on the Hearst candidacy, ignoring Ivins. Tammany officials, believing that the opposition vote would be divided, were very confident of victory.[20] The Outlook complained that the voters, unwilling to abandon Tammany, had abdicated their sovereignty.[21] But the Hearst effort gained respectability when the Tribune and the World, papers that had long despised Hearst both personally and professionally, endorsed his candidacy. As a matter of conviction Pulitzer detested Hearst's professions, principles, and purposes; however, he wrote, he did admire his courage in accepting for reasons of principle a candidacy that could not lead to his election. He would render a public service, added Pulitzer, by vigorously articulating the principles of the Democratic party which had been lost to corrupt bosses. Pulitzer made a private analysis of the factors in the election's outcome:

> If he will detach from the blind followers of the Murphy machine a large body, he will teach the voter that his first duty is to vote in accordance with his own conscience and as a freeman, he will render a service to the cause of independence and intelligence and show the way all voters should vote, free and untrammeled in accordance with their own individual convictions, not because a ticket is labelled Democratic or Republican.
> Whether Mr. Gush /Hearst/ is sincere or not in his professions is no more the question than whether Mr. Murphy is sincere

181

> in his alleged Democratic principles. The
> main question is who teaches more inde-
> pendence in voting, who awakens more indig-
> nation against corruption and misgovernment,
> who comes nearer prescribing the real truth,
> who is more against party humbug, who
> against fooling the people.
> We sincerely hope Mr. Gush will receive
> a very large vote.[22]

The _Tribune_ endorsed him because he gave the
voters a viable alternative to machine government.

Hearst labelled his campaign effort "the
Progressive movement." He would later claim
that this had been the first instance that the
term was used for a specific social or political
movement.[23] The league's platform called for
cheaper and improved municipal transportation,
for more and better public schools, for higher
wages of all city employees, and for a graduated
city income tax. Hearst was the only candidate
to support municipal ownership unequivocally.
Publicly he challenged the Tammany representatives in the Albany legislature for opposing
legislation cutting the gas rate in the city
when it was proven that the existing rates were
higher than those of other urban areas, and he
also criticized them for voting against a bill
that would have provided for the automatic re-
version of new subway lines to the city after an
initial operating period of either twenty-five
or fifty years.[24] He campaigned as a representative and champion of the poorer elements in
society. Many voters were ready to slay the
bosses and supported Hearst with almost religious
fanaticism. His campaign was less than twenty-
four hours old when Thomas Ryan, borough President of the Brooklyn Carpenters' Union, pledged
that a clear majority of the 13,000 members of
his organization would support him at the polls,
and Alfred J. Boulton, President of the Brooklyn
Labor and Citizens Union, promised the Municipal

League candidate the almost unanimous support of
the city's printers.[25]

Hearst's popularity forced McClellan to campaign more vigorously than he had planned or
desired; he had intended to give six token
speeches during the campaign but ended up delivering sixty-four speeches in twenty days preceding the election.[26] He regarded Hearst's campaign as a crusade for socialism.[27] Although
Ivins was an active campaigner and predicted
victory throughout the campaign,[28] it was a
contest between Hearst and McClellan.

Hearst attempted to strengthen his broad
appeal by involving supporters in his campaign.
He continually held open briefings to discuss
issues, campaign progress, and alternatives for
the remainder of the campaign, believing that
this involvement, if successful, would usher in
similar political "progressive movements" nationwide.[29] His campaign was remarkable given the
lack of time and organization. At first his
campaign was so erratic, not to say crazy, that
it kept Tammany officials laughing. But two
weeks into the campaign they had stopped laughing
and were frantically seeking ways to stop him.[30]
He became the greatest asset of his campaign. He
had overcome his fear of crowds and spoke with
new-found courage, determination, and enthusiasm.
He established headquarters at the New Amsterdam
Hotel and delivered an average of twelve speeches
daily.

Hearst's labor support mounted. The
Marine Trader's Council unanimously endorsed
him.[31] First Vice-President Edward Gould, of
the International Brotherhood of Teamsters, announced that forty thousand cabmen in the city
would vote for him. Gould added that 90 percent
to 95 percent of his union "regardless of political affiliations would vote for him . . .
They are as unanimous as any body of men of that
size could be."[32] The 6,000 members of the

183

Allied Printers Trade Union voted unanimously to
establish a William Randolph Hearst League of
Union Members.[33] On November 5 the 20,000 members of the Butchers and Meat Cutters' Union
unanimously endorsed him.[34] In September 1905
the female starch workers in Troy, New York, had
gone on strike. Hearst appeared before the
strikers and offered to print a special newspaper in their behalf. Over 25,000 copies were
printed and sold at ten cents apiece. He donated
all of the proceeds to the strikers' general
fund. The New York Women's Trade Union League
publicly thanked the publisher for all he had
done in their behalf, and during the campaign
endorsed his candidacy and urged all other
women's organizations to do the same.[35] Hearst
continually pointed to the anti-labor policies
of Tammany officials and emphasized his own support of organized labor, and promised unqualified support of labor laws within the
city.[36]

Hearst levelled numerous charges at Tammany
officials. He claimed that their binding commitments to the trusts made them incapable of
securing needed reforms. Tammany leaders had
realized profits, he added, by awarding the
city's gas, utility, and rail contracts to the
"right" parties. He charged that nearly half of
the funds that were budgeted for various city
developments could not be accounted for.[37]

Tammany officials' attacks on Hearst became personal and vicious. They published a
pamphlet, entitled "The Diary of an Assassin's
Accomplice," which labelled Hearst an anarchist
and accused him of inciting Czolgosz in the
McKinley assassination. Tammany workers hung
large pictures of both Hearst and Mclelland across
city streets. Under the Hearst pictures were
placed large red flags; under the McClelland
pictures were placed large American flags.
Signs posted throughout the city read, "Under
Which Flag Do You Vote?"[38]

184

McClellan himself was a more resourceful and intelligent campaigner than many Tammany cronies and sought to offset some of Hearst's immigrant support by addressing German, French, and Italian groups in their native tongues. He was relying on the intelligentsia, labor leaders, and Catholics for his strength. He viewed Hearst's efforts as a socialistic campaign appealing to only the lower, uneducated elements of society.[39]

Hearst evoked passions and a determined spirit in people who had previously been indifferent to the politics of the city. Rallies, demonstrations, and speeches all culminated in a frenzied climax as 100,000 league supporters packed into Madison Square Garden on November 5 for the final campaign rally. They gave the head of their ticket a twenty-minute ovation. In addressing them, Hearst said in part:

> . . . I greet you tonight not as Democrats or Republicans . . . I greet you not as partisans, but as citizens deeply interested with us in the welfare of our citizens and in the progress and prosperity of our great city. . . .
> I am proud of the friends who have rallied around us. They are the people's friends. I am proud of the enemies that oppose us. They are the people's enemies. We will fight those enemies together and triumph over them, no matter how powerful and unscrupulous they may be . . . We shall say with Jackson, 'Let us ask nothing but what is right and submit to nothing that is wrong.' We will fight the battle along those lines, and we will win a glorious victory if we will only trust the people.[40]

Hearst wrote privately to Brisbane that he believed his election could unite progressives against the moneyed powers:

> Our movement is disunited. It is now a movement on many levels with many leaders.

Of course business leaders are better organized. They have money and built-in
structure. They practice self-enhancement
as they profess 'progressive' solutions to
social needs. To effectively combat them,
we must begin to win at the polls. If we
shall win the mayorship despite the obvious
obstacles we will become a popular symbol
to the masses. If we win, our broad appeal
will only increase . . . [41]

Of the city newspapers, the Times was
Hearst's most outspoken critic. It labelled
his candidacy "utterly destructive" to the
city.[42] It expressed alarm at the almost fanatic
enthusiasm of his supporters:

Assaults upon the character of Mr.
Hearst and denunciations of his newspaper
methods cost him no votes . . . The vicious
element--and we suppose Mr. Hearst will poll
absolutely the whole of it--likes him all
the better for his qualities which his opponents denounce. The red flag foolishness
and quotations of violent attacks upon
Mr. McKinley from Mr. Hearst's newspapers
simply tend to make the anarchist vote
'solid' for him.[43]

The lower classes wanted to lash out at the
public service corporations and to slay the
corrupt bosses, the Times insisted, and were
using Hearst as a club because he suited them
well. Ochs named Ivins the most qualified candidate, but urged his readers to vote for McClellan
because he was the only candidate able to defeat
Hearst.[44]

Fraud and corruption marred the campaign
and election. On November 4 the Journal exposed a fraudulent Odell-Hearst petition[45] which
claimed that Hearst was endorsing several Republican candidates for municipal judges, assembly-
men, and aldermen. In return, it said, several

186

prominent city Republicans pledged to work for
Hearst. An investigation proved that one hundred and three signatures on the petition were
forged. Warrants were issued for the arrests
of George Hyman and Henry Melrose, both notaries
public who had validated the document. Commissioner of Deeds Louis Levine issued a statement that the petition indicated that Hearst and
Odell supporters had worked together preparing
it.[46] Tammany leaders planned to employ every
man that conservatism could bring to bear to
head off a Hearst victory. Corporate money
was pouring into Tammany's campaign fund, the
Evening Star reported, and the Hall's political
machinery was forced to work at high pressure.[47]

On election day Hearst voted early and spent
the remainder of the day at his headquarters
where league watchers, beaten and bleeding, stag-
gered in relating reports of Tammany thugs controlling voting booths.[48] Murphy controlled the
ballot boxes, the election officials, and the police department. Hearst was temporarily helpless.
Just before midnight, he went into action.
Police Commissioner William McAdoo allowed his
managers to remove some of the ballot boxes
from police custody. They were moved to a
private warehouse that Hearst had rented. McAdoo
retired for the evening, claiming he had a "bad
cold." The boxes were recovered within three
hours, but Tammany officials called foul.[49]

The November 8 American headlines read
"W. R. HEARST ELECTED MAYOR." The official
tally, however, showed McClellan the victor
with 228,397 votes; Hearst finishing second with
224,925; and Ivins trailing the field with
137,193 votes. The results were close enough
to warrant a recount and the actions of Tammany
workers were suspect enough to justify an investigation. Hearst was right in making a contest of the results, the Washington Star maintained, because there was ample proof that some
of his vote had been kept away from the polls by

187

familiar Tammany methods.[50] In an editorial it
postulated that in defeat Hearst's political
fortunes would be advanced:

> Defeated by a close margin, with the
> halo of a martyr to the wickedness of Tam-
> many's election methods encircling his head,
> Mr. Hearst is in first class trim to con-
> tinue his personal exploitations for poli-
> tical honors. He has run Tammany a breath-
> ing race, so close that the discarding of
> three or four off-color McClellan ballots
> in each precinct would give the municipal
> ownership candidate a plurality. He has
> laid the foundations for a political
> organization which with care and skill he
> may build into formidable proportions. He
> has demonstrated that he has a following.
> He has proved himself a factor to be reck-
> oned with in all future calculations.
> It is not often that a man wins most
> by losing, but if there was ever such a
> case here is one.[51]

The Wall Street Journal, which had opposed
Hearst throughout the campaign, urged him to
take every legal step possible to produce an
honest count. The charges of Tammany corruption were so widespread, this financial sheet
affirmed, that most New Yorkers believed that
Hearst was legitimately elected. It added:

> An agitator who can pose as a martyr to
> a cause is always dangerous. Mr. Hearst as
> mayor of New York would soon have demon-
> strated how powerless he was to put any
> of these theories into practice and to
> carry out any of his promises, but Mr.
> Hearst out of office, with the belief
> current that he was counted out, defrauded
> of his rights, may continue to be a factor
> in the political situation.[52]

The New York Times, a paper which had pre-

dicted that a Hearst victory would sweep the city
down the muddy flood of socialism,[53] played down
most of the charges of corruption and hailed the
McClellan victory.[54]   It conceded, however, that
the election results could be regarded as a
personal triumph for Hearst:

> The Hearst vote, outrunning, we ima-
> gine, even the expectations of his own
> intelligent supporters attained pro-
> portions that were not merely threatening
> but almost triumphant . . .
> A Hearst administration would have
> been a menace to the welfare and pro-
> sperity of New York . . .
> The really reckless and dangerous
> class of voters, men who if they could
> have their own way would in the most radi-
> cal and sweeping manner change not only our
> system of government but the established
> social order, were attracted to him by his
> readiness to promise pretty much everything
> they wanted . . .
> The 200,000 votes cast for Mr. Hearst
> represent not so much a political aspi-
> ration as a social exasperation.[55]

Hearst's supporters rallied behind him.
Their accusations, printed in the American, were
numerous. Tammany officials, they charged, had
openly boasted that Murphy had distributed
$1,000,000 to thirty-seven district leaders to
buy votes for McClellan.[56] These accusations did
lead to the arrest of fourteen Tammany workers
who were charged with bribery.[57] Hearst supporters claimed that election officials had
directed them to voting booths with blue pen-
cils and that all ballots marked with any color
except black were discarded.[58] They said that
Tammany thugs had used brass tacks, brass knuck-
les, clubs, and paving stones to keep them from
the polls.[59] They estimated that Tammany had
employed over 5,000 thugs on election day, and
that they had injured thousands of honest

voters.[60] Throughout the day, voters were refused their right to vote because repeaters had
already voted in their place.[61] Democratic
United States Senator John L. McLauren of South
Carolina, who was visiting in the city on election
day, witnessed "intimidation, slugging, threats,
and every other expedient to prevent men from
voting for Hearst." He told a _Times_ reporter,
"/ I / never felt greater sympathy for a man
than Hearst, after seeing these things."[62] Only
three thugs were arrested, and one of them confessed that he had voted twelve times for names
written out by a Tammany leader.[63] On these
charges the London _Times_ observed:

> There is only too good reason to be-
> lieve that Tammany obtained its victory
> by resorting to every device in its power
> to prevent the people from expressing their
> will. It is asserted, and asserted on good
> authority, that voters were intimidated into
> giving their votes for McClellan; that others
> who refused to vote for him were thrown out
> of the polling booths before they could
> vote; that voting papers for Mr. Hearst were
> deliberately mutilated; that Tammany ad-
> herents had been instructed weeks before the
> election to join Hearst clubs and to secure
> the confidence of the leaders in order to
> get appointed as watchers of the polls; that
> these men did receive appointments and not
> only closed their eyes to illegalities on
> behalf of Tammany, but aided in intimidating
> voters; and that the final count of the
> vote was unfair. . . .
>   It is no longer a question of the fit-
> ness of one candidate or the other. It is
> a question of the purity of the ballot.
> This election in New York may raise the most
> serious issue that has confronted the Ameri-
> can people for many years. The _Evening
> Post_ has been a bitter opponent of Mr.
> Hearst. For a newspaper so conservative
> it has gone to extraordinary lengths in

personal attacks, yet it says today ' . . .
Any man who condones trickery concealed,
fraud covered up, or justice denied in this
matter is a more dangerous enemy of society
than Mr. Hearst.'[64]

Hearst was enraged with the displacement of
ballot boxes on election day. Peter Cambell, a
Hearst employee, saw ballot boxes floating down
the East River.[65] On November 8 Hearst supporters spotted two more ballot boxes floating
in the North River.[66] By November 12, four boxes
were found in the 34th assembly district in the
Bronx, two were discovered at 904 Stein Avenue
in Astoria, and single boxes were found in
barber shops at 302 East Third Street and 500
West 28th Street.[67] Bernard Mayneck saw two
boxes in a Gravesend tailor shop window and
called the local police department. They would
not have made a difference in the vote, Sergeant
McGuire informed Mayneck, because "they would be
destroyed in any event."[68]

In his newspapers Hearst attacked Murphy
and Tammany officials for their unethical behavior. On November 10 the _Evening Journal_
featured a controversial Davenport cartoon
picturing Murphy in prison stripes with the
caption reading "Look out Murphy! It's a
short lockstep from Delmonico's to Sing Sing."

Local Republican leaders believed that
Hearst had been elected. Nicholas Butler,
President of Columbia University, wrote President Roosevelt: "The best opinion here is that
when the election is reviewed by the courts,
Hearst will be elected."[69] In defeat, Ivins
publicly stated:

I feel sure that if it were possible to
eliminate Tammany's corruption, Mr. Hearst
would lead the poll. In his efforts to
preserve the purity of our elections, Mr.
Hearst should have the support of every

191

true American.[70]

Roosevelt, in response to these convictions, confided to a political ally:

> . . . we should use every means in our power
> to make it evident that we will not tolerate
> either fraud or corruption in elections . . .
> if he was entitled to the seat he should
> have it.[71]

Hearst demanded a recount. McClellan and
Murphy opposed a recount. Ivins volunteered
his services to aid Hearst. Hearst decided to
take his grievance to court and hired Alexander
Bacon and F. B. Bower to serve with Ivins as his
counsel.[72] He offered a $10,000 reward for in-
formation leading to arrest, conviction, and
imprisonment of the first Tammany leader for
election fraud.[73] Former Governor Frank Black,
former President of the New York Bar Association,
Henry Howland, Dr. Charles Parkhurst, and Dr.
Felix Adler were among thousands of city voters
who wrote to the league candidate to pursue the
matter in the courts. A letter from Black to
Brisbane is typical:

> It is the bound duty of Mr. Hearst to
> demand a recount. He must fight to the
> bitter end no matter what the sacrifices
> in time and money.
> The debauching of the ballot is the
> greatest and most insidious menace to con-
> stitutional liberty in the country today.
> If the ballot box is stuffed, if intimi-
> dation, coercion, and bribery are practiced
> at the polls without interference by
> the agents of law and order a deathblow
> is struck at the very foundations of our
> system of government.
> I have been opposed politically to
> Mr. Hearst, but I am profoundly con-
> vinced that his cause lies straight and
> clear before him. If Tammany has debauched

the ballot, and in so doing trampled upon
the inalienable rights of over 225,000
freemen of this great city, Mr. Hearst is
bound by every obligation of his citizen-
ship to bring the rascals to justice and
assume duties and responsibilities of the
mayoralty.[74]

Hearst supporters took to the streets in
protest. On November 11, Senator John Ford,
Bird Coler, Alexander Bacon, Dr. Charles
Parkhurst, General James Grant Wilson, S. S.
McClure, Ernest Crosby, and Henry Siegel addressed a protest group consisting of over
5,000 city voters.[75] The following day Hearst,
who opposed mob rule, published a plea to his
supporters to refrain from mass meetings and
demonstrations.[76] The nation was watching his
actions, he wrote Parkhurst, so it was important
to seek reasonable demands through proper legal
channels.[77]

Hearst was unable to force a recount. In
1906 the state legislature voted down a recount
bill. He lost every court case on the matter
and on June 13, 1908, Justice John C. Gray,
speaking for a unanimous State Surpeme Court,
declared the recount unconstitutional on fourteen counts. Three years had expired, the court
held, and most ballots were destroyed. The court
did answer to specific complaints and lessened
the mayor's plurality by 869 votes.[78] Governor
Hughes signed these official results on July
2, 1908.[79] The proceedings cost McClellan
$83,574,44.[80]

The Hearst vote had been evenly distributed:

	Hearst	Ivins	McClellan
Manhattan and Bronx	120,491	61,785	137,077
Brooklyn	82,908	59,498	66,975

193

	Hearst	Ivins	McClellan
Queens	18,343	7,259	12,622
Richmond	2,966	4,501	6,121[81]

There was not a single district in which Ivins' total equalled the number of registered Republicans:

	Registered Republicans	Republican Votes	Registered Democrats	Democratic Votes
Manhattan and Bronx	103,239	64,354	183,025	140,978
City	221,849	138,118	321,083	229,083[82]

Both Hearst and McClellan polled a larger vote than the entire Republican enrollment. Hearst carried the 8th, 10th, and 16th districts, which were Jewish, but did so without cutting into the Tammany vote. He carried eleven assembly districts in Manhattan and the Bronx, but only two candidates on his ticket were elected.

Given a chance to vote for Hearst, the Times reported, the previously unrepresented masses had turned out in great numbers.[83] Other working class voters responded by cutting across traditional partisan lines to vote for him. He polled 37 percent of the vote in Manhattan's working class district and over 42 percent of the vote in upper Manhattan's working class district.[84] He recieved approximately 50 percent of the Republican working class vote and about 33 percent of the Democratic working class vote of the 1903 mayoralty election. Outside of the four loyal Tammany districts, he cost the Republicans 23,000 votes, and the Democrats 31,000 votes.[85] The immigrants responded to his candidacy, the Italians and Irish giving him over 35 percent of their vote,[86] the Germans giving him 47.5 percent of their votes, and the Jews delivering to him over 55 percent of their

194

vote.[87] McClellan's victory could be credited
to upper class voters as Hearst upset the appeal
that Tammany as a dispenser of social services
had traditionally made to the lower classes.[88]
Nicholas Butler wrote:

> Whatever we may think of the man, the fact
> cannot be blinked that four-fifths of his
> enormous vote . . . came from men who are
> sick and disgusted at the alliance between
> the great financiers and the bosses which
> has ruled this town for so long, and voted
> for him primarily for that reason.[89]

In retrospect, the most controversial aspect
of the election was the invalidation by Tammany
election officials of 8,139 ballots. Disregard-
ing all of the alleged corruption, the final
election results rested upon the interpretation
by these officials of the existing election laws.

The ballot used in the 1905 election listed
seven parties. Circles were located below the
party emblems for the convenience of voters
desiring to vote a straight party ticket. The
laws concerning these circles were ambiguous,
if not contradictory. The election code stated
that a voter could "not put a cross under two
party emblems under any circumstances,"[90] but
also stated several paragraphs later that if a
voter desired to vote for a majority of the
candidates from one party and split his ticket
he could make "a cross in the circle under
the emblem of the party which has nominated a
majority of the candidates for which he wished
to vote . . . putting another cross in the
square to the left of the name of each candidate for who he wishes to vote, outside his
party column."[91] The dispute arose over ballots
on which voters had placed a cross in two
circles, one of which was located below the
Jerome party emblem.[92] The only name to appear
below this emblem was William Travers Jerome,
independent candidate for District Attorney, who

was elected. The state Supreme Court suggested that these ballots count for all of the candidates except the Democratic, Republican, and Municipal Ownership League candidates for District Attorney because the intent of the voters was evident. No court orders were ever issued, however, because the election officials invalidated and destroyed the ballots.[93]

Hearst supporters argued in vain that the election officials based their decision on too narrow an interpretation of the laws. Section 110 of the New York election laws, they argued, justified the admissibility of the disputed ballots. It stated "if a crossmark is in more than one circle and if on either ticket there shall be a candidate for an office for which no other candidate is listed on the other ticket the elector's vote shall be counted for such candidate."[94] Rule 6 of section 110 was even more specific:

> If the elector for such candidate mark in more than one circle at the head of the tickets, and if on either of such tickets there shall be one or more candidates for office for which no other candidate is or are named on such other ticket or tickets so marked in the circle his vote shall be counted for such candidate or candidates.[95]

A literal interpretation of this law would have validated the ballots.

The few election officials who were not Tammany men publicly stated that Hearst had received at least 6,145 votes on these disputed ballots,[96] which would give him a total of 231,751 votes. If McClellan had received all of the remaining ballot votes, which was unlikely, his total would have been 230,445. Hearst later complimented the Tammany election officials for their foresight, observing that his first act in office would have been to imprison them.[97]

McClellan's re-election led directly to his break with Tammany Hall. The repeated Hearst attacks on Tammany's methods made a significant impact on the mayor. He awarded only two city jobs to Tammany regulars. Asspiring for greater political success. he believed that a break with Tammany while the nation watched Hearst and Ivins challenge its methods in court would award him positive national publicity. He believed that the political machine "could no longer provide him with assistance in national politics and that the time had come for him to establish a reputation as an independent."[98]

Hearst emerged from the 1905 election at the apex of his political career. A victory would have given him less publicity, Shearn wrote the defeated editor, than he received by being an honest champion of the people denied by a corrupt political machine the office to which he had been legally elected.[99] Hearst reflected on the election in an unpublished letter to Brisbane:

A tragedy to the people. The laborers and immigrants became involved--really involved . . . I believe more than ever that our movement will succeed.

The defeat is a setback . . . but we should use it to compel quicker and greater victory.

Our next effort will be the most important thus far.

A single defeat, or steal, is not the end. Bryan demonstrated that consecutive losses destroy a movement--populism. The principles behind the movement become lost and the personal qualities and political mistakes of the candidate that personifies those principles are remembered.

Let us never forget that the pro-

197

ressive principles are more important
than any election that I am involved in.
I would step aside immediately if I could
be assured that it would help the progressive cause. . . .
    The masses look to reformers like
you and me and Seabury and Hughes. . . .
    We will run for Governor as planned.[100]

Brisbane wrote to John Sleicher that he was
urging Hearst to leave politics and to devote
himself to his propaganda for the elevation of
the masses.[101] But Hearst's followers wanted
another chance and Hearst needed one. His mayoralty campaign had lasted only twenty days. He
decided to declare early and to campaign diligently for the governorship of New York State.

Footnotes

[1] Hearst to Brisbane, February 7, 1905, J.A.M.

[2] Chambers, op. cit., pp. 96-108.

[3] Ibid., p. 98.

[4] Seabury to Hearst, October 2, 1905, J.A.M.

[5] New York Times, October 4, 1905.

[6] Hearst to Shearn, October 4, 1905, J.A.M.

[7] New York Tribune, October 5, 1905.

[8] New York Evening Journal, October 5, 1905.

[9] New York World, October 5, 1905.

[10] New York American, October 6, 1905.

[11] Mayor McClellan's Speech of Acceptance at the Democratic party's New York City Convention, October 5, 1905, McClellan Papers, Library of Congress.

[12] New York Times, October 6, 1905.

[13] Hearst to Seabury, October 11, 1905, J.A.M.

[14] New York American, October 5, 1905.

[15] New York World, October 11, 1905.

[16] New York American, October 13, 1905.

[17] New York Evening Journal, October 13, 1905.

[18] New York Times, October 14, 1905.

[19] New York Times, October 11, 1905.

[20]"Tammany's Confidence Game," *Outlook*, October 7, 1905, pp. 296-297.

[21]*Ibid.*, p. 297.

[22]Pulitzer to Heaton and Cobb, Editorial Rooms, October 11, 1905, Pulitzer Papers, Library of Congress.

[23]New York *American*, October 24, 1909.

[24]Irwin Yellowitz, *Labor and the Progressive Movement in New York State, 1897-1916* (Ithaca, New York: Cornell University Press, 1965), p. 190.

[25]New York *American*, October 12, 1905.

[26]New York *American*, November 5, 1905.

[27]Harold Syrett, ed., *The Gentleman and the Tiger: The Autobiography of George B. McClellan, Jr.* (Philadelphia: J. B. Lippincott Company, 1956), p. 226.

[28]New York *Times*, November 5, 1905.

[29]New York *American*, November 4, 1905.

[30]Dennison Lindsay, "The Strange Hearst Campaign," *Ridgeway's*, October 27, 1906, pp. 23-24.

[31]New York *American*, October 19, 1905.

[32]*Ibid.*

[33]New York *American*, November 3, 1905.

[34]New York *American*, November 6, 1905.

[35]New York *American*, November 3, 1905.

[36]New York *Evening Journal*, October 14, 1905.

[37]New York _American_, October 14, 1905.

[38]New York _Times_, November 1, 1905.

[39]New York _Times_, November 6, 1905.

[40]New York _Evening Journal_, November 6, 1905.

[41]Hearst to Brisbane, November 6, 1905, J.A.M.

[42]New York _Times_, November 1, 1905.

[43]New York _Times_, November 3, 1905.

[44]_Ibid_.

[45]New York _Evening Journal_, November 4, 1905.

[46]New York _Times_, November 5, 1905.

[47]Washington _Evening Star_, November 6, 1905.

[48]New York _American_, November 8, 1905.

[49]New York _Times_, November 9, 1905.

[50]Washington _Evening Star_, November 8, 1905.

[51]_Ibid_.

[52]New York _Wall Street Journal_, November 9, 1905.

[53]New York _Times_, November 6, 1905.

[54]New York _Times_, November 8, 1905.

[55]_Ibid_.

[56]New York _American_, November 7, 8, 1905; New York _World_, November 8, 1905.

[57]New York _Times_, November 7, 1905.

[58]New York _American_, November 8, 1905;
New York _Tribune_, November 8, 1905.

[59]New York _American_, November 9, 1905.

[60]_Ibid_.

[61]New York _Times_, November 9, 1905.

[62]New York _Times_, November 11, 1905.

[63]New York _World_, November 11, 1905.

[64]London _Times_, November 9, 1905.

[65]Myatt, _op. cit._, p. 75.

[66]New York _American_, November 12, 1905.

[67]_Ibid_.

[68]New York _Times_, November 10, 1905.

[69]Butler to Roosevelt, November 9, 1905,
Roosevelt Papers, Library of Congress.

[70]New York _American_, November 9, 1905.

[71]Roosevelt to Julius Mayer, February 17,
1906, Elting Morison, ed., _The Letters of
Theodore Roosevelt_ (Cambridge: The Harvard
University Press, 1952), p. 156.

[72]New York _Evening Journal_, November 9, 1905.

[73]New York _Times_, November 10, 1905.

[74]New York _American_, November 10, 1905.

[75]New York _American_, November 12, 1905.

[76]New York _American_, November 13, 1905.

[77] Hearst to Parkhurst, November 11, 1905, J.A.M.

[78] New York *American*, June 14, 1908.

[79] New York *American*, July 3, 1908.

[80] City Auditor Accounts, June 4, 1909, McClellan Papers, Library of Congress.

[81] New York *Times*, November 8, 1905.

[82] "The New York City Vote Analyzed," *Nation*, November 16, 1905, p. 395.

[83] New York *Times*, November 9, 1905.

[84] Henderson, *op. cit.*, p. 106.

[85] *Ibid.*, p. 107.

[86] *Ibid.*, p. 110.

[87] *Ibid.*, p. 111.

[88] "The New York City Vote Analyzed," *loc. cit.*

[89] Butler to Roosevelt, November 9, 1905, Roosevelt Papers, Library of Congress.

[90] New York *Times*, November 6, 1905.

[91] *Ibid.*

[92] In re Hearst et al., 48 N.Y. Misc. Rep. 453 (1905).

[93] *Ibid.*, p. 126.

[94] Paragraph 6, Subdivision 2, Section 110, New York State Election Laws, New York *Times*, November 6, 1905.

[95] New York *Times*, November 6, 1905.

[96]New York _Times_, November 10, 1905; New York _American_, November 10, 1905.

[97]Hearst Speech, State Convention of Independence Party, May 2, 1908, J.A.M.

[98]Syrett, _op. cit._, p.26.

[99]Shearn to Hearst, November 10, 1905, J.A.M.

[100]Hearst to Brisbane, December 1, 1905, J.A.M.

[101]Sleicher to Roosevelt, October 17, 1906, Roosevelt Papers, Library of Congress.

VIII
Running for Governor

In 1906 Hearst conducted his most intense
and best organized effort for political office.
He officially opened his campaign on September
3, 1906, but it had been obvious to all political observers after the 1905 election that
he would make a serious drive for the governorship.

The members of the Independence League,
formerly the Municipal Ownership League, emerged
from the 1905 election enthusiastic, hopeful,
and determined. Five hundred league delegates
assembled in Albany on February 28, 1906, and
recognized Hearst as the leader of their movement.[1] The league was founded, Hearst told them
in his keynote address, to free "typical American citizens" from boss rule and corporation
control.[2] He explained:

> There can no longer be doubt in the
> minds of intelligent men that a powerful
> financial class is now absolutely dominant
> in the government of this nation. . . . So
> long as the corporations control both
> parties the people have no · · · relief
> except through an independent movement.
> · · ·
> It is clear that the government of the
> nation . . . is no longer a government of
> the people organized for their own better-
> ment. It has degenerated into a corpo-
> ration of organized monopoly . . . . opera-
> ting . . . for the enrichment of a small
> predatory class . . . [3]

Thousands of voters of small means responded to
his rhetoric and sent him donations of up to
one dollar urging him to enter the gubernatorial
campaign.[4]

State political leaders believed that Hearst

was organizing a statewide independent political
movement.[5] Political opponents called him a
demagogue, believing that he would do anything to
become President of the United States. Franklin
Lane, who had fallen out of Hearst's favor in
San Francisco and was now serving on the Interstate Commerce Commission, wrote bitterly:

> . . . Hearst knows public sentiment and how
> to develop it very well, and will be a
> danger to the United States, I am afraid,
> for many years to come. He has a great
> capacity for disorganization for any move-
> ment that is not his own, and an equal capa-
> city for organization for any movement that
> is his personal property. He feels with the
> people . . . He is willing to do whatever
> for the minute the people may want done and
> give them what they cry for, unrestrained by
> sense of justice, or of ultimate effect.
> He is the great American Pander.[6]

Hearst launched his gubernatorial campaign
on Labor Day, prior to any state party conventions. He addressed 3,000 people in Syracuse,
demanding improved labor conditions in the nation
and urging Congress and the President to make
Labor Day a national holiday.[7] Within hours he
addressed a crowd of 5,000 at the Fairgrounds in
Watertown, urging the nation's producing classes
to unite in the progressive movement to upgrade
social conditions in America.[8]

The Independence League was the first political party to hold a state convention for the
1906 elections.[9] League delegates met at Carnegie
Hall on September 11. Their rallying issue was
a demand for the free vote and an honest count.
The adopted platform called for a constitutional
amendment for the direct election of United
States Senators, revised election laws, investigations of state agencies, public ownership of
public utilities, and fair railroad rates.[10]

Hearst's nomination was a foregone conclusion. Other nominees included Lewis Chanler from Dutchess for Lieutenant Governor; John Ford of New York City for Attorney General; John Whalen of Monroe for Secretary of State; George Fuller of Jefferson for State Treasurer; Charles Auel of Erie for State Comptroller; and Frank Getman of Tompkins for State Engineer and Surveyor.

Hearst, who was developing as the nation's foremost media politician, was a legitimate threat to both parties. He was himself an active candidate and his eight newspapers promoted their publisher daily. "I am well satisfied to use the power of my publications," he told supporters, "to drive out of office the white slaves of the trusts and to promote the fortunes of honest servants of the people."[11] In numerous speeches he pointed, somewhat erroneously, to successes of third party movements, among them the Independence party of 1776, the Jeffersonian movement, and the Jackson movement, when a new party was founded on the principle of popular rule.[12]

State law dictated that the two dominant parties in the gubernatorial election gained control of the state's election machinery. Democratic party leaders realized that a Democrat against both Hearst and the Republican nominee could mean a third place finish.[13] W. G. Connors, a Tammany officer, contacted Hearst's political manager suggesting a fusion between the Democratic party and the Independence League:

> . . . A united front against a common enemy . . . can be accomplished by honest fusion between the Independence League and the Democratic party. . . . An overwhelming number of the delegates elected to the Democratic state convention will vote for the nomination of William Randolph Hearst for governor, and I assure you, without hesitation that he will be nominated.[14]

Most old line Democratic party regulars opposed a Hearst gubernatorial nomination because they believed he was too unpredictable and to independent of party desires.[15] But Hearst's popularity made it obvious that the party's only chance of success would be to nominate Hearst and to run a fusion ticket with the Independence League.[16]

Hearst instructed his political adviser not to seek the Democratic party's nomination, but informed him that he would accept an honest draft if a fusion ticket was agreeable to both parties and if the Democratic convention adopted in its platform the progressive planks of the Independence League's platform.[17] It would be awkward for Hearst to accept a nomination so intimately associated with Tammany, but he realized that he could be elected more easily with a major party's backing. Victory was important because he entertained hopes for the 1908 Democratic party's presidential nomination. Ihmsen advised him that it would be in his best interest[18] to campaign alongside state Democratic leaders. "I will work with most Democrats," Hearst responded, "but I will not sacrifice everything I represent and work with Tammany men."[19] When informed that State Senator Patrick McCarren, Tammany's Brooklyn boss, endorsed his nomination, he told reporters, "McCarren may be for me. as reported, but I am not for McCarren. I repeat now that I am absolutely . . . opposed to the Murphys and McCarrens, the Sullivans, the McClellans, and the kind of politics they represent."[20]

The Democrats opened their convention in Buffalo on September 25. State Senator Thomas Francis Grady was elected permanent chairman. The frontrunning announced candidates for the gubernatorial nomination were Jerome, Mayor James Noble Adam of Buffalo, and Mayor Thomas Mott Osborne of Auburn.[21] Most delegates expected Hearst to make a serious bid.[22] In an

irony of political fate, Tammany officials
maneuvered to insure his nomination.[23]   The
convention's Credential Committee refused to
seat sixty anti-Hearst delegates, including the
entire Queen's delegation that had been elected
by a popular majority of over 3,000 votes.[24]
Grady's systematic elimination of Hearst's opposition resulted in his nomination. Indicating
his own unhappiness with the bosses' decision,
at the day's end Grady told reporters, "Boys,
this is the dirtiest day's work I have ever done
in my life."[25] On the first ballot Hearst tallied 309 of the 450 delegate votes. Protesting
against the methods used to get this nomination,
the Independents, Osborne and Jerome, bolted the
convention calling for a "democratic" convention
to meet in Albany.[26] For similar reasons,
McClellan organized an Independent-Democratic
movement and raised money for the Republican
nominee.

Hearst accepted the nomination and adopted
the party platform, which was in essence a
restatement of the Independence League's platform.[27] A minor attempt at a fusion ticket was
made. Chanler and Whalen were carried over
from the league's ticket, but all the other
league candidates were dropped. "Hearst has
caused the Democratic party to become once
again the party of the people," the American
announced in an effort to justify its chief's
treatment of the Independent movement he had
initiated and led; the paper reaffirmed that
"his appeal is to the people and his reliance
is upon them."[28] Initially many of his followers seemed to agree. The German-American
League and the Italian-American League, parts
of the Independence League, endorsed his candidacy.[29] The Democratic-Republican General Committee of New York County, consisting of anti-
Tammany voters, issued a pamphlet stating in
part:

The Democratic candidate for Governor,

209

> William Randolph Hearst, stands in the pub-
> lic estimation as . . . the embodiment of
> the people's protest against monopoly in
> every form. He has done more than any
> other man to expose the dishonesty and crimi-
> nality of these great trust combinations
> and has spent years of effort and a large
> part of his own personal fortune in a
> determined effort to bring them to justice.
> And he may be depended upon, if elected, to
> employ all the powers of government to cor-
> rect these abuses and to punish those re-
> sponsible for them.
>
> The officials and directors of the
> Coal Trust, Beef Trust, Ice Trust, Gas
> Trust, Woolen Trust, Railroad Trust, and
> other Trusts are bitterly arrayed against
> him.
>
> A vote for William Randolph Hearst is
> a vote against monopoly in every form.[30]

In campaign speeches Hearst repeatedly told
voters that he was not advocating a political
revolution, but instead spoke of a "plan to
put into practical operation the principles of
Jefferson's policy of government."[31] He continued to denounce Murphy and the methods he
employed, but, because he was a Tammany candidate for the third time in four years, the denunciations were less frequent and of a milder
nature than they had been the previous year.

Several labor unions endorsed the Democratic nominee and platform. Within three
weeks, he had received unanimous resolutions
of support from the Bricklayers, the New York
City Central Labor Union, the Typographical
Union, the Central Federated Union of New York,
and several other unions.[32] A typical resolution, from the Batavia Typographical Union
No. 511, declared:

> . . . that no workingman of intelligence
> has any cause to question the sincerity of

William Randolph Hearst. For twenty years
he has proved his friendship to labor . . .
We only seek and expect of Mr. Hearst that
he shall continue to be the same William
Randolph Hearst that he has been as an
employer of labor, as Congressman, as editor
of a great chain of influential newspapers.
A vote for Mr. Hearst is a vote to hasten
the time when the people themselves, through
the instrumentality of government, shall
abolish wage slavery, civilize the slums,
take control of monopolies and give to
the men who do the world's work a decent
share of the world's wealth and a fair
chance for the education of their children
and the establishment of happy homes which
present day civilization affords.[33]

On October 18 state labor leaders John Whalen,
A. J. Boulton, Joseph Buchanan, P. J. Donnelly,
Peter Bohre, Peter Keefe, Daniel Russell, T.
O'Connor, Charles Kinsley, and William Moshier
organized the "Flying Wedge," an organization
through which labor could work solidly as a
phalanx to secure his election.[34] These leaders
hosted a mass meeting at Madison Square Garden
on October 25 to endorse their candidate and to
make a public demonstration of labor's support
for him.[35]

The New York Republicans held their convention in Saratoga. Governor Frank W. Higgins
attempted to name Lieutenant Governor Linn
Bruce to be his successor, but Herbert E.
Parsons, President of the New York County
Republican Committee, endorsed Charles Evans
Hughes, a dignified and upright reformer who had
recently gained popular acclaim for his victory
over insurance company frauds; Hearst had been
ready to endorse him in 1905. President
Roosevelt telegrammed the delegates his endorsement of Hughes, urging them to remain
united against Hearst.[36] By acclamation party
leaders on September 26 nominated Hughes for

governor and Bruce for lieutenant governor. The
platform included reformist planks dealing with
trust restriction and land conservation.[37]

Hughes, a forty year old political new-
comer, was a commanding figure with impressive
credentials. A member of the New York Bar Association and a former professor of law at Cornell
University, he had served in 1905 as chief counsel on the Stevens Investigating Gas Commission,
established by the New York State legislature.
His exposures of numerous instances of fraud,
which led to the creation of a state commission
to regulate gas and electric utilities, made
him a widely admired figure. In September 1905
Higgins appointed him chief counsel of the
Armstrong Insurance Commission, established to
investigate the state insurance companies. His
sensational exposure of corruption, given favorable front-page coverage in Hearst's New York
newspapers, shocked the public and spurred
regulatory legislation. In early 1906, during
the coal inquiry, Roosevelt appointed him special
assistant to Attorney General William Moody, in
charge of federal investigations of combinations
in restraint of trade and of alleged illegal
corporate practices. Grave abuses had grown up
in the American system, he believed, so like
his Democratic opponent he was engaging in an
effort to eliminate them.[38] He had never held
an elective office, or been a candidate for one,
and was the most respected candidate available.

Hearst initially spoke well of Hughes, but
as the campaign progressed Hearst's camp attacked
Hughes. The Hearst press dealt with him savagely
as a corporation lawyer, charging him with being
an agent of the lighting trust, the shipbuilding
trust, the whiskey trust, the sugar trust, the
tobacco trust, the street railway trust, and the
insurance trust.[39] Hearst's cartoonists portrayed him as an animated "featherduster" behind
which the pirates of high finance hid.

In early October Hughes received a lengthy

letter from the politically moderate Charles
Sprague Smith, editor of the People's Institute,
in New York, relating his impressions of the
Hearst campaign and the Hearst movement. Hughes
mailed copies of the letter to Republican and
reform leaders nationwide. It is worth quoting
at length because it describes Hearst as a dangerous demagogue who sought to lead a central-
ized and regimented autocratic government:

> . . . If Mr. Hearst wins, he will become a
> formidable candidate for the national leader-
> ship of the Democratic Party. This means
> that not merely the doctrines that he
> espouses, but also his demagogue methods
> of presenting them, may become accepted as
> those approved by the Progressive movement.
> While I believe thoroughly in the Progres-
> sive movement, it seems to me of the highest
> importance that it should be led by men of
> consecration and broad intelligence, and
> I do not find in Mr. Hearst either of
> these qualities. To combat him successfully
> to win among the people a sufficient fol-
> lowing, it is however necessary to recognize
> clearly the source of his power.
> . . . we are at the beginning of what
> can, without exaggeration, be called a
> Social Revolution, which appears to be
> world wide in scope. Whoever would have
> the people on his side must in principle
> accept the progressive programme. The
> common people are becoming ever more
> conscious of their power and ever more
> united in their resolution to remove all
> obstacles which stand in the way of what
> they conceive to be the attainment of Social
> Justice. They feel that there has grown
> up within recent years a vicious partner-
> ship between the so-called Trusts and men
> in public office, which has transferred our
> government into one that aids in the
> building up of a moneyed oligarchy and is
> defeating the very purpose of its organi-
> zation, which was to provide equal oppor-

213

tunities for all and the protection for the many against the aggressions of the few.

Locally the demand is that special privileges in whatever manner secured be done away with, that monopolies which today oppress the people and prevent the just distribution of the results of production should be put under sufficient governmental control; in so far as such control proves ineffective, that the principle of government ownership be admitted. . . . . I believe that the masses of our people are sufficiently self restrained, patient and broadminded to be willing to accept that leadership which counsels slow procedure through experiment and gradual change from the old to the new, rather than that which urges revolutionary processes.

I am confident that the time for hesitation is past, that men of action listed on the people's side are the only ones who will command a large following. Therefore whoever would be a helpful guide in the present situation, must frankly recognize the essential justice of the people's position, and must seek to persuade them to adopt temperate methods rather than extreme ones.

Papers like the New York _Times_ assail Mr. Hearst, thinking to condemn him for what they call his semi-socialistic views. Such condemnation with the masses of the people acts contrariwise. It is just this recognition that the power is passing into the people's hands and that this passage should be admitted and formulated in due legislation that gives Mr. Hearst his strength.

. . . There should be no division between masses and classes. Of course Mr. Hearst would be very willing that such separation be made and that he appear as the sole defender of the people's interest. It will be made if the Republican campaign is conducted from the conservative stand-

214

point. . . .

> The main issue in the people's mind is economic. No popular following can now be maintained, unless this is recognized. The old issue of personal integrity and nonpartisanship in office are no longer sufficient as rallying cries. Constructive statemanship along progressive lines is demanded. . . .[40]

This statement catches something of a mentality common among well-to-do progressives: reformist, but liking a certain sober propriety in the effort for reform.

In the early campaign Roosevelt became increasingly concerned at Hearst's support among religious and ethnic groups. "No people like to be ignored, even unintentionally," wrote the President, advising Hughes to get two or three Catholics on his campaign committee, and to balance his speeches to Protestant groups with others before Catholic organizations.[41] Roosevelt proposed a revision of the New York Republican judiciary ticket; no Catholic had been placed on the Brooklyn ticket and "an excellent East Side Jew," Judge Rolasky, had been passed over in the Manhattan choices.[42]

Roosevelt expressed to Hughes disappointment and concern over Hearst's command of labor's support.[43] On October 23 the President, in what the Brooklyn _Eagle_ called a desperate move to save New York and the nation from Hearstism,[44] appointed as Secretary of Commerce and Labor Oscar Solomon Straus, a life long Democrat who had acquired a national reputation for his philanthropic aid to the New York City poor.[45] This demonstrated the Republican party's commitment to place personal worth above party affiliation, the President wrote his newest appointee, adding that he hoped his appointment would attract Democrats and Jews to Hughes' camp.[46]

215

The Straus appointment caused a feud, between Oscar and his brother Nathan, a leading
Democrat, former Park Commissioner of New York
City, leader of the national campaign for the
compulsory pasteurization of milk, founder of
a system of lodging houses and relief stations,
and a distributor of coal and food to the poor
in New York City. Nathan urged the Jews and
laborers to remain united in their support for
the Democratic ticket. In a letter to Brisbane,
printed in the American, he wrote:

> I am going to vote for William Randolph
> Hearst for Governor and advise all my
> friends to vote for him because . . . I
> believe the time has come to put a curb
> on those dangerous influences which are
> arrayed against him. I am aware that those
> who oppose him raise the cry of 'demagogue,'
> 'breeder of discontent,' and 'dangerous
> element.'
>   Every new idea that is honest and every
> new leader that is honest are attacked that
> way . . . As a citizen proud of New York
> and proud of the Nation, I am proud of the
> public spirit shown by Mr. Hearst, and his
> courage in attacking the biggest and most
> powerful men of his own class. . . . [47]

Adlai Stevenson actively campaigned for
Hearst. Hearst's loyalty to the Democratic
party and to his own principles, the former
Vice-President stated, were unequalled. He
wrote:

> Mr. Hearst is a strong personality--
> a man of recognized ability, of strict in-
> tegrity, and has, in a marked degree, the
> courage of his convictions. . . . His
> cause is that of the people. His election
> would be the triumph of the people and a
> just condemnation of the corrupt methods
> and practices that have brought Democrats
> defeat in late Presidential contests. [48]

It is noteworthy that Stevenson used the word
integrity in describing Hearst's attributes. Although the term was commonly used to describe the
publisher, recent biographers find little integrity in Hearst's activities.

Hughes proved himself to be an effective
and vigorous campaigner. He travelled widely,
frequently attending five or six rallies a day[49]
and made as many as twenty speeches in a day.
Hearst, he observed, was a corporation boss, the
representative of the greatest newspaper trust
in the world, who hid behind a rhetoric denouncing monopolies. He pointed to the Hearst-
Tammany alliance and questioned his opponent's
public denunciation of Tammany Hall.[50]

Roosevelt took an increasingly active interest in the campaign. Hearst had a large
following, the President wrote, "among the
ignorant and unthinking people"; all "decent
thinking men" supported Hughes.[51] Hearst's
election, he wrote in early October, would be a
"very bad thing" for the Republican party in
1908.[52] He noted that any Hearst success would
be "a smashing defeat for the administration."[53]
All presidential help would be appreciated,
Hughes wrote Roosevelt, and he noted that the
support would be necessary to beat Hearst.[54]

Roosevelt, going as far as he believed he
could without bringing charges against his ad-
minstration of federal intervention in local
elections, sent three members of his Cabinet to
New York to campaign for Hughes. Secretary of
State Elihu Root proved to be the most effective
campaigner.

On September 17 Roosevelt had asked Root
to go to New York to give "a rousing speech"
supporting Hughes.[55] The Secretary of State
initially balked at the request, confiding in
his father that he believed Hearst would be
elected and that his election would be good for
the Republican party because once in power he

217

would not be able to make good on his radical
promises and would be forever discredited as a
progressive politician.[56]   Root's reluctance to
campaign for Hughes prompted Willard Bartlett,
Justice on the New York State Court of Appeals,
to write:

> I do not think that /national7 Repub-
> lican leaders are sufficiently alive to the
> danger of the Hearst movement . . . it is
> astonishing to find how many men who declare
> themselves Republican also declare their
> intention of voting for Mr. Hearst. . . .
> the working people in the smaller cities
> are pretty well united in their sympathy
> to the Hearst movement.[57]

Root reluctantly agreed to campaign in New
York, believing that he could not do anything
to curb the Hearst momentum.[58]   Several state
Republican leaders had by this time come to
question the administration's commitment to
Hughes' cause and were hesitant to have Root
come to the state.   In response Root wrote:

> Lord only knows what is going to be
> the result in New York. Party lines are
> so broken up and the campaign is off to
> such a curious character that there does
> not seem to be anything on which to base a
> forecast. There seems to be rather a
> disposition on the part of the state mana-
> gers to fight shy of administration help
> for the reason that they want to get Demo-
> cratic votes. I think they make a mis-
> take because, after all, what the President
> has done in the principal argument with the
> great body of voters against turning the
> country over to people of the Hearst type.[59]

Root appeared at Utica on November 1, and
delivered a speech directed at Hearst:

> I say to you, with the President's

authority, that he greatly desire the election of Mr. Hughes as Governor of the State
of New York.

I say to you, with the President's
authority, that he regards Mr. Hearst to be
wholly unfit to be Governor, as an in-
sincere, self-seeking demagogue, who is
trying to deceive the workingmen of New York
by false statements and false promises.

I say to you, with the President's
authority, that he considers Mr. Hearst's
election would be an injury and a discredit
alike to all honest labor and to honest
capital, and a serious injury to the work
in which he is engaged of enforcing just and
equal laws against corporate wrong-doing.

President Roosevelt and Mr. Hearst
stand as far as the poles asunder. Listen
to what President Roosevelt himself has
said about Mr. Hearst and his kind. In
President Roosevelt's first message to
Congress, in speaking of the assassin of
McKinley, he spoke of him as inflamed 'by
the reckless utterances of those who, on the
stump and in the public press, appeal to
the dark and evil spirits of malice and
greed, envy and sullen hatred. The wind is
sowed by the men who preach such doctrines,
and they cannot escape their share of responsibility for the whirlwind that is
reaped. This applies alike to the deliberate
demagogue, to the exploiters of sensationalism, and to the crude and foolish visionary
who, for whatever reason, apologizes for
crime or excites aimless discontent.'

I SAY, BY THE PRESIDENT'S AUTHORITY,
THAT IN PENNING THESE WORDS, WITH THE HORROR
OF PRESIDENT McKINLEY'S MURDER FRESH BE-
FORE HIM, HE HAD MR. HEARST SPECIFICALLY
IN MIND.

And I say, by the President's authority,
that what he thought of Mr. Hearst then he
thinks of Mr. Hearst now.[60]

The public's initial reaction to Root's

219

speech was mixed. He received numerous telegrams some calling the speech a disgrace to the nation and to the Roosevelt administration,[61] others praising him for his service to Hughes, the President, and the entire Republican party.[62] He had created controversy that could damage Hearst's credibility. "Roosevelt Calls Hearst Inciter of Assassin," the New York _Times_ charged in a front-page headline.[63] Charles Allan, a Hughes supporter, wrote that the speech had forced voters to re-examine the Hearst methods, the power he wielded through his sensationalistic newspaper methods, and his ruthlessness with that power.[64]

Numerous newspapers and periodicals throughout the state were very critical of Hearst and his candidacy. James Gordon Bennett, owner of the New York _Herald_, was his most outspoken critic. A feud had developed between the two publishers following a Hearst investigation that produced sufficient evidence to convict Bennett on a charge of sending obscene matter through the mails. Hearst was printing lewd personals and addresses of houses of ill repute, retaliated Bennett in an effort to discredit his rival's moral and political character. Bennett led the anti-Hearst press that included the _World_, _Times_, _Evening Mail_, _Independent Review_, _American Review of Reviews_, _Outlook_, _Nation_, and _Harper's Weekly_. Hughes was endorsed by a majority of the state's newspapers.[65]

Hearst also witnessed a slow erosion of support from Independence League members who believed that he had betrayed them. He appeared to be substituting personal power for progressive principles as he campaigned for the Democratic ticket, ignoring the Independence League's ticket. The Independence labor party, created to support Hearst, ceased to function as an organization after October 13.[66]

The Hearst campaign was part of the progressive movement, Hearst told Lincoln Steffens, and American progressivism was part of a world wide movement for individual rights and liberties. Journalism was the power that should express and guide the movement, suggested the publisher of the world's largest newspaper chain. He said that while no single individual yet personified progressivism in America, he was one of the identifiable regional leaders.[67] To make inroads into the traditional Republican strongholds in upstate New York, he travelled the state widely, telling voters that if elected he would direct through the legislature the passage of progressive measures and would clean up corruption in government on the New York City and State level. The North American Review, singing his praises in its columns, said: "There is no doubt that Hearst will be elected President of the United States . . . He is the most popular individual in the United States today."[68]

Hearst intensified his attacks on Tammany Hall in an attempt to dispel the talk of an alliance between himself and Tammany. Boss McCarren was "corrupt and a tool of the standard oil /company7," he charged while campaigning in Brooklyn, adding, "I will not tolerate McCarren after the election whether he is for me or against me."[69] The Tammany leader subsequently supported the entire Democratic ticket except its head, issuing instructions on election day that under no circumstances was Hearst to be elected.[70]

Hearst and Hughes, both confident of victory as election day approached, ran active, organized, "modern" campaigns.[71] Hearst forced a media campaign, breaking down party affiliations and urging voters to examine issues rather than personalities.[72] This expanded influence of the press in politics actually aided the previously little known Hughes.[73]

On election day, November 6, the entire
Democratic ticket, with the single exception of
Hearst, was victorious. McCarren had found his
revenge in the votes.[74] "I congratulate the
bosses on their insight in defeating me," Hearst
publicly stated, "for my first act as governor
would have been to lift the dishonest officials
by the hair of their unworthy heads."[75] Hughes
was elected with less than a 60,000 vote plurality:

	New York State	New York City
Hearst	691,105	338,513
Hughes	749,002	261,455

New York City totals:

	Manhattan and Bronx	Brooklyn	Queens	Rich-mond
Hughes	124,318	106,932	13,881	6,518
Hearst	181,120	109,816	22,047	7,310[76]

Hearst had again fared well with laborers,
immigrants, and the lower classes.[77] He made
a strong showing in upstate New York, carrying
several cities and significantly cutting the
Republican majority in many others.[78] He carried
Buffalo, Syracuse, Rochester, and Troy. He won
Troy by 200 votes, reversing a 4,000 vote Republican majority of 1904.[79] He won New York City
by 77,000 votes; he had expected to take it by
over 200,000.[80] He ran between 60,000 and
70,000 votes behind the rest of his ticket.
The results reveal that clearly McCarren had
knifed him, but the returns do not demonstrate
that Murphy had. He did recieve over 72 percent of the lower Manhattan working class district's vote, 67 percent of the upper Manhattan
working class district's vote, 64.7 percent of
of the Harlem Jewish vote, and 73 percent of the
Yorkville German vote.[81] But he lost the vote of

more affluent Democrats at the same time that he
won the lower class vote--the same situation that
had occurred in the 1905 mayoralty race.

Many Democrats had voted for Hughes and many
Republicans for Hearst, reflected the Washington
Evening Star, and in both cases the votes had
been for reform.[82] The World expressed the views
of a large number of citizens who could not
make up their minds to vote for Hearst: "By
an unexpectedly small plurality they have elected Mr. Hughes to do the work that Mr. Hearst
was clamoring to do; but there can be no
question as to their demand that the works shall
be done."[83] The Press, a Republican organ which
had persistently judged Hearst to be a formidable candidate, reflected:

>   But Mr. Hughes has won by so narrow
> a margin, with Republican wreckage
> strewing all the state, that we think those
> who have been wont to defy public sentiment
> will at last realize that this is a final
> warning.[84]

Hughes had appealed to the moderate and conservative voter and to several respectable reformers in both parties.[85] His stands against
trusts and monopolies were not radical, wrote
a New York Republican, but represented the
essence of moderation.[86] Throughout the campaign he had projected an image of respectability, honesty, and moderation, and he was
elected in what a student of the era has called
"an eruption of respectability."[87] The fundamental issue of the campaign, the Governor-elect
reflected to a Times reporter, had been "whether
New Yorkers wanted to have a rule of reason based
on fundamentals or mob rule based on caprice and
passion."[88]

The result was a bitter defeat for Hearst,
who had spent over $500,000 during the campaign
while Hughes invested only $619.[89] His poli-

tical future, following three unsuccessful bids in three years, was very much in doubt. Major party leaders and reform leaders nationwide had mixed opinions on whether he should continue to seek public office.[90] Some were saying that Hearst and Hearstism had been stopped,[91] while others were not yet willing to write him off as a powerful and appealing candidate.[92] The Tribune believed that Hughes' election was a "stern rebuke to Mr. Hearst's demagogy."[93] The Times did not agree with the Tribune:

> A plurality of 63,000 against Mr. Hearst is not enough. Satisfaction there may be, and heartfelt thankfulness that we have escaped at all, but in the margin of our deliverance there is no cause for enthusiastic rejoicing; rather for a reason of humiliation and searching of minds and hearts, that the people of this great commonwealth may discover how it came about that this strange and reckless desire for overthrow and dangerous adventure has possessed so many of them.[94]

Oscar Straus told reporters that Hearst had convinced the masses that they were victims of an unjust system:

> To this class his is the attitude of a martyr, the defender of a cause that is almost secured.[95]

Opponents generally conceded that both New York defeats were attributable to Tammany.[96] Thomas Chappell wrote Taft that the Hearst press would continue to advance liberal policies and programs regardless of Hearst's political plans.[97]

Republican party leaders believed Hearst would be a presidential candidate in 1908.[98] He had proved himself "an active, bold, broadminded progressive," wrote the Baltimore Sun, "who is in touch with the people, in touch with

224

the times--who will inspire public confidence."[99]
Paul Branact, a New York Republican, warned
Roosevelt not to let up in his fight against
Hearstism:

> The fact that Hearst came so near to
> being elected is very disheartening. It
> means that Hearst will continue to be an
> important factor and probably that the
> Hearst propaganda will continue with re-
> newed vigor.
> The adjustment of the misunderstandings
> between the rich and the poor which have
> made Hearstism possible, will, it seems to
> me, be the important political work for the
> next few years.[100]

Hearst initially believed his political career was over, publicly stating:

> . . . I will serve in the lead or the ranks,
> just exactly as the people desire, and as
> earnestly and as loyally in one place as in
> the other.
> The people have decided to retain the
> Republican party in power. I will make my
> fight in the ranks, therefore, and as a
> private citizen, to do my best to pro-
> mote the interests of my fellow citizens.[101]

Two weeks later, he was more emphatic:

> I shall never again be a candidate. I
> shall continue to live in New York and to
> advocate and support the principles of re-
> form which I have always stood for.[102]

Hearst had become more paternalistic than
most other progressive leaders, believing that a
progressive had to be elected president to insure nationwide social legislation.[103] Realizing
that he would not be that president, he decided
to do his part in promoting "progressive" principles and endorsing "progressive" candidates on

every level nationwide.[104] He told friends at a
banquet in his honor that the progressives' par-
tial victory in 1906 foretold of greater victories, that when voters thoroughly understood
progressive rhetoric they would accept it. In
closing he said:

> My sincerity is vindicated, for the
> best proof in my sincerity in opposing
> trusts and bosses and machines has been
> their sincerity in opposing me.[105]

Declining a re-election bid for Congress in
1906, Hearst ceased to be an elected official on
March 3, 1907. In his losing efforts he over-
came many obstacles and ran formidable campaigns,
but because of his unorthodox methods and his
stance as an outsider he was as effective in
arousing opposition as he was at attracting support. Because he appealed--and with success--to
the lower class, his opponents labelled him a
demagogue. He made an impact on politics, but
continually lost to respectable, moderate candidates. He was, however, a successful vote
getter who proved that urban immigrant workers
could be won from the machine and a recognized
leader of a movement to clean up government and
to upgrade social conditions. During his two
New York campaigns respectable reformers, including Bryan, Watson, Upton Sinclair, Ida
Tarbell, Lincoln Steffens, Robert LaFollette,
William Allen White, and Adlai Stevenson were
attracted to him, wrote for his newspapers, and
in written communications aided him in his
formulation of progressive thought. Yet his on-
again, off-again relations with Tammany Hall, his
direct appeal to the lower classes to unite as
a unit to wrest the power of government from
the upper classes, his sensationalistic newspaper methods which at times exaggerated the
truth, his unwarranted vicious personal attacks
on Hughes, and his desire to do everything his
own way alienated many respectable reformers as

226

well as some machine politicians and forced others who believed in the principles and policies that he was advocating to become indifferent to his candidacies.

Footnotes

[1]New York *American*, March 1, 1906.

[2]New York *Times*, March 1, 1906.

[3]"Hearst Address to The Independence League Convention," February 28, 1906, J.A.M. Also in Older, *op. cit.*, pp. 287-289.

[4]J.A.M.

[5]Abbot, *op. cit.*, p. 152.

[6]Swanberg, *Citizen Hearst*, *op. cit.*, pp. 239-240.

[7]New York *American*, September 4, 1906.

[8]New York *Evening Journal*, September 4, 1906.

[9]New York *American*, September 12, 1906.

[10]New York *Tribune*, September 12, 1906.

[11]New York *Times*, September 13, 1906.

[12]New York *American*, September 13, 1906.

[13]Edwin P. Kilroe to Miss M. Margaret, November 19, 1940, Kilroe Papers, Columbia University.

[14]Conners to Ihmsen, September 11, 1906, J.A.M.

[15]New York *Times*, September 12, 1906.

[16]New York *Times*, August 22, 1906.

[17]Hearst to Ihmsen, September 12, 1906, J.A.M.

[18]Ihmsen to Hearst, September 13, 1906, J.A.M.

[19]Hearst to Ihmsen, September 14, 1906, J.A.M.

[20]New York _American_, September 13, 1906.

[21]New York _Times_, September 26, 1906.

[22]New York _World_, September 26, 1906.

[23]New York _Times_, September 27, 1906.

[24]Eleanor Piller, "The Hearst-Hughes Gubernatorial Campaign of 1906" (M.A. Thesis, Columbia University, 1937), p. 24.

[25]Kilroe to Miss M. Margaret, November 19, 1940, Kilroe Papers, Columbia University.

[26]New York _Times_, September 28, 1906.

[27]New York State Democratic party's 1906 Platform, Kilroe Papers, Columbia University.

[28]New York _American_, September 27, 1906.

[29]New York _American_, September 26, 1906.

[30]J. Sargeant Cram, "Hearst," October 1906, Kilroe Papers, Columbia University.

[31]Hearst speech at Madison Square Garden, September 28, 1906, J.A.M.; Also in New York _American_, September 29, 1906.

[32]Other unions included The Sandy Hill Trades and Labor Assembly, the Rochester Cigarmakers, the Rochester Amalgamated Sheet Metal Workers International Alliance, the Oswego International Brotherhood of Electric Workers, the Port Jervis Central Labor Union, the Commercial Telegraphers Union of America, the Watertown

Central Labor Union, the Ogdensburg I.L.M., the Ogdensburg Teamsters, the Ogdensburg Central Labor Union, the Harbor Boatsmen, the Utica Loom Fixers' Union, the Rochester Machinists' Union, the Italian-American Builders' Union, the German-American League of Kings Union, the William Randolph Hearst Allied Printing Trade Clubs, and the Buffalo Printers' Union. New York _American_, October 19, 1906.

[33]Batavia Typographical Union No. 511, Resolution Endorsing Hearst, November 2, 1906, J.A.M.

[34]New York _American_, October 19, 1906.

[35]New York _Times_, October 26, 1906.

[36]"Entry Into Politics," Hughes Papers, Library of Congress.

[37]New York Republican Platform, 1906, Kilroe Papers, Columbia University.

[38]Ida Tarbell, "How About Hughes?" _The American Magazine_, March 1908, p. 464, Hughes Papers, Library of Congress.

[39]William Allen White to C. J. Lamb, October 11, 1906, White Papers, Library of Congress; White to Roosevelt, October 18, 1906, White Papers, Library of Congress; Beveridge to Roosevelt, October 16, 1906, Beveridge Papers, Library of Congress; Charles Gates to Roosevelt, October 17, 1906, Roosevelt Papers, Library of Congress; Hughes to Roosevelt, October 21, 1906, Roosevelt Papers, Library of Congress; Charles Doerflinger to John Spooner, October 26,1906, Spooner Papers, Library of Congress.

[40]Smith to Hughes, October 3, 1906, Hughes Papers, Library of Congress; Roosevelt Papers, Library of Congress.

[41]Roosevelt to Hughes, October 4, 1906, Roosevelt Papers, Library of Congress.

[42]Roosevelt to Hughes, October 5, 1906, Roosevelt Papers, Library of Congress.

[43]Roosevelt to Hughes, October 2, 1906, Roosevelt Papers, Library of Congress.

[44]Brooklyn Eagle, October 24, 1906, Straus Papers, Library of Congress.

[45]Brooklyn Times, October 24, 1906, Straus Papers, Library of Congress.

[46]Roosevelt to Straus, October 31, 1906, Straus Papers, Library of Congress.

[47]Straus to Brisbane, October 30, 1906, printed in New York American, October 31, 1906.

[48]Stevenson to Joseph Foster, October 25, 1906, New York American, November 3, 1906.

[49]Merlo J. Pusey, Charles Evans Hughes, vol.1 (New York: Macmillan Company, 1951), p. 176.

[50]New York Tribune, October 9, 1906; New York Herald, November 2, 1906; New York World, October 22, 1906.

[51]Roosevelt to Henry Cabot Lodge, September 27, 1906; Morison, ed., op. cit., p. 129.

[52]Roosevelt to Lodge, October 1, 1906; Ibid., p. 436.

[53]Roosevelt to Timothy Lester Woodruff, October 14, 1906, Roosevelt Papers, Library of Congress.

[54]Hearst to Roosevelt, October 4, 1906, Roosevelt Papers, Library of Congress.

232

[55]Roosevelt to Root, September 17, 1906, Root Papers, Library of Congress.

[56]Root to Oren Root, October 25, 1906, Root Papers, Library of Congress.

[57]Bartlett to "Felix," October 3, 1906, Root Papers, Library of Congress.

[58]Root to Oren Root, October 25, 1906, Root Papers, Library of Congress.

[59]Root to Whitelaw Reid, American Embassy, London, October 24, 1906, Root Papers, Library of Congress.

[60]"Root's Speech at Utica," November 1, 1906, Root Papers, Library of Congress.

[61]H. M. Cougar to Root, November 4, 1906, Root Papers, Library of Congress.

[62]George Ambrose to Root, November 3, 1906, Root Papers, Library of Congress.

[63]New York _Times_, November 2, 1906.

[64]Henry Brown to Root, October 2, 1906, Root Papers, Library of Congress.

[65]Piller, _op. cit._, p. 50.

[66]New York _Times_, October 14, 1906.

[67]Steffens, "Hearst, The Man of Mystery," _op. cit._, p. 14.

[68]_North American Review_, September 21, 1906, J.A.M.

[69]Older, _op. cit._, p. 310.

[70]Piller, _op. cit._, p. 60.

[71]Washington _Evening Star_, November 6, 1906.

[72]New York _American_, November 5, 1906.

[73]The anti-Hearst press dredged up both
fact and fiction in the campaign. The _Tribune_,
reminding voters of Hearst's attack on the employment of cheap Chinese labor, ran a picture
showing Chinese coolies working on the "Hearst
estate" in California. Hearst did not own any
California estates in 1906. New York _Tribune_,
October 9, 1906. The _World_ charged that the
"pro-union," "eight-hour" Hearst forced 2700
workers at the Homestake mine in South Dakota
to "slave" under open-shop conditions. Hearst
had no financial interest in the Homestake. New
York _World_, October 22, 1906. The _Herald_, _Sun_,
and _Post_ ran attacks, suggesting his moral un-
fitness for office.

[74]Thomas Chappell to Taft, November 8, 1906,
Taft Papers, Library of Congress.

[75]Older, _op. cit._, p. 315.

[76]New York _Times_, November 7, 1906.

[77]William Howard Taft to Root, November
10, 1906, Taft Papers. Library of Congress.

[78]Hector Hutchings to Roosevelt, November
7, 1906, Taft Papers, Library of Congress.

[79]New York _American_, November 8, 1906.

[80]Hearst speech, November 5, 1906, printed
in New York _American_, November 6, 1906.

[81]Henderson, _op. cit._, p. 112.

[82]Washington _Evening Star_, November 7, 1906.

[83]New York _World_, November 7, 1906.

[84]New York _Press_, November 7, 1906, J.A.M.

[85] John Coit Spooner to Root, November 9, 1906, Spooner Papers, Library of Congress.

[86] Thomas Chappell to Taft, November 9, 1906, Taft Papers, Library of Congress.

[87] Frank Kilroe, "The Governorship of Charles Evans Hughes: A Study in Reform, 1906-1910" (M.A. Thesis, Columbia University, 1934), p. 24.

[88] New York Times, October 13, 1924.

[89] Sworn statements to the New York Secretary of State, November 16, 1906, Hughes Papers, Library of Congress.

[90] London Times, November 8, 1906.

[91] Thomas Chappell to Taft, November 8, 1906, Taft Papers, Library of Congress; Hector Hutchings to Roosevelt, November 7, 1906, Taft Papers, Library of Congress; Oscar Straus statement, Washington Herald, November 16, 1906, Straus Papers, Library of Congress; H. Parker to Superintendent, Delaware, Lackawanna, and Western Railroad Company, November 9, 1906, Root Papers, Library of Congress.

[92] Thomas Chappell to Taft, November 9, 1906, Taft Papers, Library of Congress: New York World, November 7, 1906: New York Times, November 7, 1906.

[93] New York Tribune, November 7, 1906.

[94] New York Times, November 7, 1906.

[95] Washington Herald, no date, Straus Papers, Library of Congress.

[96] John C. Spooner to W. T. Lewis, November 9, 1906, Spooner Papers, Library of Congress.

[97] Chappell to Taft, November 9, 1906, Taft Papers, Library of Congress.

[98]Taft to Root, November 10, 1906, Taft Papers, Library of Congress; Spooner to Root, November 9, 1906, Spooner Papers, Library of Congress.

[99]Baltimore *Sun*, November 9, 1906, Taft Papers, Library of Congress.

[100]Branact to Roosevelt, November 7, 1906, Roosevelt Papers, Library of Congress.

[101]New York *American*, November 7, 1906.

[102]New York *Tribune*, November 19, 1906.

[103]Interview with William Randolph Hearst, Jr., September 25, 1978.

[104]Hearst to Brisbane, November 11, 1906, J.A.M.

[105]New York *American*, November 13, 1906.

IX

The Independence Party

Defeat in 1906 led Hearst to believe that the Democrats refused to represent the masses of American citizens. Having already reached this conclusion about the Republicans, he presumed that a new political party pledged to return the power of the government to the people could succeed. Following unsuccessful attempts at fusion in 1905 and 1906, he decided to form a truly progressive party, and on April 13, 1907 announced the formation of the Independence Party.[1] Ihmsen again served as Hearst's political adviser and organizer. Between April and November he established over one hundred Independence party clubs in New York state claiming a membership of 250,000 voters.[2] Ihmsen made his appeal to dissident leaders, both Republican and Democratic,[3] but the backbone of the new party, Hearst wrote, would be organized labor.[4]

The New York state Independence party's first annual convention opened in Manhattan on September 28, 1907. Hearst told delegates that the decision making process in America was continuously shifting up and away from the grass roots voters:[5]

> It is not a popular government, it is not a responsible government, it is a government beyond the control and independent will of the people.[6]

Hearst charged that business and professional leaders were organizing to protect their selfish interests, and that they were preaching social reform while practicing political and social conservatism. He pledged that the Independence party would be a vehicle for progressivism, that it would become "not only a national party, but the one dominant, patriotic, incorruptible, invincible party of the United States of America."[7]

237

The Independence party's platform, drafted
by Hearst, Ihmsen, Shearn, and Bourke Cockran,
was in large measure a restatement of the 1906
Municipal Ownership League's platform.[8] Party
leaders believed it essential not to change
issues from year to year.[9] Answering charges
that the Independent movement was too radical
to succeed, Hearst told a _Times_ reporter:

> The radicalism of today is the con-
> servatism of tomorrow, if it is sound radi-
> calism. My radicalism has been a demand
> for the punishment of the guilty, whether
> they be important and powerful, or weak and
> insignificant, for practice of the equality
> before the law which we profess; for the
> maintenance of the liberal conditions which
> have given opportunity to all, and which
> have resulted in the astonishing develop-
> ment of this great country of ours.[10]

Independent party candidates made few impressive victories in the 1907 elections.
Tammany's "Big" Tom Foley was easily re-elected
Sheriff over Ihmsen. Independent candidates for
the New York County Court of Appeals polled over
110,000 votes, but this represented only 10 percent of the total vote. The Independents did
have success with fusion tickets, combining with
Democrats to oust the Republican machine in
Rochester and fusing with Republicans to defeat
the Democratic boss in Albany. They also made
respectable showings, running straight tickets,
in Syracuse, Buffalo, and Brooklyn.[11]

The scanty but promising results of the
1907 elections encourage Hearst to mount a
national independent political movement.[12]
Since the major parties were betraying the
people, he wrote, the masses of voters were
eager to align themselves to an honest independent movement.[13] "I do not expect to win
in 1908," he confided, "but do expect to control
the executive branch following the 1912

238

election."[14] Ihmsen was given unlimited travel
money and a bonus for increasing membership totals. The new party was publicized in every
Hearst paper. Ihmsen initially sent forty-five
Hearst employees nationwide, each to a different
state, to establish Independence League Clubs.[15]
They set up over five hundred clubs with a
membership outside of New York of 2,500,000.[16]
Within five months the number of clubs had
tripled.[17] Hearst supported these clubs financially, and reported their activities in his
newspapers. He sent out weekly newspapers to
each club and he spoke before hundreds of them.[18]

In 1908 the Independence party held several
national rallies. The first, on January 11,
in Indianapolis, drafted a list of principles
similar to the Populist platform of 1896, but
without the silver issue.[19] A second rally
was held in Chicago on February 22. Perhaps
disciplining his rhetoric to his larger ambitions, Hearst told party members that the purpose
of an independent movement was neither to revo-
lutionize the American political system nor to
insert violent innovations or theories into the
system.[20] The proposed transfer of the power
of government back to the people, he added
reassuringly, was intended to conserve the form
of popular government that the founding fathers
had planned for when they drafted the constitution.[21] His conclusion was equally bland:

I believe that there is ample reason
and opportunity for a party that is uni-
formly and universally progressive and is
devoted to these principles . . .
I define a party as a collection of
individuals devoted to certain definite
principles and active in politics to promote these principles, and I declare that
according to that definition there is no
national party in the United States today.
Let us inaugurate a party that is not a
class party; that is not a sectional party;

that is founded on American principles, and
will adhere to those principles consistently.
Let us inaugurate a party that will be
a national party in the true sense of the
word, and let us call it THE National
party, if you will.
It will be the only one worthy of the
name.[22]

The New York State Independence party's annual convention was held on May 2 at Carnegie
Hall. The party had organizations in every
community in New York with a total membership
of over 500,000,[23] and the large and enthusiastic
turnout was an impressive show of strength.[24]
Hearst told the delegates that he believed that
the independent movement embodied the principles
of the progressive movement.[25] Independents
were taking the lead in American progressivism,
asserted Temporary Chairman Henry A. Powell,
and neither major party could write a platform
more loyal to the American people than the Independence party's platform.[26]

In his membership drive, Hearst made an
extensive effort to attract organized labor.
During the first few months of 1908, he wrote
hundreds of letters to local labor leaders
nationwide. All favorable responses were published in the American. But most union leaders
were reluctant to form an independent labor
party. In 1872 the National Labor Union, the
predecessor of the A. F. of L., had entered
politics on a national scale by nominating
Thomas Hendricks for President. Hendricks mus-
tered less than 1 percent of the popular vote
and the National Labor Union never held another
convention. The labor movement in general was
demoralized until the reorganization of the
workers in 1880. Gompers later observed, "Many
delegates may feel the desirability of forming
a third political party; but in view of recent
experience I can only say that such action would
be extremely unwise."[27] He held the same opinion

in the twentieth century.

On March 16 the National Labor Conference convened in Washington, D.C. to discuss labor's options for the upcoming elections. The conferees drafted a list of labor grievances that were forwarded to Charles W. Fairbanks, President of the United States Senate, and Joseph Cannon, Speaker of the United States House of Representatives. They wrote the Congressional leaders:

> We come to you as representatives of the wage-workers of our country whose rights, interests, and welfare have been jeopardized and flagrantly, woefully disregarded and neglected. We come to you because you are responsible for legislation, or the failure for legislation . . We must now hold you responsible.[28]

Both the Republican administration and the Republican controlled Congress chose to ignore the list of labor's grievances. President Roosevelt wrote:

> . . . the labor people are causing all the trouble they can. I do not think that Congress last year did all they might have for these labor people; but their position is so extreme that they have left us no alternative but to come out squarely against some of their demands.[29]

The Executive Council of the A. F. of L., therefore, voted to send representatives to both major national conventions to present labor's grievances and to lobby for the enactment of labor planks in their party platforms. If these parties should reject labor's grievances and requests, Gompers telegrammed Hearst, the Executive Council of the A. F. of L. would unanimously vote to throw the support of the organization behind the Independence party.[30]

When Hearst made the telegram public, the labor leader denied ever having sent it.[31] Republican party delegates ignored labor's grievances and demands when drafting their platform.

Congressional Democratic party leaders indicated to labor representatives that if they controlled Congress they would initiate and pass legislation to alleviate most of labor's grievances.[32] The Democratic party delegates incorporated most of labor's requests into their party platform, an indication that the party was receptive to progressive issues that had been considered radical in 1904.[33]

Gompers boldly employed his position to advance Bryan's candidacy and urged laborers to vote against Republican candidates in November. "Both Parties Have Spoken--Choose Between Them," he wrote in an _American Federationist_ editorial in which he spelled out the offenses that the Republican administration, the Republican-controlled Congress, and the Republican National Convention had committed against labor. Ignoring the Independence party, he urged laborers to unite in support of the Democratic party in order to repudiate the Republican party:

> We desire to repeat here that we believe the whole mass of workers of this country will respond in hearty sympathy with the Democratic Party in the coming campaign as a result of its actions on the labor planks of its platform. They will be of practical benefit to the workers.
> We have no hesitation in urging the workers and our friends throughout the country to support the party in this campaign which has shown its sympathies with our wrongs and its desire to remedy them and to see that the rights of the people are restored.[34]

Gompers assured Bryan, who was heading the Demo-

242

cratic party's national ticket for the third
time, that organized labor would support his
candidacy.[35] This was the first time in A.
F. of L. history that members were urged to give
their votes to a specific political party in a
presidential election.[36]

At this time, of course, the Independent
party had not yet held its convention, but
Gompers was already worrying about Hearst.
Early in July Gompers urged the publisher to
withhold his party from the campaign. He expressed concern that a split in the labor vote
would insure Taft's election.[37] Gompers again
denied communicating with Hearst and urged him
to be true to his principles and support Bryan:

> . . . fundamental principles and personal
> rights and human liberty were involved in
> this campaign, and that those that aimed to
> align themselves to contest for the re-
> assertion and re-establishment of those
> principles ought to cooperate for their
> absolute achievement rather than 'play'
> politics by a so-called third party move-
> ment, and out of this evidently the story
> was made and the message sent to Mr. Hearst.
> Men are not necessarily earnest or
> sincere because they boldly proclaim that
> they are. They are to be taken for what
> they endeavor to do.[38]

Hearst believed that Gompers' actions and utterances were justifying his long time suspicions
of the labor leader: that Gompers was conservative and afraid to take chances. Gompers
was not a true representative of the American
laborer, Hearst confided to Brisbane, adding:

> According to my personal standards a
> purer patriotism consists in laboring to
> establish a new party which will be con-
> sistently devoted to the interests of the
> citizenship, and particularly to the advan-
> tage and advancement of the producing classes.

I do not think that the path of patriotism lies in supporting a discredited and
decadent old party which has neither con-
scientious convictions nor honest intention, or endorsing chamelot candidates who
change the color of their political opinion
with every varying hue of opportunism.

I do not think that the best benefit
of laboring men lies in supporting that old
party because of a sop of false promise,
when the performance of that party while
in power did more to injure labor than all
injunctions ever issued before or since.

I have lost faith in the empty professions of an ingenerate /sic/ Democracy.
I have lost confidence in the ability, in
the sincerity, and even in the integrity
of its leaders.

I do not consider it patriotism to
pretend to support that which, as a citizen,
I distrust, and detest, and I earnestly
hope that the Independence party will give
me an opportunity to vote for candidates
that are both able and honest, and for a
declaration of principles that is both
sound and sincere.[39]

Addressing five hundred delegates assembled at
Chicago's Orchestra Hall on July 27, Hearst
urged the nomination of a truly independent
and truly progressive ticket:

Let us nominate candidates from among
the many men here present whose lives and
deeds are a guarantee of genuineness, a
pledge of the sincerity of our profession.
Then let us go forth to an honorable effort
for a righteous cause, to battle and to
victory.[40]

On July 28, the Independence party nomi-
nated Thomas L. Hisgen of Massachusetts for
President and John Temple Graves of Georgia for
Vice-President. A fifty-two year old businessman

from West Springfield. Hisgen had run for
governor of Massachusetts in 1906 as an Independent, finishing a respectable second to
Governor Guild and running well ahead of the
Republican candidate. He had gained local notoriety for successfully checking a Standard Oil
Company attempt to establish an axle grease
monopoly in Massachusetts.[41] Graves was a Hearst
employee, former Populist, and long time col-
league of Thomas Watson.[42] They did not make
a strong ticket.

Hearst and Shearn drafted the platform.[43]
It was much like the Populist platform of
1896, though of course it contained no silver
plank; and it championed labor.[44] Platform
planks called for the direct nomination of all
candidates; the initiative, referendum, and recall; government regulation of capital; jury
trials in all cases of contempt; creation of
central government banks; government regulation
of the railroads and telegraph lines; effective
anti-trust laws; parcel post and postal savings
bonds; a national system of roads; creation of
a National Health Bureau; exclusion of Asiatic
labor; a national conservation program and ex-
tension of inland waterways; popular election of
United States Senators and state and federal
judges; and a graduated income tax. Pro-labor
planks petitioned for legislation preventing injunctions before trials in labor cases, removal
of farmers' co-operatives and labor unions from
the restrictions of the Sherman anti-trust law,
the eight-hour work day, legislation outlawing
the employers' right to blackball employees,
employer liability laws, prohibition of child
and convict labor, creation of a Department of
Labor, and tariff revision.[45] The platform incorporated the many facets of Hearstism over
the past thirteen years.[46]

Throughout the month of August the Hearst
newspapers encouraged the formation of Independent Clubs and urged their readers to join

the Independent movement. Records and membership
lists are scarce, but Ihmsen assured his chief
that over 3,000 clubs, enrolling nearly three
million voters, were meeting weekly, and that
the number of new clubs was increasing daily.
Conceding a Taft victory, he promised that Hisgen
would make a respectable showing, perhaps matching Bryan's vote.[47]

On Labor Day, September 4, Hearst and
Hisgen opened their first joint campaign speaking
tour in Davenport, Iowa. Both insisted that reform leaders nationwide were disappointed with
many fundamental provisions of the major party
platforms and many omissions.[48] The contest between special privilege and the common good,
Hearst warned, was drawing close and becoming
ever more critical. Accusing Bryan and all
Democratic leaders of waivering on issues, he
claimed to have jumped parties in a determined
effort to cling to progressive principles.[49] He
very much overshadowed Hisgen when they appeared
in public together.[50]

Two weeks into the speaking tour, Hearst
questioned Ihmsen's estimate of the strength
and appeal of the Independence party. No respectable reformers except Shearn were endorsing
it. Hisgen was creating no enthusiasm, and local
and national labor leaders were pledging their
support to Bryan.[51] Now desperate, Hearst, in
a September 17 speech at Columbus Ohio, disclosed documentary evidence linking major political party leaders to the Standard Oil Company. The letters, the political effect of
which would continue for years, put life and interest into the campaign. Hearst charged that
there was vast corruption in American politics,
the Democrats eagerly competing with the Republicans for favors from the trusts;

> I am not here with empty assertions
> but with legal evidence and documentary
> proof.

246

> I am now going to read copies of let-
> ters written by Mr. John D. Archbold, Chief
> Agent of the Standard Oil, an intimate
> personal representative of Mr. Rockefeller
> and Mr. Rogers. These letters have been
> given me by a gentleman who has intimate
> association with the giant of corruption,
> the Standard Oil . . . [52]

He proceeded to read ten letters in which the
Standard Oil Company rewarded Congressional members for, in effect, lobbying for its interests
in Congress. The letters had come into the publisher's possession shortly after the 1904
presidential election. William Winkfield and
Charles Stump, employed as messengers and file
clerks in a Standard Oil Company office in New
York City, had removed the letters from the
files at night, made photocopies of them, returned them to the files, and then attempted to
sell them.[53] It was the first of a number of
exposés that Hearst made in speeches during the
1908 campaign. He would continue to print letters over the next four years.

The several thousands of voters gathered at
Memorial Hall on September 17 were hardly stirred
by Hearst's speech and were unaware of the importance of his revelations. Reporters, however,
did recognize the sensation and his coup caused
nationwide excitement. He was given front-page
coverage on nearly every daily newspaper in
America.[54]

On September 18 Senator Joseph B. Foraker,
an Ohio Republican, conceded that he had corresponded with Archbold, but claimed that there
was never mention of Congressional matters.[55] He
was obviously unaware of the number of letters
containing damaging evidence that the publisher
possessed.[56]

During a political rally on September 18
at St. Louis, Hearst revealed two letters, one

247

telling of the transfer of $500,000 to Senator
Foraker asking him to intercede to prevent passage of an anti-monopoly bill being considered,[57]
the other indicating that Democratic Governor
C. N. Haskell of Oklahoma had secured official
state acts favorable to the Standard Oil Company.[58] The following day, while appearing with
Hisgen at a rally in Memphis, Hearst made another letter public, this from Republican Congressman Joseph Crocker Sibley of Pennsylvania
to Archbold. Sibley, "the miserable little
Standard Oil spy in the House," expressed a desire to recruit Democratic Senator Joseph Bailey
of Texas, who, he believed, would be "a tower of
strength and safety" for the Standard Oil interests.[59] Hearst and Hisgen returned to the East
Coast and the publisher released another letter
indicating that Archbold was sending Foraker
large sums of money for his efforts in behalf of
Standard Oil. On September 22 President
Roosevelt suspended Foraker from the Taft campaign.[60]

At political rallies in New York, Denver,
El Paso, and Los Angeles, Hearst revealed more
damaging letters. He disclosed that Standard
Oil had been a large contributor to Roosevelt's
1904 presidential bid; that Archbold had pur-
suaded Mark Hanna to help defeat a candidate for
the Ohio Attorney General who had campaigned
against the corruption of Standard Oil; that
Archbold had manipulated judicial appointments
in Pennsylvania and had sent large sums of
money to Pennsylvania Republican Senators
Boise Penrose and Matt Quay; and that Archbold
and Democratic Senator John L. McLaurin of
South Carolina were intimate friends.[61]

Roosevelt summoned Hearst to the White
House to question him on whether or not he had
any letters damaging to the administration.
Hearst assured the President, in a forty-five
minute meeting, that he had none. Following the
meeting, Roosevelt told reporters:

Mr. Hearst has published much interesting and important correspondence of the
Standard Oil people, especially that of Mr.
Archbold with various public men. I have
in times past criticized Mr. Hearst, but in
this matter he has rendered a public service
of high importance and I hope he will pub-
lish all the letters dealing with the matter which he has in his possession. If Mr.
Hearst or anybody else has any letter from
me dealing with Standard Oil affairs, I
shall be delighted to have it published.[62]

Answering opponents critical of his "nose-
gay journalism," Hearst repeatedly said that he
was using the letters to prove to the masses of
plain American citizens that both major parties
were composed of corrupt individuals. He would
continue, he promised, to expose letters that
revealed actions threatening the public interest
and welfare.[63]

An immediate and positive result of the
Hearst exposures was that corporations and
trusts drastically cut back on their traditional lavish campaign contributions. In
addition to losing campaign funds, the Democratic party replaced its National Chairman and
pledged to disclose by October 15 all contri-
butors to the presidential election. Ida
Tarbell, Ray Stannard Baker, Lincoln Steffens,
and John Phillips praised Hearst for exposing
corruption in government. These four recognized
muckrakers investigated his allegations, and over
the next five years published fifteen articles
in McClure's Magazine on Standard Oil Corruption.

Many reformers were critical of Hearst's
methods. If he was interested in cleaning up
corruption in government, they asked, why would
he not release at once all of the remaining
letters that he possessed and why had he waited
nearly four years to begin releasing them? He

could have released them in 1905 when the muckraking movement was at its height and the public
was reading exposures with excitement. Reform
was advancing boldly and public revelations
might have spurred the revolt against monopoly.[64] Many believed that his reason for not
revealing the letters in 1905 or 1906 had been
that individuals associated with his campaigns
were involved, people who, after disclosure,
would have done little to aid his efforts in
New York and might have dismissed him from a
Democratic presidential nomination in 1908.
Being a newspaperman, he knew that he had a great
news story that he could use against both major
parties. Presenting them as his party was
struggling for recognition, he appeared to be a
political opportunist interested mainly in ac-
quiring power for himself. The creation of his
own political party was his greatest political
gamble, and the letters were the biggest news
story of the campaign. He succeeded in attracting a considerable amount of national publicity and coverage, but it did nothing to aid
Hisgen. The letters were enlightening and controversial, but were four years old. Many of
the individuals involved had died or were out
of office. His decision to wait to release them
had watered them down as effective political
weapons.

Having succeeded in getting national publicity for his party, Hearst made every effort
possible to attract the labor vote to Hisgen,[65]
but by August, an alliance between the American
Federation of Labor and the Democratic party had
been sealed. Gompers met on August 27 with
Norman Mack, Chairman of the Democratic Committee, and the two representatives worked out a
fourteen point agreement whereby the A. F. of L.
and the Democratic party would co-operate with
each other. Throughout the rest of the campaign
Gompers held strategy and policy conferences with
Bryan, who publicly offered him a cabinet post
in the new administration. Through August,
September, and October, the A. F. of L. leader

250

led a contingent of labor leaders on a whirlwind speaking tour of industrial states.[66]

Already disturbed at Hearst's presence in the campaign, Gompers was now vocal. He feared that the publisher's wide appeal to laborers would result in a divided labor vote that would negate labor's first nationwide effort in a presidential campaign. Because he saw Hearst as a threat, he condemned Hearst and denounced his party.[67] While posing as a philanthropist and a leader of progressivism, Gompers charged, Hearst was destroying the efforts of organized labor. "We are forced to believe," Gompers wrote, "that Mr. Hearst is not desirous of helping the workers to a redress of their wrongs," but instead, was more interested in upstaging Bryan.[68] The Republicans were rejoicing in the Hisgen candidacy, he added, because every vote for him would be a vote less for Bryan.[69]

Bryan, urging progressives and Independence party members to support the Democratic ticket, made a concerted effort to convince them of the futility of the new party. Pointing to the similarities between his party's platform and the Independence party's platform, he warned voters that no progressive planks would be enacted if the non-Republican vote was split:

> The question that must confront every member of the Independence party is this: Will he assist in the defeat of the Democratic party, which stands for so much what he favors, merely because he cannot get all that he would like?[70]

Gompers, Bryan, Hearst, and most political observers grossly overestimated the strength and appeal of the Independence party. Hearst had attracted attention, but he was not a candidate. Hisgen lacked voter appeal on the national level. Opponents portrayed him as a Hearst puppet, much the same as the Hearst cartoonists had portrayed

251

McKinley as Mark Hanna's creature. The widely
popular Roosevelt had endorsed Taft, who had an
excellent reputation; the Republicans were content and united. Bryan conducted his most pru-
dent campaign, but it lacked enthusiasm. Taft
polled 52 percent of the vote and was easily
elected. Hisgen polled 82,537 votes out of
nearly fifteen million cast, finishing behind
Taft, Bryan, Socialist Eugene Debs, and Pro-
hibitionist Eugene Chafin, and ahead of Populist
Thomas Watson and Social Laborist August
Gillhaus.

The Independence party did not split the
Democrats' vote, but non-union laborers had
proved again to be apathetic toward Bryan's
candidacy. Louis F. Post, editor of the Public,
perceived that organized labor had voted solidly
for Bryan, but he observed that the union worker
was only a minority of the labor force.[71] C. T.
Callahan, a local Democratic party leader from
Holyoke, Massachusetts, observed:

> I am deeply disappointed and chagrined
> at the folly of the laboring man. In our
> great manufacturing centers of our state
> they failed us utterly. . . . while we were
> fighting labor's enemies, labor itself re-
> fused to participate in the contest. In
> view of our experience, it is a grave
> question in my mind whether in the next
> campaign we ought to jeopardize the pro-
> motion of great principles of democracy by
> taking up the industrial cause of people
> who have so little interest as to act with
> its enemies.[72]

James B. Weaver wrote that "the trust and monopoly magnates, having made their peace with
Roosevelt and Taft, united to intimidate the
so-called businessmen, from peanut vendor to
country bankers."[73] More damaging than coercion,
Louis Koenig has observed, was the widespread ex-
pectation of the business community that pros-

perity would flourish more under Taft than
Bryan, an impression that moved the work force
to vote for Taft.[74]

If organized labor did not put the Democrats over in the presidential race, it may
have contributed to the party's success in
Congressional elections. The Democrats did well
in the 1908 Congressional elections--possibly
because of organized labor. Bryan praised
Gompers and his fellow leaders and expressed his
belief that labor would be an effective weapon
for the Democratic party in the future.[75]
Gompers, agreeing with Bryan, wrote:

> Labor's political work is just begun.
> The future is ours. Labor will continue the
> work of this campaign until those who are
> hostile or neglected towards its demands
> are willing to accord us justice.[76]

He argued that labor's entry into the campaign
was the single most important political event in
the 20th Century. Politicians, regardless of
party, would have to recognize labor demands or
take their chances at the polls:

> Labor will make its political power
> more effective as time goes on. It ac-
> quires wisdom from experience; it realizes
> that in most things the unorganized are in
> full sympathy with its policy and it must
> aid them to throw off the unjust conditions
> and assert their manhood . . . Labor moves
> forward with renewed hope and confidence
> . . . The outlook was never more hopeful.
> . . . This campaign was unsuccessful if
> judged only be the number of votes cast.
> We say with conviction that its moral in-
> fluence can hardly be accurately esti-
> mated at this time, yet even now Labor's
> political activity is recognized as a great
> movement to protect the liberties of the
> people and restore to them their natural

and constitutionally guaranteed rights.[77]

Although the Independence party had failed to garner labor support, Hearst had taken a significant part in labor's complete reversal of attitude toward political involvement, through organization, action, publicity, and negotiations. Some labor leaders had reasons more practical than ideological for their reluctance to support the movement that offered them most. Hearst was suspect as a reform leader. Having attacked corruption in politics, he had run as a Tammany candidate three times in four years. He had served as President of the National Democratic Clubs, had served as a Democratic Representative in the United States House of Representatives, and had been a serious contender for the 1904 Democratic presidential nomination, yet when he was opposed in the party in 1905 and 1908, he actively campaigned against it. He urged labor leaders to align themselves to the Democratic party and once they had done so he labelled it corrupt and condemned them for not taking a chance with a new party that offered little more. His actions were too erratic and unorthodox for organized labor, which had slowly and cautiously entered politics.

Hisgen had fared much more poorly than anyone had expected. Running on a popular progressive platform, receiving an enormous amount of positive national publicity in the Hearst press, and being in the headlines nationwide daily as Hearst revealed Standard Oil letters, he received a puzzlingly small vote. Voters in the thirty-nine states cast their ballots for him, but he tallied only .55 percent of the popular vote, attaining only the slightest respectability in California, Massachusetts, Illinois, and Rhode Island. He polled 35,000 votes in New York City, preventing Bryan from capturing the traditional Democratic stronghold, yet the vote was not very impressive in comparison to independent candidates' totals in 1905 and 1907.

254

Convinced that both parties were corrupt and believing that an independent political party could succeed in America,[78] Hearst had great difficulty believing just how poorly the Independence party had fared.[79] He had been politically humiliated in 1908. Still believing that his movement and the progressive movement were one and the same, he was worried, he wrote Brisbane, that the Hisgen defeat could seriously affect the progressive movement. To offset this, he wrote, the American and the Evening Journal would continue to advocate reform measures and to endorse progressive candidates regardless of party affiliation:

> The progressive battle is long from over. The people have been awakened to the injustices and inequities in American society. They are ready to act, I believe, to force change.
> We need reform men not afraid to act to bring about this change.
> We must continue to do our part in informing the plain people and we must intensify our efforts to elect progressives, true progressives that is, to office.
> The Progressive Movement will fall to the rhetoric of big business, I fear, unless, of course, we can unite the honest masses and elect a progressive President.
> We have done our share of action on the local level and we have effectively advocated progressive principles to the entire nation. We know that a vast majority of Americans are progressive in thought. We must do our part to put that thought into constructive political action.
> Let us put respectability and sincerity into a movement that can and will succeed. There is so much that needs to be done to insure the success of progressivism-- let us do our share to insure its success.[80]

Concerned about respectability, Hearst was ready

to give up his independence and co-operate with progressive politicians.

Footnotes

[1] New York *American*, October 14, 1907.

[2] Ihmsen to Brisbane, November 1, 1907, J.A.M.

[3] Hearst to Ihmsen, October 16, 1907, J.A.M.

[4] Hearst to Ihmsen, November 1, 1907, J.A.M.

[5] New York *World*, September 29, 1907.

[6] New York *American*, September 29, 1907.

[7] *Ibid*.

[8] New York *American*, September 30, 1907.

[9] Hearst speech, October 19, 1907, New York *American*, October 20, 1907.

[10] New York *Times*, September 15, 1907.

[11] Older, *op. cit.*, p. 319.

[12] Hearst to Brisbane, January 10, 1908, J.A.M.

[13] *Ibid*.

[14] Hearst to Ihmsen, November 17, 1907, J.A.M.

[15] Ihmsen to Hearst, November 24, 1907, J.A.M.

[16] Ihmsen to Hearst, January 10, 1908, J.A.M.

[17] Ihmsen to Hearst, June 2, 1908, J.A.M.

[18] Hearst to Brisbane, January 11, 1908, J.A.M.

[19] New York _American_, January 13, 1908, J.A.M.

[20] Chicago _American_, February 23, 1908, J.A.M.

[21] New York _American_, February 23, 1908, J.A.M.

[22] _Ibid_.

[23] New York _American_, May 3, 1908.

[24] New York _Times_, May 3, 1908.

[25] New York _Evening Journal_, May 3, 1908.

[26] New York _American_, May 10, 1908.

[27] _Annual Report of The A. F. of L. Convention_, St. Louis, 1888.

[28] Samuel Gompers, _Labor and The Common Welfare_ (New York: E. P. Dutton and Company, 1919), p. 136.

[29] Roosevelt to Elihu Root, August 18, 1906, Root Papers, Library of Congress.

[30] Gompers to Hearst, May 10, 1908, J.A.M.

[31] _American Federationist_, September 1908, p. 735, J.A.M.

[32] All except women's suffrage and the establishment of a government postal savings bank, _Annual Report to the A. F. of L. Convention,_ Denver, Colorado, November 1908.

[33] New York _Times_, July 22, 1908

[34] *American Federationist*, August 1908, p. 603.

[35] Gompers to Bryan, June 27, 1908, A. F. of L. Papers, Library of Congress.

[36] Karson, *op. cit.*, p.59.

[37] Gompers to Hearst, July 6, 1908, J.A.M.

[38] Gompers to G. W. Perkins, July 24, 1908, A. F. of L. Papers, Library of Congress.

[39] Hearst to Brisbane, July 14, 1908, J.A.M.

[40] New York *Evening Journal*, July 28, 1908.

[41] New York *American*, July 29, 1908.

[42] New York *Times*, July 29, 1908.

[43] New York *Evening Journal*, July 29, 1908.

[44] Chicago *American*, July 29, 1908, J.A.M.

[45] New York *American*, July 29, 1908.

[46] New York *World*, July 29, 1908,

[47] Ihmsen to Hearst, September 1, 1908, J.A.M.

[48] New York *American*, September 5, 1908.

[49] New York *Evening Journal*, September 5, 1908.

[50] New York *American*, November 5, 1908.

[51] Hearst to Brisbane, September 16, 1908, J.A.M.

[52] New York *American*, September 18, 1908.

[53] John Kennedy Winkler, _William Randolph Hearst: A New Appraisal_ (New York: Hastings House, 1955), p. 157.

[54] New York _Times_, September 19, 1908.

[55] New York _American_, September 19, 1908.

[56] New York _World_, September 19, 1908.

[57] New York _American_, September 19, 1908.

[58] New York _Times_, September 19, 1908.

[59] New York _American_, September 20, 1908.

[60] New York _Times_, September 23, 1908.

[61] Swanberg, _Citizen Hearst_, op. cit., p. 262.

[62] Carlson and Bates, op. cit., pp. 170-171.

[63] Winkler, _William Randolph Hearst: A New Appraisal_, op. cit., p. 60.

[64] Fuller, op. cit., p. 139.

[65] Hearst speech in Atlanta, September 12, 1908, New York _American_, September 13, 1908.

[66] Karson, op. cit., p. 60.

[67] Samuel Gompers, "Mr. Hearst's Political Toy," _American Federationist_, November 1908, p. 734.

[68] _Ibid_., p. 735.

[69] Samuel Gompers, "Labor Duty in Politics," _American Federationist_, November 1908, pp. 783-784.

[70] New York _Times_, July 31, 1908.

[71]Post to Bryan, November 2, 1908, Bryan Papers, Library of Congress.

[72]Callahan to Bryan, November 7, 1908, Bryan Papers, Library of Congress.

[73]Weaver to Bryan, November 13, 1908, Bryan Papers, Library of Congress.

[74]Koenig, op. cit., p. 445.

[75]Commoner, November 20, 1908, J.A.M.

[76]Samuel Gompers, "Influence of Labor's Great Campaign Now and For the Future," American Federationist, December 1908, p. 970.

[77]Ibid, p. 973.

[78]Hearst to Shearn, November 17, 1908, J.A.M.

[79]Hearst to Ihmsen, November 15, 1908, J.A.M.

[80]Hearst to Brisbane, November 18, 1908, J.A.M.

X

Once Again a Democrat

Although Hearst had decided, following the
1908 election, to give up his attempt to lead his
own "progressive movement," during the 1909 campaign he was thrust into the leadership of yet
another independent political movement in New
York State. He realized that his Independence
party had failed and had no chance for future
success. Speaking at a non-partisan banquet five
weeks following the election, he expressed his
conviction that an independent party could succeed. But he argued that until a truly progressive party came along, Independents should support whatever movement came closest to their
ideas.[1]

In 1909 Hearst again centered his political
activity on the New York elections. He did not
intend to seek public office but planned to be
active in support of progressive candidates.[2]
Addressing four hundred guests at the New York
County Independence League's third annual dinner
in his honor, he stated that he would never again
be a political candidate. The guests shouted
their disapproval, to which he responded: "I am
not going to give up fighting, but I want to
fight for someone else."[3] A _Times_ editorial
speculated that if he was drafted to run for
mayor, he would again pose a serious threat to
Tammany Hall.[4] His city newspapers, which still
sold for a penny, began in early April a six-
week editorial campaign acquainting readers with
issues and urging voters to nominate progressive
candidates.[5]

Hearst in early September came out in full
support of Judge William Gaynor for mayor. The
Hearst press had supported Gaynor, who, in
turn, had backed Hearst's gubernatorial bid.[6]
The publisher was attempting to form a Gaynor-
Republican Fusion ticket.[7] Murphy, realizing
Gaynor's strength among the city's independents
approached him suggesting a Tammany nomination.[8]

263

This attempt to draft Hearst's hand-picked candidate was a public insult to the newspaperman, and he pledged that Gaynor would lose the support of his newspapers if he accepted the Tammany nomination.[9] Hearst wrote:

> I believe that the people fully understand the situation and that they are thoroughly disgusted with the Tammany misgovernment. I think they only want an opportunity to place in office honest and trustworthy men with a satisfactory program of reform.[10]

Hearst lashed out at Gaynor for even considering Murphy's offer.[11]

Former Hearst supporters and local reform leaders, who remembered that Hearst had accepted three Tammany nominations yet claimed to remain true to his reform principles, criticized him for turning against a reform candidate whom he had long supported on the stump and in his newspapers.[12] Samuel Seabury accused him of being incapable of cooperating with other politicians and reformers when he could not direct and control their actions.[13]

Gaynor wanted both to accept the nomination and to remain a Hearst ally. He publicly stated:

> I value Mr. Hearst's support more highly than I can express. . . . He has done great good in this community and it will never be lost.[14]

In early October Gaynor accepted the Tammany nomination. Hearst, taking Seabury's advice, came out in support of Gaynor. He told a World reporter:

> I believe that Judge Gaynor is a good man and would make a good mayor, but I am sincerely sorry that Tammany is allowed to use his good name as a cloak for another raid upon this pillaged city.

With all I am for Judge Gaynor, but
not for Tammany, I think the Independents
should do their best to elect Judge Gaynor
and to defeat Tammany Hall.[15]

"I can support Gaynor," he wrote Brisbane, "because he is running on a platform made up almost
exclusively of Independent League demands."[16]
Hearst was, in fact, quite pleased that so many
progressive planks had been incorporated into
both party platforms. Commenting on the platforms
to a reporter, he said:

. . . In fact they are largely denials of
their former platforms and affirmations of
the principles of the Independents.
If the Independents have done nothing
else they have at least compelled the old
parties to pay some attention to the demands
of the people.[17]

Satisfied with the candidate and with the platform, on October 5 he again publicly declared
that he would not be a candidate:

. . . it would not be best for our principles for me to be continually a candidate
for office.
The public would soon conclude that I
was active in politics, not for principles,
but to hold office. While this is far from
true, and while my friends know well that I
consider office-holding the most arduous and
onerous task that can fall to the lot of
any citizen, still the suspicion that I was
a chronic office seeker would certainly injure me, and what is more important, would
probably injure our cause.
Let us consider the success of our
principles rather than personal or individual vindication.[18]

A Republican Fusion element nominated a
complete ticket headed by Otto Bannard, President of the New York Trust Company and treasurer
of the Republican County Committee.[19] He im-

mediately alienated Hearst by coming out against
municipal ownership.[20]

The Independence League held its annual convention on October 6 at Cooper Union Hall. The
3,000 delegates assembled expressed opposition
to both Bannard and Gaynor and shouted for a
Hearst nomination.[21] Sylvester L. Malone nominated him, and William Ivins, the Republican
candidate four years earlier, seconded the nomination.[22] He was unanimously selected and a
delegation was chosen to notify him at his home
on 86th Street and Riverside Drive of the convention's action.[23] Within thirty-six hours of
being notified he appeared before the convention
and accepted the nomination.[24] The league nominated a Fusion ticket, including Democrats,
Republicans, and Independents. On October 10 he
was named head of the Civil Alliance ticket.[25]

Hearst believed that he had no chance of
victory. He knew, he told Brisbane, that Gaynor
would win and could benefit the city. He was
concerned, however, with the rest of the Democratic party's ticket, which featured many
Tammany regulars. He was running for mayor to
give his Fusion ticket an honest chance. If
Gaynor was the only candidate on the Democratic
ticket to win, Tammany's stronghold over the
city would be shaken. Hearst's campaign motto
was "If Tammany is defeated the citizens win."[26]
He ran on a Declaration of Principles that was
almost identical to his 1905 platform.[27] Throughout the campaign he delivered a daily average of
four public addresses.[28]

Shearn on the stump, Ihmsen behind the
scenes, and Brisbane in the American and Evening
Journal ran Hearst's campaign. Several well-
known local progressives, inlcuding women's
suffrage advocate Maude Malone,[29] Dr. Ward,
Ben S. Hampton, S. S. McClure, William Lamar,
and John A. Sleitchter,[30] endorsed the Civil
Alliance ticket and campaigned for its head.

266

McClure, addressing a political rally, said that
Hearst "labored consistently, and I think, sin-
cerely, for the interests of the city as against
Tammany."[31] Hundreds of businessmen, from all
sections of the city, formed the Businessmen's
Municipal League to conduct an independent and
aggressive campaign for him.[32] Ivins campaigned
actively, warning city voters that Gaynor was unpredictable,[33] and describing Hearst as consistently progressive.[34] In a statement to the
press at the Civil Alliance headquarters, Ivins
predicted:

> Hearst will lose none of his old Repub-
> lican and Democratic vote and will get half
> of the McClellan Republicans and half, or
> 10,000 of the new vote, which will give him
> the difference or balance--say 243,000.
> I look then for this result: Hearst,
> 243,000; Gaynor, 183,000 to 185,000;
> Bannard, 167,000--a total of 595,000--the
> difference of 5,000 in the total of four
> years ago being the socialist vote, which
> will go to Gaynor.
> If I am right, Mr. Hearst will be
> handsomely elected and if there is full
> realization of this before /the/ election
> I look for a landslide which will give him
> a majority of all the votes cast.[35]

The Hearst newspapers were the only city
newspapers to support the entire Civil Alliance
ticket.[36] The _Times_ endorsed Bannard,[37] and did
not mention Hearst by name in a single editorial
during the month of October. Pulitzer's _World_
endorsed Gaynor and the entire Civil Alliance
ticket except its head, noting that the alliance
was more than a Hearst party--that it had a
serious chance all along and had popular candidates independent of Hearst. Pulitzer was sympathetic to Hearst, allowing Brisbane to write a
World editorial in his behalf.[38]

Tammany Hall leaders, again more concerned

with the challenge from Independents than with that from Republicans, led the campaign in opposition to Hearst.[39] They wrote, published, and widely circulated a pamphlet entitled "The Life of William R. Hearst." It charged Hearst with being a dangerous self-seeking demagogue who disregarded the rights of others and whose journalistic methods were based on exaggerations and falsehoods unprecedented in American journalism:

> . . . He wanted power and questioned not the means by which it would be gained. In order to attract attention and gain a following, he posed as a friend of the masses. . . . the positive bad that he accomplished was in using the friendship which he had gained among the masses to divide the people at the critical elections and cruelly lead them into the traps of the common foe . . . /He/ appeals to the evil passions of the weak and the malignant and strives to ruin that which he cannot rule . . . nothing has been too mean, too bitter, nothing too low or scurrilous for for him to say about men who refused to be coerced by his newspapers or corrupted by his dollar . . . In an attempt to destroy those whom he cannot control, no cesspool has been so deep that he would not dive to its bottom for sagacious scandal and depravity with which to fill the journalistic sewers over which he presides.
>
> Such is the pampered pet of fortune who scorned his bribes, betrayed every cause he has espoused, turned traitor to democracy and dastard to his political comrades and whose criminal journalism may boast of its most conspicuous achievement, the assassination of President McKinley by one of his feebleminded dupes.[40]

On November 2 voters elected Gaynor mayor of New York City with a 73,000 vote plurality.

Gaynor polled 250,387 votes; Bannard finished second, polling 177,304 votes; and Hearst trailed the field, polling 154,187 votes.[41] All of the other Civil Alliance candidates, however, were elected.[42] Tammany was thus left with only four of the sixteen seats on the Board of Estimates and with the mayoralty, and it was questionable to what extent it could influence or control Gaynor.[43]

Local reform leaders, Civial Alliance candidates, and anti-Tammany candidates praised Hearst for his accomplishments.[44] Bannard told supporters, "Hearst pulled the whole Fusion ticket through."[45] John Purroy Mitchel, President of the Board of Aldermen, observed:

> The candidates on the Fusion ticket owe their election to Mr. Hearst. I cannot express too emphatically my appreciation of his public spirit in entering the campaign. All decent citizens of New York owe Mr. Hearst a debt of gratitude for the success he has rendered them.[46]

William A. Prendergast, Comptroller-elect said:

> Without the aid which he rendered the Fusion cause it would not have been possible to have secured this victory.
> It has been generally conceded that in accepting most of the nominees of the Fusion conference Mr. Hearst acted with an unselfishness that is stateslike.[47]

Even a *Times* editorial congratulated him for accomplishing his objectives:

> For that he is entitled to the gratitude of the community. . . . Mr. Hearst now learns what has often been learned by others who have stacked their political fortunes upon appeals to the passions of the people, that there is always danger that another may come to the fore with louder appeals and more

extravagant promises. Every community has
its mindless part, and the mindless always
run after the man who makes the most noise.
That is what happened to Mr. Hearst, that
is what has cut his vote of four years ago.
But he has done a good service to the city,
and that thought must console him.[48]

Hearst publicly stated that he was very much
satisfied with the results.[49]

An _American_ editorial claimed that New York
City citizens were the true victors in the campaign. Hearst was successful, it read, because
he had entered the race to give the Civil Alliance ticket an honest chance.[50] A Brooklyn
Eagle editorial expressed a similar view:

> The results indicate that Mr. Hearst
> was sincere in his statement that he did not
> want to be mayor of New York. . . .
> He could know of no such autocracy in
> any public office. The powers of the mayor
> of New York are large, but they are not un-
> limited; and Mr. Hearst would be sure to
> find in their limitations a hindrance and
> a severe annoyance.
> Outside of the mayoralty he will con-
> tinue to do the work which has made him a
> person to be reckoned with in this city,
> and he will do it far more happily than he
> could do the checkered and hampered work
> of mayor.[51]

Carrying only 6th, 26th, and 31st assembly
districts,[52] Hearst did not fare nearly as well
in 1909 as he had in 1905. Gaynor ran strongly
in ever section of the city:

	Kings	Queens	Richmond
Hearst	45,622	12,871	2,279
Gaynor	87,448	14,998	6,458
Bannard	69,153	10,139	4,440 [53]

He polled 61.8 percent of the lower West Side Irish vote, 55.6 percent of the vote of the Hell's Kitchen Irish, 66.1 percent of that of the Greenwich Village Italians, 52.2 percent of the Italian vote in East Harlem, and 51.1 percent of the Manhattan working class vote.[54] Hearst's popularity at the polls had dropped among all these groups. He maintained his 1905 popularity only among the Jews.[55]

At a December non-partisan banquet held in his honor at the Hotel Astor, Hearst declared that the results of the election were advances for progressivism. Predicting greater victories, he urged independents to cling to progressive principles. The major political parties, he insisted, were no longer extensions of public sentiment but were instead controlled by business and professional elites. He again envisioned the formation of a National Progressive party:

> I do know that when the Progressive party is formed and its principles clearly defined, elections will be contested upon live issues, and vital questions will be decided by the results of the elections.[56]

In December Hearst in the American exposed confidential letters written between Murphy and Tammany lieutenants, concerning city jobs in the Gaynor administration for the Tammany faithful. He charged that the Mayor-elect was surrendering progressive principles.[57] Murphy admitted the authenticity of the letters, but said of the publisher:

> It is pretty low down for a man who has run once for the nomination for President of the United States, once for mayor of New York, and once for governor to hire an agent to enter a man's room and steal his correspondences.[58]

He correctly noted that the letters were not very damaging.

Hearst realized that he could not captain
the Independent's cause in 1912 so he decided to
combine forces with respectable reform leaders
and seek out a suitable candidate for the 1912
presidential election.[59] During the spring of
1910 he and Brisbane corresponded regularly with
several liberal Congressmen, including Victor
Murdock of Kansas, George Norris of Nebraska,
Henry Allen Cooper of Wisconsin, Everis Hayes of
California, and Champ Clark of Missouri. In New
York they received accounts, which they printed
in the American and Evening Journal, that Speaker
of the House Joe Cannon of Illinois was exploiting
nearly every prerogative of the office that he
held.[60]

A hard-shelled Republican, Cannon appeared nearly invincible. He enjoyed the power
to appoint committee members, to appoint committee chairmen, to determine the schedule of
business in the House, and to recognize members
on the floor. He controlled the Rules Committee, the Republican caucus, and the Republican floor vote. He shuffled both committee
assignments and committee chairmen.

Several Republican Congressmen, realizing
the possiblity of getting national publicity,
expressed to Hearst their opposition to Cannon's
rule.[61] They were of progressive persuasion, all
of them favoring the regulation of employment of
women and children in factories, the regulation
of hours of a work day, the reduction or removal
of all tariffs, the creation of an equitable tax
system, and the adoption of minimum wage laws.[62]
Agreeing with Hearst editorials, they believed
it vital to the nation's survival to enlarge
and revise the powers of government in dealing
with social and economic inequities. Their
immediate intention was to break the Speaker's
procedural stronghold.

On January 7, 1910, Progressive Congressmen,
led by Norris, a Republican, and Clark, a Demo-

crat, challenged the Speaker's customary practice of appointing committee members.[63] The conflict reached a climax between March 16 and March 18 when House members curbed Cannon's power to control the Rules Committee. The revolt, Norris wrote, signified promise for future progressive legislation.[64] Hearst wired a congratulatory telegram to Clark.[65]

The revolt against Cannon was the first major instance of reform in the modern Congress. Additional changes in committee assignments and the selection of committee chairmen were quick to follow. The progressive-insurgents did not become the leaders of a procedural majority following the curbing of the Speaker's powers. Norris, in floor debate, emphasized that they had challenged not Joe Cannon but the powers he wielded as Speaker. By pioneering procedural change, Hearst wrote Norris, they opened the way for substantive change. [66] The way to achieve lasting change was not to switch office-holders but to transform the office. Hearst, being a former progressive Congressman, realized the significance of the events in the House.[67] He was so impressed with the actions of Norris, LaFollette, and Clark that he suggested to Brisbane the possibility of promoting one of them for the presidency.[68]

In the spring of 1910 Hearst again turned his attention to the New York elections. On May 5 the New York State Independence League held a strategy conference. Addressing the delegates from fifty-six assembly districts, Hearst said that the progressive voters in the state held the balance of power and should unite in the upcoming elections.[69] In his plea of unity, he called his long time opponent Theodore Roosevelt to return from England to campaign for progressive candidates:

Come home to New York Mr. Roosevelt and honestly take the warpath against the bosses.

273

> We Independents are whetting our tom-
> hawks /sic/ for the fray. There is no
> jealousy in our ranks. We do not care who
> leads, if only he leads aright.
> We do not care who gains the glory[70]
> as long as the people gain the victory.

Traditional party support was eroding, he told
a World reporter, as a tremendous number of
progressives became disillusioned with their
parties:

> . . . the vast majority of the citizens of
> the United States are not only in favor of
> progress and reform in politics, but have
> made up their minds to secure progress and
> reform and to secure them now.[71]

Pointing to progressive advances in Kansas,
Nebraska, Iowa, Wisconsin, New Hampshire, Michi-
gan, Tennessee, and New York, he predicted that
if progressives could unite, regardless of party,
they could, in 1912, elect a president from
within their ranks.[72]

On October 7 the New York State Independence
party held its annual convention. Hearst sent
a message to the delegates assembled in Webster
Hall, predicting that the state's progressives
would unite behind the league candidates. He
wrote:

> Our straight ticket will give pro-
> gressives the only opportunity that they
> will have in this campaign to vote for a
> platform that sincerely expresses their
> ideas and for candidates that honestly
> represent their principles. Our straight
> ticket offers the only refuge to our pro-
> gressive citizens who were shrewdly tricked
> in the Republican convention and boldly
> driven out of the Democratic convention.[73]

A full ticket was nominated, headed by John Jay

Hopper for Governor. Hopper, a well-known civil engineer, had joined the Independence League in 1905, managing Hearst's Harlem campaign.[74] He had since served as Harlem's Independence League leader.[75] Hearst ran for lieutenant-governor. Following Hopper's acceptance speech, the delegates chanted: "We'll go it alone and smash both machines!"[76] Shearn, giving the acceptance speech for Hearst in the editor's absence, quoted from a letter Hearst had written the previous day:

> The Independence League has done exactly as it pledged itself to do. It has made an honest effort to support progressive principles and progressive candidates, regardless of party, and, having failed to find them in the old parties, it has bravely determined to make an independent campaign of its own.[77]

Hearst consented to run as a candidate and to support the Independence League because he was dissatisfied with the major party nominees.[78] He had publicly challenged the Republican state delegates to overthrow their party's oligarchy and to take a stand for direct primaries and pure elections.[79] But the Republicans had nominated Henry Stimson, a Harvard Law School graduate, former counsel in Elihu Root's law firm, United States Attorney General for the southern district of New York, and Roosevelt's hand picked candidate. A Wall Street lawyer, he was entering politics as one of Roosevelt's trust busting liberals. He would later serve in the cabinets of four presidents.[80] Labelling Stimson a representative of Wall Street and high finance, Hearst urged the Democratic state delegates to nominate progressive candidates and to draft a progressive platform.[81] The Democrats nominated John Dix, a lumber merchant. Upon graduation from Cornell, he had worked as a farmhand and mechanic to learn about labor conditions. He was an important but not powerful figure in state politics. He was Chairman of the State Demo-

275

cratic Committee and, in 1908, had run as the
party's candidate for lieutenant-governor. Although he was an ardent advocate of conservation
and labor unions, he had been at odds with
Hearst since 1906, when he bolted the party instead of supporting the editor.[82]

During the campaign R. G. Davis wrote
articles in the Westminster Review and the
London Review of Reviews denouncing the middle
class and urging reformers to devote their efforts to the lower and working classes:

> As a class, they /the middle class7
> are too selfish to incur any social risks,
> and they think themselves too superior, and
> too wise to be influenced by modern poli-
> tical thought . . . Anything of a serious
> nature produces ennui . . . In truth, the
> working classes are forming a higher con-
> ception of art and music and of science
> and literature than the middle classes.
> Reformers should devote their atten-
> tion rather to the working class than to
> the almost hopeless task of converting the
> middle class.[83]

Hearst was not appealing solely to the working
class, but the article did make an impact on him.
He quoted from it frequently in campaign speeches
and sent copies of it to numerous reformers,
including LaFollette, S. S. McClure, and Clark.[84]
He also sent copies of it to his editors, cred-
iting them for the part they were playing in
the elevation of the working class.[85]

Without Hearst at the head of the Independence League's ticket, its chances for victory
on any level were nil.[86] In 1910 the progressives divided the Republicans, and Murphy was
able to win not only the governorship again but
both houses of the state legislature.[87] Dix
polled 689,700 votes, or 48 percent of the total,
outdistancing Stimson by over 67,000 votes.
Hopper tallied about 45,000 votes. In the

lieutenant-governor election Hearst finished a distant third, polling 48,208 votes in New York City[88] and just 60,000 votes statewide.[89]

In defeat Hearst came to realize the voters were as tired of him as they were of Bryan. In a letter to Brisbane, he pledged never again to seek political office.[90] He claimed that the Democrats had come to power in New York not for what they were doing but because of what the Republican had failed to do while in power,[91] and the American cited elections of progressive candidates whom his newspapers had supported, including Governor Robert Bass in New Hampshire, Governor Judson Harmon in Ohio, Senator John Cummins in Iowa, Governor Joseph Baldwin in Connecticut, Governor Hiram Johnson in California, Governor Eugene Foss in Massachusetts, and Governor Ralph Plaisted in Maine.[92] Within hours of their election, both Plaisted[93] and Foss[94] sent telegrams to Hearst thanking him for his "invaluable aid" in their campaigns, each adding that he was the most important factor in the victory. An American editorial credited both major parties for adjusting to progressivism in the drafting of platforms and the selections of candidates.[95]

Since it was obvious that Hearst was in no position to mount a presidential drive, Shearn advised him to support either Roosevelt, LaFollette, or Clark "to insure that a progressive secure at least one of the major party's nominations."[96] Hearst's political and social philosophy could have justified his endorsement of each of Shearn's suggested candidates. But he could not yet bring himself to support Roosevelt, who had publicly denounced him and had actively campaigned against him. From the start he leaned towards Clark, a long time friend and former Congressional ally. Clark, a lawyer and former college president, had first been elected to the 53rd Congress, had served as House minority leader during the 60th and 61st

Congresses, and became Speaker of the House
during the 62nd Congress. Hearst still had
ties with Democratic party leaders--especially
in New York, Illinois, and California--and knew
that he could influence the 1912 national convention. It may have also occurred to him that
he could be a progressive compromise candidate
in the event of a deadlocked convention. He
wrote that if he could not become president, he
would do his part to insure the nomination of a
successful and viable politician whose views
were similar to his own--Champ Clark.[97] On
April 11, 1911, he announced in his newspapers
his formal endorsement of Clark for President.[98]
A self-appointed leader of a campaign to secure
for Clark the party's presidential nomination,
Hearst was again a Democrat.

In 1912 Hearst acquired his ninth newspaper,
the Atlanta Georgian, enlarging again the world's
largest newspaper chain. Democrats had suffered
through four consecutive presidential election
losses and were, for the most part, willing to
accept the support of his newspapers. He started
early and made a concerted effort to rule the
1912 Democratic convention.

On October 19, 1911, Hearst publicly announced his intentions to re-enter the folds
of the Democratic party. Speaking before a
county Democratic party convention at Carnegie
Hall, he said:

> Mr. Murphy and his kind drove me out
> of the Democratic party, but the commendable
> causes of the national Democracy has /sic/
> brought me back into the fold.
> I am registering as a Democrat, I am
> speaking as a Democrat, and I am going to
> fight the undemocratic principles of Murphy
> and Tammany Hall.[99]

The New York Independence League did not die at
this point, but without its biggest supporter it
declined in prestige and power. Members did not

278

accept the announcement well.[100]

Newspapers generally looked favorably on
Hearst's announcement, an indication that they
had opposed him more for his methods than his
beliefs. A Washington Post editorial, "Public
Life Bettered Through W. R. Hearst," read:

> The people of the United States did not
> require the personal statement of William
> Randolph Hearst that he is a Democrat to
> assure themselves as to his political con-
> victions. . . .
> The public life of the United States
> has been bettered through the persistent
> efforts of William Randolph Hearst.
> He has fought the battle of the masses
> of the people bravely and nobly, often at
> great cost to himself in time, money, and
> friends. . . .
> His announcement at New York last
> night adds a mighty factor to the aggressive
> power of Democracy in the ensuing cam-
> paign . . .
> Not only in New York, but throughout
> the union Mr. Hearst has the confidence of
> an independent and progressive electorate
> that stands for the highest ideals in
> public life, and loves to follow the stan-
> dard of a champion so tireless in his ef-
> forts to attain them. . . . [101]

Every New York City newspaper carried stories,
most giving front-page coverage and editorials
to his actions. Every paper gave him positive
coverage. The World[102] and Sun[103] decided that
his reason for returning to the party was to
wage war on Murphy. Even the Tribune, his most
outspoken critic for more than a decade, featured
a sympathetic front-page article on the address,
adding in an editorial, "New York State and New
York City are suffering from too much Murphy . . .
He can be humbled and overthrown if every voter
who resents political jobbery enlists to fight
him at the polls on election day."[104]

Within twenty-four hours of making his announcement, Hearst received congratulatory telegrams from national Democratic party leaders[105]
including Champ Clark and Oscar Underwood.
They welcomed him back and saw in his actions
an omen that the Democratic party was setting
aside factional differences for the common
good. Clark expressed a belief that the nation's
progressives were uniting under the Democratic
party's banner.[106]

New York's independent Democrats were also
receptive to Hearst. John Purroy Mitchel, elected
President of the New York City Board of Aldermen
in 1909, praised him for his efforts towards
municipal ownership in New York City and progressive advances nationwide.[107] William
Prendergast, elected Comptroller in 1909,
stated that Hearst's press was the greatest tool
for the nation's progressives.[108] State Senator
Robert Owen observed:

> William Randolph Hearst has been advocating
> the essential principles of Democracy for
> years, and I rejoice to know his magnifi-
> cent papers will continue to stand for these
> doctrines. He has done a great work in
> promoting genuine progress and deserves
> the appreciation of all who stand for
> honest and efficient government.[109]

In his newspapers Hearst urged all Inde-
pendent-progressives to form Fusion tickets with
the Democratic party,[110] promising that his[111]
newspapers would support all such tickets.
The 1911 New York Fusion attempts were quite
successful. Boss government received a stinging
rebuke in nearly every part of the state and in
nearly every county and borough in New York
City.[112] Tammany was left with only forty-
eight seats of the one hundred and fifty seats
in the New York Assembly.[113] On the elections
Hearst reflected:

. . . a great victory has been won. Honest government has triumphed in nine-tenths of the districts of the city and of the state.

I said the day before the election that the wave of reform which had been sweeping across the continent would break in New York in this election.

It has broken and big and little bosses are carried away in its flood.

The victory is with Fusion and with the cause that Fusion represents . . . [114]

From out of the state the publisher received telegrams of appreciation. In a representative telegram the Democratic State Central Committee Chairman for New Mexico, where the entire Democratic progressive's ticket had been elected, wrote to Brisbane of Hearst's resourcefulness:

I wish to thank Mr. Hearst for the magnificent assistance he gave us for our fight for good government and progress.

Our problem was to place the issue before our Spanish speaking voters, nearly one half of the voters of our new state. This was solved through the Spanish edition of the Los Angeles _Examiner_. In making this magnificent contribution to our success, Mr. Hearst showed anew both his often-exhibited friendship for New Mexico, and his interest to fight for good government, wherever that fight is waged. [115]

On the New Mexico elections, State Central Committeeman J. D. Hand reflected:

New Mexico Democrats and Progressives have won this fight practically alone, except for the splendid help of William Randolph Hearst.

I was sent to seek aid from the Eastern Democrats. I beat over the whole field. The National Committee gave us $100. I spent it for stamp money. But with Mr. Hearst it was different. I had a three-

> hour conference with him in New York, and
> found that he knew nearly as much about
> general conditions here as we did.
> He gave us real help, and when the
> Spanish editions of his Los Angeles _Examiner_
> reached us--when I saw it in every pre-
> cinct where I campaigned, I knew we couldn't
> be beaten, because it presented twelve
> pages of truth to our Spanish speaking
> friends.[116]

Massachusetts Governor Eugene Foss, Boston Mayor
John Fitzgerald, New Mexico Governor William
McDonald, New Mexico Secretary of State Samuel
Bell Thomas, and Massachusetts Lieutenant-
Governor-elect David Walsh sent letters of
praise and gratitude to Hearst.[117]

Following the 1911 elections, Hearst intensified his efforts to name a presidential
nominee in 1912. He clearly favored Clark, but
confided that he would endorse Democratic Congressman Oscar Underwood of Alabama, or, if the
Democrats did not endorse a progressive, would
support LaFollette, either as a Republican or as
a third party candidate. The early frontrunners
were Clark and Woodrow Wilson.

In 1910 Wilson had been elected Governor
of New Jersey, with the endorsement and full
support of the Hearst newspapers. Wilson was
the first Democrat to carry the state in over
two decades. Hearst had rejoiced in his victory,
writing:

> Through his interesting personality,
> as through a deep channel, the university
> with its high-sourced mountain springs of
> art and science will have a chance to pour
> itself upon the arid plains of public life.
> For Dr. Wilson is no isolated school
> man descending into the political arena.
> His accepted mission and the whole meaning
> of his career as a political historian and
> college president has been the democratizing

of knowledge . . . Wilson may perform before
the eyes of politicians a Galilean mir-
acle.[118]

When Wilson's name began to circulate as a
possible progressive presidential candidate,
however, Hearst opposed him.[119] By late January,
1912, the Hearst newspapers had come to lead the
anti-Wilson forces. Hearst's attitude came of
Wilson's earlier conservatism[120] and his remarks
on the new immigrants.[121] Hearst's method of
attack was to quote Wilson's passages expressing
his opposition to the populist and progressive
movements and making critical remarks about the
Hungarians, Poles, and Italians. Hearst wrote:

> The world knows what Wilson thinks
> of the Hungarians, Poles, and Italians--
> he has told them very plainly, if not too
> courteously in his fifth volume of his
> History of the American People. Governor
> Wilson says that one of the curses of this
> country is to quote his exact words, 'men
> of the lowest class of the South of Italy
> and men of the meanest sort out of Hungary
> and Poland, men out of the ranks where there
> was neither skill nor energy, nor any
> initiative of quick intelligence.' Most
> interesting of all, perhaps, is his frank
> confession that he thinks Chinese labor
> would be better for this country than the
> Hungarians, Poles, and Italians.[122]

Hearst, having directed a great amount of his
political, social, and newspaper appeal to the
immigrant masses, refused to support a candidate who opposed them.[123] He also attacked
Wilson for waivering on issues. In his gubernatorial campaign Wilson had opposed the initiative, referendum, and recall while as a progressive presidential candidate he supported
them.[124]

Hearst endorsed Clark in all of his newspapers, public addresses, journals, and public

interviews. As the main speaker at a gathering
of Democratic leaders in January 1912 in Washington, D.C., Hearst attacked Roosevelt, who was
mounting his own drive for the presidency, for
attempting to steal the thunder of progressivism. He suggested, claiming to be a regional
leader and a spokesman for the progressive
movement, that the nation's Independent-pro-
gressives would cast the deciding votes in the
November elections and that his newspapers could
influence their decisions. He pledged if the
Democrats nominated a progressive like Clark for
President, they would have their best chance of
victory in two decades.[125] He continuously insisted that the 1912 election would be decided
on progressive principles:

> Principle has become . . . important
> . . . with the majority of the people in
> this country. The era of education has
> passed. The era of conviction and action
> has come. The people have discovered what
> is wrong and have devised what is necessary
> to set it right. Parties must proceed in
> accordance with the public will or they will
> receive no public support.[126]

Throughout January and February Hearst was
once again often mentioned as a potential candidate for the Democratic party's presidential
nomination. In mid-February, M.F. Tarpey, member of the California State Democratic Committee,
sent to Hearst a copy of a letter written by
Clark offering to withdraw his name from the
California primary and support Hearst if he
ran.[127] Hearst replied to Tarpey that he was
not interested in entering any state primaries
and would urge Californians to endorse Clark:

> The Democratic party was founded as a
> progressive party. To survive it must
> continue as the progressive party of the
> nation. To succeed it must declare boldly
> for prgressive principles and must nomi-
> nate for the presidency a Democrat whose

284

progressive sentiments are sound and sincere.[128]

Realizing that Wilson was Clark's major opposition for the nomination, Hearst conducted an extensive newspaper campaign against him. He hired John Temple Graves and Alfred Henry Lewis to write a series of newspaper and magazine articles intended to stir opposition to Wilson. He labelled the New Jersey Governor a Federalist,[129] and argued that Wilson's public addresses and writings indicated that he distrusted the plain citizens.[130] Hearst charged that Wilson, in his histories of the nation, had given more credit to Hamilton than to Washington in the struggle for independence, and had dismissed every popular leader and every popular people's movement. Wilson, Hearst observed, had described the country as "young and foolish" when Jackson came to power, adding that "few can believe it would again approve or applaud childish arrogance and ignorant arbitrariness like his."[131]

Hearst and his editors praised Clark as much as they attacked Wilson. Hearst's Magazine featured a full-page portrait of Clark. "Universally popular," "a man's man," "rugged personality," and "masterful sincerity" were the kinds of phrases with which Hearst's writers referred to Clark. Portraying him as a progressive capable of leading a national movement for social reform, Hearst asserted that Clark had succeeded in uniting Democratic Congressmen for the first time in a generation.[132]

In late June, Andrew Lawrence and Mayor Carter Harrison of Chicago accompanied Hearst to the Democratic National Convention in Baltimore. As a leading supporter of the frontrunning candidate for the presidential nomination, Hearst entered the convention in the strongest position he had ever enjoyed in a Democratic convention.[133] Progressive delegates, with the strength to determine a major party's nomination for the first time, were enthusiastic and confident.[134] On June 26 Hearst telegrammed Brisbane:

> I am definitely and positively and finally in favor of a progressive candidate and a progressive platform carried to victory by the enthusiastic support of a united Democracy. I know there is no more genuine progressive in the length and breadth of this land of ours than Champ Clark.[135]

On the convention floor he told reporters:

> In my opinion the vast majorities of the delegates of this convention are progressive, and the convention will demonstrate its own progressive character in the preparation of the platform and the nomination of a candidate. . . . [136]

The Hearst-Murphy feud, ongoing since 1905, continued into the convention. Murphy controlled New York's ninety member delegation, which was pledged, by the unit rule, to Governor Judson Harmon of Ohio. He opposed Clark because of his close alliance with Hearst.[137] The _Times_ predicted that if Clark were elected President, Hearst would be the next Democratic Governor of New York, a member of the new Cabinet, or an ambassador.[138] Hearst and Murphy had made another "deal," the _Tribune_ speculated, in which Murphy would swing the state's delegates to Clark at a climactic moment during the balloting, and would, in return have Hearst's pledge of newspaper support in the New York City and State elections.[139]

Hearst, although not himself a convention delegate, had an enormous influence over a great number of delegates.[140] Bryan was a delegate and, to a greater degree than Hearst, could in-

fluence party delegates,[141]   The Nebraskan was
still the most hailed and attended Democrat at
the convention.[142]   He favored the nomination of
either Underwood or Wilson.[143]   Once again, wrote
Hearst, Bryan was sacrificing progressive principles for personal advantage. Charging that
Bryan had made an alliance with Underwood and
Wilson, neither of whom he believed could defeat
either Taft or Roosevelt, he speculated that
Bryan's aim was to deadlock the convention and
run as a compromise candidate, promising
Underwood and Wilson cabinet positions.[144]

     Bryan's first political maneuver in Balti-
more was to mount a challenge to Alton Parker,
the national committee's selection, who was
seeking the convention's temporary chairmanship.
Lined up in support of Parker were the city
bosses and the community of financiers and
lawyers that writers then and since have known
as Wall Street.[145] Wilson delegates pledged
their support to Bryan but Clark men believed
that Bryan, if elected, would exploit the per-
quisite of that office and direct the nomination
to himself.[146]   In the ensuing roll call, Harmon,
Underwood, and many Clark followers voted for
Parker, who defeated Bryan 579 to 510.

     The next day a committee of progressive
delegates offered Bryan the chairmanship of the
Resolution Committee. Bryan declined the offer
but agreed to serve on the committee and to appoint its chairman; he chose Senator John W.
Kern of Indiana. In the first committee meeting
Bryan proposed that the platform be withheld from
the convention until after the presidential nomination.[147] The eventual platform, which would
be acceptable to Clark, Wilson, Underwood, and
Bryan,[148] confirmed the dominance of progressive forces in the party: direct elections
for United States Senators, direct primaries for
all candidates, government regulation of railroad rates, commission government for all
cities, initiative, referendum, and recall, reasonable immigration restriction, improved labor

287

conditions, union recognition, and a one-term limit on the next Democrat elected president.[149]

Clark controlled a clear majority of the delegates in the early balloting but could not reach the necessary two-thirds required for the nomination. On the tenth ballot Murphy, as the Tribune had predicted, swung the New York delegation to Clark. This gave him a clear majority with 556 votes to Wilson's 350½ and Underwood's 117½.

Not since 1884 had a Democratic candidate with a majority in the convention failed to win the nomination by the required two-thirds.[150] But the stampede for Clark never developed. The Times speculated that Clark's dependence on Hearst hurt the Congressman.[151] Even more damaging to Clark was Bryan's unwillingness to declare for him. Bryan charged that Clark's inaction during the fight for temporary chairman made his commitment to the progressive sentiment suspect. Nebraska employed the unit rule and Bryan voted for Clark on the first thirteen ballots, but he refused to support Clark publicly and spread criticism among the delegates that the Missourian was too easy going to manage the government.[152]

Prior to the balloting Wilson had written to Bryan:

It is the imperative duty of each candidate for the nomination to see to it that his own independence is beyond question. I can see no other way to do this than to declare that he will not accept the nomination if it is secured without the aid of that delegation (the Ryan-Murphy-Belmont-Hearst delegation from New York). For myself, I have no hesitation in making that declaration.[153]

The note may have had an effect on Bryan, who

288

took the floor and introduced a resolution preventing the convention from nominating any candidate who would be "the representative of or under obligation to J. Piermont Morgan, Thomas F. Ryan, August Belmont or any other member of the privilege-hunting and favor-seeking class."[154] It carried overwhelmingly, 883 to 201.

On the fourteenth ballot, following Murphy's shift of New York's votes to Clark, Bryan pledged his support to Wilson.[155] Bryan, Clark wrote, "wanted to create a deadlock and grab off the nomination for himself. He had no more idea of nominating Governor Wilson for President than he did of nominating him as Ahkoond of Swat. His well-considered plan was to kill off both Governor Wilson and myself. As I was leading, I must be killed off first . . . "[156] Wilson's managers expressed a similar belief when Bryan on June 30, while the momentum was shifting to Wilson, declared that the delegate should nominate a ticket within twenty-four hours. He suggested only minor candidates, with not the least chance for nomination.[157]

On the thirtieth ballot Wilson moved past Clark. In a pragmatic move on the forty-third ballot, Sullivan broke with Hearst and Clark and delivered Illinois' fifty-eight votes to Wilson. Virginia followed the lead and Wilson secured the nomination on the forty-sixth ballot. In a rush to make the nomination unanimous, Murphy cast New York's 90 votes for Wilson.[158]

Hearst had once again been rebuked by the Democratic party. Charging that Bryan had done everything conceivable to prevent Clark's nomination, Hearst claimed that the party had missed its opportunity to have a genuinely progressive leader.[159] While Wilson was not Hearst's kind of progressive, Hearst misunderstood the mood of the delegates. Wilson's nomination could not, the World argued, be construed as a defeat of progressivism.[160] Wilson had campaigned for the

289

nomination as a progressive, and pledged in his acceptance speech, to campaign for the presidency as a progressive.[161] Many party leaders believed that he was the strongest candidate available and would be able to unite the nation's progressives.[162] J. L. Cleveigh, editor of the Perth Amboy Evening News, wrote to him:

> I realize fully that it is also a great victory for the progressive principles in which the great majority of the people in this country today believe. As you are the one leader, however, who best represents these principles, the result at Baltimore today is as much a personal triumph for you as it is endorsement of the things for which you stand.[163]

Still doubtful that Wilson was dedicated to progressive principles, Hearst challenged him to rewrite the party platform in such a way as to insure the restoration of governmental power to the people. In a public address, he said:

> The whole progressive programme is based upon a genuine and sincere policy of restoring the power of government to the hands of the people. Without this power of government reposed in the hands of the people to accomplish any of the reforms which this platform or more genuine platforms declare for. . . . This platform as a whole is no platform for a progressive to stand on . . . Whether it is due to ignorance or insecurity it is immaterial. It deprives the progressives of all hopes in the Democratic party. It deprives the citizens of the country of all confidence in the Democratic party.[164]

This utterance is a measure of how Hearst as a politician had changed in a decade. As a Congressman he had rarely confined himself to such generalities.

In this year the Republicans, who had remained united behind party presidential candidates over the previous two decades, fought
harder than the Democrats over the selection of
a candidate. The Republican hopefuls included
Robert LaFollette, former President Roosevelt,
and the incumbent Taft.

On January 21, 1911, Robert LaFollette had
established the National Progressive Republican League. This nationally recognized reformer had first contacted Hearst in 1909 with
a proposal for progressives to unite. He wrote
to Hearst:

> . . . through the . . . Progressive League
> the Republican and Democratic progressive
> leaders can gather together the men and the
> women who are progressive and educate them
> as to what should be the next step, so that
> when the times come for the contest within
> the primaries there will be (1) a unanimity
> of opinion and of action (2) through an
> organization whereby (a) the issues will be
> squarely raised (b) in just the shape they
> want them and (c) then about 75 percent of
> the voters within the party will probably
> support the issues, because they plan to
> increase their political power, also termi-
> nate the monopolists robberies and to re-
> vise public taxes.[165]

In the course of 1911 he appealed to Hearst,
Louis Post, Tom Johnson, Lincoln Steffens, and
other reform leaders nationwide to unite to
elect progressive candidates to office.[166]
During the year he mounted a personal drive to
wrest the Republican nomination from Taft. His
chances dwindled, however, when in December,
during a press conference, he reportedly suffered
a nervous breakdown.

When Roosevelt, in the summer or 1911, decided to challenge his hand picked candidate for

291

the Republican party's presidential nomination
he assumed that Hearst, because of his commitment
to progressive principles, would support him despite their differences.[167] But Hearst, describing him as a "late blooming progressive
trying to steal the thunder of the movement,"[168]
did not support him. This was more than just a
personality conflict, as most Hearst biographers
suggest.[169]

Hearst was disturbed precisely because the
ex-President had become a symbol of progressivism
without having the substance. Roosevelt had become more of a symbol of progressivism out of
office, Hearst wrote Brisbane, than he had been
in office.[170] Speaking at a Democratic banquet
in Jefferson's honor in 1907, he had attacked
Roosevelt for presenting the image of a trust
buster while actually being quite conservative in
his attitudes and actions toward the trusts.[171]
Congressman Charles Littlefield from Maine
wrote to Hearst that in six and one-half years
Roosevelt, for all his talk, had secured only
seven convictions through the enforcement of
trust laws. They resulted in $96,000 worth of
fines paid to the government, and the litigation
had cost the taxpayers $386,242. Roosevelt had
acted in the 1902 coal strike, Littlefield
argued, only because the people demanded presidential action.[172] Hearst observed:

> The better part of the proposals that
> Mr. Roosevelt would now of a sudden enact
> into law were introduced by me in Congress
> during Mr. Roosevelt's presidential terms
> without the slightest assistance from Mr.
> Roosevelt to make them laws.[173]

He believed that Roosevelt was, in fact, a
pragmatic politician, doing what was required
to protect himself, and having acted as a progressive during his presidency only until he
met the slightest resistance.[174]

Taft was generally considered to be a more

292

conservative president, but, as Hearst pointed out in a letter to Brisbane, Roosevelt's progressive policy had produced only forty-four anti-trust injunctions in seven years while Taft's conservatism had produced eighty-eighty injunctions in less than four years.[175] Taft, the *American* observed, had also formulated a national conservation program and set aside more land for preservation than Roosevelt had.[176] But by 1912 progressive principles were much more readily accepted than they had been a half decade earlier. Neither Taft nor Roosevelt was progressive enough, Hearst wrote, to assume the presidency under its banner.[177]

Roosevelt won every popular Republican primary election that he entered. He had proved his appeal to his party's progressives, Hearst wrote, and Taft should thus step aside. If he was denied his party's nomination, the people would be denied their right to select candidates.[178] Taft controlled party regulars, however, and was able to steer the nomination to himself. Bryan, who covered the convention for the New York *World*, observed that the convention proved that organized interests could easily subdue the progressive cause.[179] Roosevelt supporters left the Republican National Convention in disgust and moral outrage and went to Chicago, where they established the Bull Moose Progressive party and nominated Roosevelt for President.

Following the three conventions, Hearst travelled to Europe, where he contemplated the course of action that he should take in the campaign. Roosevelt claimed to be the most progressive candidate,[180] but Hearst continued to believe that he was an opportunist.

Returning to the states, Hearst reluctantly threw his support and that of his newspapers behind Wilson.[181] He endorsed the Democratic party's platform, which Clark delegates had drafted, and favored the progressive principles that Wilson was advocating during the campaign.[182]

In the election Wilson amassed 6,296,547 votes, or 41.9 percent of the total, and was easily elected. Wilson carried forty states and 435 of the 531 Electoral College votes. Roosevelt finished second with 27.4 percent of the popular vote, taking six states and 88 Electoral College votes. Carrying only Vermont and Utah, Taft finished third with 23.2 percent of the popular vote. Socialist candidate Eugene Debs made an impressive showing, polling 6 percent of the popular vote.

Following the election Hearst publicly advised Wilson of his new responsibilities and obligations. Pointing out that Wilson had received fewer votes than Bryan had in 1908, he wrote that this political reality should instill in the President-elect a profound sense of responsibility. Newspapers had educated the American people to become a restless, intelligent, and exacting jury, he reasoned, and because they demanded a progressive president, Wilson was now obligated to live up to his party's platform and to his campaign promises.[183]

Reflecting on Roosevelt's failure, Hearst told members of the New York Young Republican Club that the former President was not as progressive as a majority of American voters had come to be. His platform, Hearst charged, was the same as the 1908 Independence party's platform. The editor also noted that Roosevelt's National Progressive party had never become a national political party of progressives. He had "committed the distinct error of making his third party movement almost entirely Republican," staffed with Republican officeholders and appealing almost entirely to the progressive wing of that party. Hearst assured his audience that progressivism had not peaked with Roosevelt's showing, though it was another indication of its appeal.[184]

Wilson was only the second Democrat to occupy the White House since 1860. He was determined to unite both his party and the nation's progressives.[185] In both efforts, Hearst would serve as a public watchdog and obstacle.

Footnotes

[1] New York _American_, December 15, 1908.

[2] Hearst to Morrill Goddard, April 30, 1909, J.A.M.

[3] New York _Times_, April 18, 1909.

[4] New York _Times_, October 3, 1909.

[5] The _American_ called for municipal owner-ship, for ballot reform, for an eight-hour work day for all city workers, for an improved city school system, and for a city conservation pro-gram. New York _American_, April 17 - May 29, 1909.

[6] Carlson and Bates, _op. cit._, pp. 160-161.

[7] New York _American_, September 12, 1909.

[8] New York _Tribune_, September 12, 1909.

[9] New York _American_, September 13, 1909.

[10] _Ibid_.

[11] New York _American_, September 21, 1909.

[12] New York _Tribune_, September 14, 1909.

[13] Chambers, _op. cit._, p. 125.

[14] Swanberg, _Citizen Hearst_, _op. cit._, p. 267.

[15] New York _World_, October 5, 1909.

[16] Hearst to Brisbane, October 3, 1909, J.A.M.

[17] New York _American_, October 6, 1909.

[18] New York _World_, October 5, 1909.

[19] New York *Times*, January 17, 1909.

[20] New York *American*, October 4, 1909.

[21] New York *American*, October 7, 1909.

[22] New York *Times*, October 7, 1909.

[23] New York *Times*, October 8, 1909.

[24] New York *Times*, October 9, 1909.

[25] New York *American*, October 11, 1909.

[26] New York *American*, October 8, 1909.

[27] New York *American*, October 12, 1909.

[28] New York *American*, October 23, 1909.

[29] Malone to Hearst, October 12, 1909, J.A.M.

[30] New York *American*, October 24, 1909.

[31] *Ibid*.

[32] New York *American*, October 25, 1909.

[33] New York *World*, October 30, 1909.

[34] New York *Tribune*, October 30, 1909.

[35] New York *American*, October 30, 1909.

[36] New York *American*, October 21, 1909.

[37] New York *Times*, October 13, 1909.

[38] Pulitzer to Editors, October 7, 1909, Pulitzer Papers, Library of Congress.

[39] New York *American*, October 21, 1909.

298

[40]Tammany Hall, "The Life of William R. Hearst," Kilroe Collection, Columbia University.

[41]New York _Times_, November 3, 1909.

[42]New York _American_. November 3, 1909.

[43]New York _Times_, November 3, 1909.

[44]New York _American_, November 3-10, 1909.

[45]New York _American_, November 3, 1909.

[46]_Ibid_.

[47]_Ibid_.

[48]New York _Times_, November 3, 1909.

[49]New York _American_, November 3, 1909.

[50]_Ibid_.

[51]Brooklyn _Eagle_, November 3, 1909, J.A.M.

[52]New York _Times_, November 3, 1909.

[53]New York _World_, November 3, 1909.

[54]Henderson, _op. cit._, p. 113.

[55]New York _American_, November 4, 1909.

[56]New York _American_, December 15, 1909.

[57]_Ibid_.

[58]New York _Tribune_, December 16, 1909.

[59]Hearst to Brisbane, November 17, 1909, J.A.M.

[60]Norris to Hearst, March 10, 1910, J.A.M.; Murdock to Hearst, May 6, 1919, J.A.M.; Clark to

Brisbane, March 19, 1919, J.A.M.

[61]Norris to Hearst, March 17, 1919, J.A.M.

[62]Benjamin Parke DeWitt, _The Progressive Movement_ (New York: Macmillan Company, 1915), p. 24.

[63]Washington _Evening Star_, January 8, 1910.

[64]Norris to Brisbane, March 24, 1910, J.A.M.

[65]Hearst to Clark, March 22, 1910, J.A.M.

[66]Hearst to Norris, March 20, 1910, J.A.M.

[67]Hearst to Brisbane, March 19, 1910, J.A.M.

[68]Hearst to Brisbane, September 17, 1910, J.A.M.

[69]New York _American_, May 6, 1910.

[70]Hearst to Roosevelt, September 7, 1910, J.A.M.

[71]New York _World_, September 11, 1910.

[72]New York _American_, September 12, 1910.

[73]New York _American_, October 8, 1910.

[74]_Ibid_.

[75]New York _Times_, May 17, 1923.

[76]New York _American_, October 5, 1910.

[77]Hearst to Shearn, October 7, 1910, J.A.M.; New York _American_, October 8, 1910.

[78]New York _American_, October 7, 1910.

[79]New York _American_, September 27, 1910.

[80] New York _Times_, October 21, 1950.

[81] New York _American_, September 29, 1910.

[82] New York _Times_, April 10, 1928.

[83] R. G. Davis, "Down On The Middle Class," London _Review_ _of_ _Reviews_, October 1910, p. 367, J.A.M.

[84] Hearst to LaFollette, Hearst to McClure, Hearst to Clark, October 31, 1910, J.A.M.

[85] Hearst to Editors, October 31, 1910, J.A.M.

[86] New York _Times_, November 8, 1910.

[87] Henderson, _op_. _cit_., p. 114.

[88] New York _American_, November 9, 1910.

[89] New York _Times_, November 9, 1910.

[90] Hearst to Brisbane, November 10, 1910, J.A.M.

[91] New York _American_, November 9, 1910, J.A.M.

[92] New York _American_, November 10, 1910.

[93] Plaisted to Hearst, November 8, 1910, J.A.M.

[94] Foss to Hearst, November 8, 1910, J.A.M.

[95] New York _American_, November 10, 1910.

[96] Shearn to Hearst, December 1, 1910, J.A.M.

[97] Hearst to Brisbane, April 10, 1911, J.A.M.

[98] New York _American_, April 11, 1911.

[99]New York *American*, October 20, 1911.

[100]New York *Times*, October 20, 1911.

[101]Washington *Post*, October 21, 1911.

[102]New York *World*, October 20, 1911.

[103]New York *Sun*, October 20, 1911.

[104]New York *Tribune*, October 20, 1911.

[105]Hearst also received congratulatory tele-grams from Thomas Hickey, Gavin McNab, Frank Gould, Edwin Newman, George Chamberlain, Cotter Bride, Albert Burleson, William Brantley, Justice W. Martin, William Sulzer, John Cox, Judge Lockwood Honore, Charles Lopicka, Francis Walker, John Echart, and James Bowers. All dated October 20, 1911, J.A.M.

[106]New York *American*, October 21, 1911.

[107]New York *American*, July 2, 1911.

[108]*Ibid*.

[109]New York *American*, August 24, 1911.

[110]New York *American*, October 21, 1911.

[111]New York *American*, August 24, 1911.

[112]New York *Times*, November 9, 1911.

[113]New York *Tribune*, November 9, 1911.

[114]New York *American*, November 9, 1911.

[115]A. A. Jones to Brisbane, November 8, 1911, J.A.M.

[116]Hand to Brisbane, November 8, 1911, J.A.M.

[117]All dated November 8, 1911, J.A.M.

[118]Older, op. cit., p. 344.

[119]John Tebbel, The Life and Good Times of William Randolph Hearst (New York: E. P. Dutton and Company, 1952), p. 225.

[120]New York American, January 15, 1911.

[121]New York American, April 11, 1911.

[122]San Francisco Examiner, February 10, 1911, J.A.M.

[123]New York American, February 11, 1912.

[124]New York Daily Chronicle, September 25, 1911, J.A.M.

[125]New York Times, January 9, 1912.

[126]New York American, November 26, 1911.

[127]Tarpey to Hearst, February 18, 1912, J.A.M.; Clark to Tarpey, February 17, 1912, J.A.M.

[128]Hearst to Tarpey, February 18, 1912, J.A.M.

[129]New York American, February 10, 1912.

[130]San Francisco Examiner, February 10, 1912, J.A.M.

[131]Washington Post, March 14, 1912,

[132]New York American, May 1, 1912.

[133]Washington Post, June 27, 1912.

[134]New York American, June 27, 1912.

[135]Hearst to Brisbane, June 26, 1912, J.A.M.

[136] New York _American_, June 27, 1912.

[137] New York _Times_, June 27, 1912.

[138] New York _Times_, June 28, 1912.

[139] New York _Tribune_, June 29, 1912.

[140] Washington _Post_, June 27, 1912.

[141] New York _Times_, June 27, 1912.

[142] Koenig, _op. cit._, p. 485.

[143] New York _American_, June 27, 1912.

[144] Hearst to Brisbane, June 28, 1912, J.A.M.

[145] Koenig, _op. cit._, p. 484.

[146] New York _Times_, June 24, 1912.

[147] New York _Times_, June 25, 1912.

[148] New York _American_, July 1, 1912.

[149] Wilson's notes on the platform, July 2, 1912, Wilson Papers, Library of Congress.

[150] Koenig, _op. cit._, p. 491.

[151] New York _Times_, June 28, 1912.

[152] William Jennings Bryan and Mary Bryan, _The Memoirs of William Jennings Bryan_ (Chicago: Winston Publishing Company, 1925), pp. 335-337.

[153] Lundberg, _op. cit._, p. 215.

[154] New York _World_, June 28, 1912.

[155] New York _American_, July 1, 1912.

[156] Champ Clark, My Quarter Century of American Politics, vol. 2 (New York: Harper and Brothers, 1920), p. 424.

[157] Bryan suggested John W. Kern, Ollie James, James O'Gorman, Charles A. Culberson, and Isador Rayner. New York Times, July 1, 1912.

[158] New York Times, July 3, 1912.

[159] New York American, July 3, 1912.

[160] New York World, July 2, 1912.

[161] Washington Evening Star, July 2, 1912

[162] Perry Belmont to Wilson, July 2, 1912, Wilson Papers, Library of Congress.

[163] Cleveigh to Wilson, July 2, 1912, Wilson Papers, Library of Congress.

[164] New York American, August 5, 1912.

[165] LaFollette to Hearst, no month or date, 1909, LaFollette Papers, Library of Congress.

[166] Hearst to Ihmsen, January 28, 1912, J.A.M.

[167] Roosevelt to Oscar Straus, June 7, 1912, Roosevelt Papers, Library of Congress.

[168] Hearst to Brisbane, June 1, 1912, J.A.M.

[169] Swanberg, Citizen Hearst, op. cit., p. 275; Older, op. cit., p. 341; Carlson and Bates, op. cit., pp. 176-177.

[170] Hearst to Brisbane, September 26, 1910, J.A.M.

[171] New York American, April 14, 1907.

305

[172]Littlefield to Hearst, April 14, 1907, J.A.M.

[173]Hearst to Brisbane, September 26, 1910, J.A.M.

[174]_Ibid_.

[175]Hearst to Brisbane, June 1, 1912, J.A.M.

[176]New York _American_, November 26, 1911.

[177]Hearst to Brisbane, June 1, 1912, J.A.M.

[178]New York _American_, May 30, 1912.

[179]Josephus Daniels, _The Wilson Era--Years of Peace, 1910-1917_ (Chapel Hill: University of North Carolina Press, 1944), p. 50.

[180]Roosevelt to Beveridge, July 27, 1912, Beveridge Papers, Library of Congress.

[181]New York _American_, August 5, 1912.

[182]New York _American_, October 10, 1912.

[183]New York _American_, November 6, 1912

[184]_Ibid_.

[185]Arthur Link, _Woodrow Wilson and the Progressive Era, 1910-1917_ (New York: Harper and Brothers, 1954), p. 34.

XI
The Wilson Years

Woodrow Wilson was a political party leader in the classic English parliamentary style. He believed that he should direct party members in Congress and, if necessary appeal over their heads to the American electorate. Realizing that the progressives had their best chance thus far of seeing favorable legislation enacted, Hearst decided to support the President-elect as long as he remained dedicated to his platform and campaign promises.[1]

In his inaugural address Wilson, addressing the Hearst-Clark wing of his party, observed of the nation's haste over the previous two decades to succeed and become great:

> Our thought has been 'Let every man look out for himself, let every generation look out for itself,' while we reared giant machinery which made it impossible that any but those who stood at the levers of control should have a chance to look out for themselves. . . . we were heedless and in a hurry to be great.[2]

The nation had now come to a sober second thought, he claimed, and the government was ready to alleviate social and economic inequities.[3]

Following Wilson's inauguration, Hearst and his editorial writers outlined progressive demands much in the manner that they had after the 1900 presidential election. Hearst urged progressives in the cities to control urban growth and development with city plans, to provide for community ownership and operation of public utilities, to initiate conservation programs, and to expand community recreation facilities.[4] For the states he favored direct primaries for all candidates, electoral reform, corrupt practices legislation, the short ballot, the Massachusetts

307

ballot, effective voter registration systems,
and the initiative, referendum, and recall.[5]
He urged voters to pressure Congress and the
President to revise downward to nation's tariff
policy, to enforce trust regulations, to enact a
graduated income tax, to limit a president's
tenure to two terms, and to recognize and encourage labor organizations.[6]

Hearst continued to battle several trusts
in New York City. His most noted effort in 1912
was his revelation that Mayor Gaynor and Borough
President George McAnney and Comptroller
Prendergast had awarded the Traction trust complete control of the city's subway system for
the next fifty years, and had guaranteed it an
annual 8.76 percent profit.[7] Hearst loudly pro-
tested the agreement and played a significant
role in blocking the proposed Gaynor-Prendergast-
Interborough Enabling Act in the state legislature.[8]

Once in office Wilson responded to the Progressives' pressures and called for a special
session of Congress to revise the nation's tariff
policy.[9] In May 1913, he maneuvered through
Congress the Underwood-Simmons Tariff, which
reduced the ad valorem rates about 11 percent,
added a number of consumer goods to the free
trade list, and eliminated tariff protection
of iron, steel, and various other trust pro-
ducts. Congress also levied a modest graduated income tax. Wilson, in an attempt to
create public support for the measure, appealed
to progressive newspapermen nationwide, including Brisbane, to endorse it.[10] With a new
sensitivity to public opinion, Congress adopted
the measure. It was an impressive show of party
loyalty, progressive influence, and presidential
leadership. Hearst, who had advocated tariff revision could not give his total support to it
since, he believed, in allowing sugar and wool and
other farm commodities to remain on the free trade
list, it was unfair to American farmers.[11]

Wilson also urged Congress to upgrade the
nation's anachronistic money and banking system.
He favored passage of his Federal Reserve bill.
Bank leaders desired a central bank with auxiliary
banks privately controlled but authorized and
protected by the federal government. Hearst opposed Wilson's proposal, again because of the
hardships that it would put on the farmers. He
urged Congress to prohibit interlocking directories for public control of regional banks, to
permit reserve banks to discount agricultural
paper, and to prevent the use of commercial
paper as a basis for currency.[12] Throughout
August and September his papers pressured Wilson
to pledge his support to allow reserve banks to
discount agricultural notes and to regulate interlocking directories. Wilson agreed to these proposals and in September the revised bill passed
the House of Representatives. As the Senate considered it, Wilson again took his case to the
people, claiming that the bankers, in order to
insure its defeat, were creating artificial
fears of impending panic. But Hearst and other
progressive spokesmen nationwide supported the
Federal Reserve bill and it passed the Senate in
December. The creation of a Federal Reserve
Board and regional banks made for an improved
and more efficient banking system. Government
control over currency and credit provided a
flexibility of short-term credit that was urgently
needed. The regulatory power of the Board, Hearst
wrote, assured a greater degree of public control over banking than ever before.[13] He believed,
however, that there was still a need to ease long-
term agricultural credit to provide the average
farmer with the means necessary to increase the
production of his land.[14]

In 1913 Wilson supported three progressive
measures. He directed through Congress legislation to establish the parcel post system.
Hearst supported it, having advocated its establishment both in his newspapers and on the
political stump for a decade and a half. Two

constitutional amendments that he had long
supported were ratified. The Sixteenth Amendment, ratified on February 3, 1913, provided
for a graduated income tax. The Seventeenth
Amendment, ratified on April 8, 1913, required
direct election of United States Senators.

In the fall of 1913 Hearst again turned his
efforts to the New York City elections. The
Independence League drafted a progressive platform and appealed to him for help.[15] It was
logical for him to support the League against
Tammany. Before a political rally at Cooper
Union on October 21, he lauded radical politics,
but in the vague terms he had been using since
1907:

> . . . there are more room and reason for
> a radical party today than ever before.
> Each new day there is opportunity for
> a new radical advance, for a further forward
> step in the direction of social justice and
> political progress.
> The progress of the world has been
> wrought by radicals--by men who had the
> imagination to see, the devotion to sac-
> rifice, the determination to succeed.
> Conservatism, of course, has its value,
> but it is at best a negative value . . .
> it too often acts as a bar to progress.
> Radicalism is the motive power of
> progress, the impulse and the inspiration
> to human advancement.[16]

On July 31, 1913, the Independence League's
mayoralty nomination went to John Purroy Mitchel,
a thirty-three year old lawyer who, upon being
appointed special counsel to the city of New York
in 1901, had uncovered the graft of the Manhattan
borough president and forced him out of office.[17]
Mitchel's record in public office commended him
to municipal reformers, and he also won the su-
port of the Wilson administration.[18] Hearst supported Mitchel because of his pledge to oppose
Tammany during the campaign and in office.[19] He

had gained Hearst's favor by being the only member of the Board of Estimates to vote against the city's dual subway contracts.[20] Hearst and Shearn supervised the drafting of Mitchel's platform, which denounced Tammany's methods and stressed the need to eliminate the corruption in city government.[21] Hearst actively campaigned for Mitchel, addressing political rallies daily for weeks before the election.[22] Mitchel's was a Fusion candidacy that Republicans, Independent Democrats, and reformers generally supported.[23]

The Times, voicing conservative opposition to the alliance between Mitchel and Hearst, labelled their views socialistic. An editorial read:

> Of what use is it to waste time considering the candidacy of . . . Mitchel . . . . Men of sober minds and common sense . . . would vote . . . for any honest and able man nominated by Tammany rather than embark the municipality on a sea of Socialistic adventure by entrusting Mr. Mitchel with the power of the mayor's office.[24]

The Times, Herald, and Tribune all opposed Mitchel, while most of the local reform leaders, and the Wilson Administration, supported him.[25]

"On the Tammany side of the political fence," reported the Tribune, Mitchel's nomination was generally considered one that would "make things easier for the Democratic machine organization."[26] The Herald reported that Tammany politicians had expressed the belief that any individual they nominated could defeat Mitchel.[27] Murphy and the Brooklyn organization had been at odds with Gaynor because the mayor had not given the machine as much patronage as some Democrats would have liked. Believing that he could afford to accede to the wishes of Gaynor's opponents and yet triumph over a divided

311

opposition, Murphy engineered the party's nomination to Edward E. McCall, chairman of the Public Service Commission.[28] McCall had been named to a fourteen-year term on the Supreme Court in 1902 and had, in January 1913, resigned from this position and accepted the chairmanship of the Public Service Commission at a reduced salary. The Times,[29] Tribune,[30] and World,[31] prophesized that his selection would prove to be a blunder.

Gaynor's supporters opened campaign headquarters on August 28 and urged the mayor to run as an Independent. A day later he declared himself a candidate and, on September 4, he officially launched his candidacy at a meeting on the steps of City Hall.[32] On October 12, while on a cruise to Europe, Gaynor died.[33] Most of Gaynor's supporters preferred Fusion to Tammany, so they supported Mitchel.[34]

With only two tickets in the field, the chief campaign issue became control of the city by Tammany.[35] Because of the Hearst press, Tammany had become so identified with corruption in the mind of the public that McCall made the assertion of his independence a major part of his campaign strategy.[36] He accused Mitchel of being Hearst's candidate:

> We hear the cry of 'Tammany' and we
> hear the cry of 'Bossism.' Such cries are
> tawdry; they are childish and silly. It
> would seem needless for me to repeat after
> the life I have lived that I am no man's man,
> but this is one thing that you can count
> on; that I am no newspaperman's man.[37]

The impeachment of Governor William Sulzer increased Mitchel's chances. Sulzer, a Tammany regular who had served as an Assemblyman and as a Congressman, had been elected Governor of New York in 1912. Once in office he angered Tammany officials because of his continued efforts to push the passage of a direct elections bill.

312

In 1913 the state legislature appointed the
Frawley Investigating Committee to investigate
financial irregularities of state institutions.
The committee, staffed by Tammany regulars, revealed that Sulzer had violated the New York
State Corrupt Practices Act by failing to report
all of the campaign contributions he had received.[38] This information led to his impeachment, and he was succeeded in office by the
lieutenant-governor, Martin A. Glynn. The trial
and removal of Sulzer caused ill feelings throughout the state. Mitchel made the impeachment a
first-rate campaign issue.[39]

On Election Day, Mitchel outpolled McCall
by 121,000 votes, the largest margin since the
formation of Greater New York City in 1897.[40]
The negative reaction to Tammany's impeachment of
Sulzer was evident in the Fusion victory in the
city and in the composition of the State Legislature. An anti-Tammany majority controlled
the Board of Aldermen and, with the exception of
the Borough President of Queens, all members of
the Board of Estimates had received Fusion support.[41]

The New York City newspapers interpreted
the election result as a blow against corruption.
"New York is infinitely better for yesterday's
triumph for righteousness," said a _Times_ now
sympathetic to the candidate; "it stands higher
in the world's estimation."[42] The _Tribune_, another
former opponent of Mitchel, declared of the city
that it "has never done so good a day's fighting
against corruption and for the cause of right
government."[43] "Tammany had been beaten," the
World commented, "but with unlimited corporation
money and influence behind it, and when a quarter
of a million voters cast their ballots for
Tammany's candidate, these ballots are a shocking
manifestation of popular indifference to honesty
and decency in government."[44]

In the wake of Tammany's defeat, Hearst

313

urged voters and elected officials to initiate electoral reforms, including direct nominations, the Massachusetts ballot, and the initiative, referendum, and recall, to complete the destruction of the city's machine system. Tammany had been beaten, but, he promised, without new legislation Tammany would return to power. He wrote:

> The people have fought a long ten year struggle against the political boss and the political machine. The forces of corruption have been routed. They must not be allowed to reform, merely under a new general. They must be pressured and destroyed and the fortresses that they occupied must be razed to the ground. In their place should rise strongholds of popular rights to protect the people's liberties and to perpetuate the people's power.[45]

When, in December, Governor Martin Glynn pushed a direct primaries bill through the state legislature, Hearst wrote:

> It is a further victory for the aroused and intelligent public sentiment, which manifested itself so vigorously that members of the legislature saw . . . that their political future was dependent upon their support of this measure. . . . In the long years of preaching the American has addressed itself to the people, knowing well that once they were awakened to the needs of the reform the politicians would be compelled to concede it.
> The result has proved that no appeal made to the people intelligently, fairly, convincingly, and persistently urged will ever fail . . . /The/ fundamental force behind its passage was the vigorous public excitement aroused and expressed by the American.[46]

Throughout 1914 Hearst sustained, mainly by

314

newspaper crusades, his battle against trusts. In the Los Angeles _Examiner_, he campaigned for municipal ownership and operation of the city's light and power.[47] In the _American_ he continued to advocate municipal ownership and operation of public utilities and he successfully challenged the city's bread trust, restoring the price of a loaf of bread to five cents.[48] In Chicago he was the driving force in securing a two-platoon system for the city's fire department, was responsible for lowering electric rates, and was instrumental in a crusade for the pasteurization of milk.[49] In all of his newspapers he urged government ownership and operation of the railroads,[50] and of the telegraph and telephone lines.[51] But these domestic programs were overshadowed by Wilson's foreign policy.

During the 1912 campaign few, if any, of the nation's progressives challenged or considered Wilson's views on foreign policy. His program of "moral principle," suggesting an American duty to work for peace both by example and through open and honest diplomacy, was generally acceptable. Most progressives trusted Secretary of State Bryan, who launched, in 1913 and 1914, a program of negotiating treaties with Great Britain, France, Italy, and twenty-seven lesser powers, calling for the submission of all disputes among the signatories to permanent commissions of arbitration.

Wilson had campaigned exclusively on a domestic program of reform which he titled the New Freedom. He had sidestepped foreign affairs and did not mention them in his inaugural address. On the eve of his inauguration he confided to a friend, "It would be the irony of fate if my administration had to deal chiefly with foreign affairs."[52] He assumed the presidency with no diplomatic experience, yet no progressive spokesman, including Hearst, made any mention of a lack of fitness in that regard.

Hearst was an expansionist until Wilson

315

became concerned with the European hostilities.
Throughout 1913 and 1914 the Hearst press advocated war with Mexico, claiming that an
American takeover would bring progressive
civilization to the average Mexican citizen.
Writing to Brisbane, he presented the outdated
manifest destiny argument:

> Righteous wars seem superficially to
> be made by men, but they must surely be
> destined by God. They are part of the
> scheme of civilization, part of the plan of
> progress. . . . Progress and civilization
> must be forced into Mexico.[53]

But he opposed American involvement in the
European struggle. From the declaration of war
by Austria-Hungary on Serbia on July 28, 1914,
until America declared war on Germany on April
6, 1917, he consistently urged the President
and Congress to keep the nation out of the
struggle. He viewed the war as purely an
economic struggle with which America should not
be concerned. Believing that the press had the
power to stop the war, he wrote to Lord
Northcliff, publisher of the London _Times_, and
Lord Burnham, publisher of the London _Telegraph_:

> The longer the war continues the
> more civilization will suffer.
> Can the war be stopped? I think it
> can.
> I think the press can appeal to the
> people, as no other influence can. I
> feel that if the appeal is made now to
> the press of all nations, and by the press
> of all nations, the war can be stopped and
> will be stopped.
> Appeal to the people for one united
> effort to compel peace.[54]

Hearst believed that Wilson's loyalties
were with the English, and that their leaders
could influence his presidential actions. Hearst
warned his readers:

Mr. Wilson gained his degree of Doctorate of Philosophy by an essay which contended flagrantly in the face of fact that the English Parliamentary form of government was superior to the American Congressional system. . . . The London _Times_ proudly advertises that . . . 'Some short time ago,' President Woodrow Wilson, when speaking at the annual dinner of bankers in New York said, 'To get the news of the world, I subscribe for the weekly editions of the London _Times_' . . . Mr. Wilson is an English free trader.[55]

The World War dominated both the Hearst press and the Wilson administration from 1914 through the end of the war. It did not, however, cause Hearst to abandon his progressive views. He confided to Brisbane that he would have supported the war effort if it had been a progressive's war like the Spanish American War.[56] He did support the Bolshevik Revolution of November 7, 1917, and, in a telegram to Andy Lawrence, editor of the New York _American_, urged America to recognize the Russian Soviet Federated Socialist Republic established on July 10, 1918:

Why are we in this war? We are in it for Democracy. Then, for Heaven's sake, why not recognize a democratic government? We recognize the imperial government of Russia, but when Russia secures a democratic government we have so far not recognized it. Does not this seem to discredit our professions of war for democracy? If this imperialistic government of Russia could be restored, we would not hesitate to recognize that. . . . We must not lose the ideals of war, because if we do, we will lose the war--as far as our American objectives are concerned. . . . Let us recognize the truest democracy in Europe, the truest democracy in the world today.[57]

317

In the early years of the European conflict, Hearst made a stand for non-involvement qualified by preparedness. Clinging to progressive domestic policies through a period of horror and fear, he criticized Wilson for allowing foreign policy to overshadow domestic policy and thus effectively slowing the tide of progressive legislation.[58]

Hearst continued to battle for progressive programs. In 1915 he took on the nation's water trusts and Chicago's electric trust. Eighteen companies had come to control all of the nation's developed water power, he charged in editorials, and they were lobbying for legislation to provide for government protection.[59] In a letter of December 15, 1915, Brisbane suggested that Hearst's efforts had blocked the passage of the Shields Bill, which would have given natural resources to private interests under the so-called leases which were virtually grants in perpetuity.[60] Attempting to curb rising electric rates in Chicago, Hearst publicly threatened to install his own electric plant to supply power to his buildings and surrounding buildings. The Insull Electric Company, succumbing to the exposure, offered him a new contract supplying electricity at half the present rate. He accepted the contract with the stipulation that every other consumer in the city using a like amount of energy would be supplied electricity at the same reduced rate.[61]

Millicent Hearst publicly joined the progressives' cause during the Mitchel campaign and remained an active public figure throughout Wilson's presidency. Mitchel would appoint her to the Chair of the Mayor's Committee of Women on National Defense. She was to become the driving force in establishing emergency relief and civic aid in New York. She supervised the establishment of canteens where volunteers served food to Army and Navy recruits. Her greatest public effort was to found and serve as President of Free Milk for Babies, Incorporated, which between 1918 and 1936 provided

more than seven million quarts of milk to under-
nourished and sick babies in their homes.[62]   She
would remain an active social worker throughout
World War II and became increasingly concerned
with progressive legislation, becoming an active
force in securing social welfare laws and playing
a significant part in the creation of the Child
Welfare Board in New York.

While Wilson had directed progressive legislation, Hearst was outspokenly critical of him
for not pushing most of the planks of his 1912
platform.[63]   In May 1915, a Hearst editorial
warned the President that unless he made a
concerted effort to direct progressive legislation through Congress, the Republicans would
regain control of Congress in 1916.[64]   Responding
to progressive sentiment in Congress and outside, Wilson in 1916 pushed through a number
of progressive measures. He secured legislation for a non-partisan Tariff Commission,
for credit aid to highway construction, for the
federal government to guarantee a living wage
and workmen's compensation, for regulation of
child labor, and for various other social reform measures.[65]   His appointment of Louis
Brandeis to the United States Supreme Court in
1916 was a further indication of the President's
intent to appease the nation's progressives.
To cover the increased costs of the defense
programs, Wilson also advanced revenue legislation, including increased income and inheri-
tance taxes. Thus he attempted to give the
preparedness issue a progressive stamp and to
identify the Democratic party with national
defense.[66]

Looking to the 1916 presidential election,
the Republican party had the task of reassimi-
lating members of the National Progressive party.
Hearst again believed that Roosevelt, who was
generally recognized as a progressive, was the
Republican's logical choice for president.[67]
Hearst and Roosevelt had come to overlook past

differences and were on friendly terms.[68] Believing progressive domestic policy to be more
important than foreign policy, Hearst supported
the interventionist Roosevelt and attended the
1916 Republican National Convention in Chicago
to influence delegates to nominate the former
President.[69] Hearst was disappointed when the
Platform Committee rejected the proposed progressive planks for women's suffrage, government
ownership of public utilities, and initiative,
referendum, and recall.[70] In a frantic last-
minute attempt to swing the nomination to
Roosevelt, Hearst sent a telegram to the former
President at Oyster Bay:

> I urge you to come to Chicago to use
> your splendid ability and mighty influence
> . . . to establish a permanent patriotic,
> radical party.[71]

Roosevelt did not go to the convention. He had
no desire to seek the nomination and had already
made an appeal to the progressive wing of the
party to nominate Senator Henry Cabot Lodge of
Massachusetts.[72] But the very first ballot revealed a strong trend to Associate Justice of
the United States Supreme Court Charles Evans
Hughes, who was easily nominated on the third.

The Republican progressives had gone to
Chicago with the sole intention of nominating
Roosevelt and were dissatisfied with the Hughes
nomination.[73] As a two-term governor of New
York Hughes had instituted many political reforms, including welfare and pro-labor legislation, but his close association with Taft,
who had appointed him to the Supreme Court in
1912, alienated them, as did the semi-progressive
platform he had agreed to run on.[74] They had
previously announced that they would not accept
Hughes as a compromise candidate.[75] The party
regulars, stated the Nation, had made virtually
no attempt to appease the progressive wing of
the party:

A veritable tragi-comedy was the play
by the progressives at Chicago. . . . One
can hardly resist a feeling of melancholy
at the plight of the sincere and impassioned
progressive delegates who went to Chicago
fired with holy zeal, and who little by
little discovered that they were being toyed
with, deceived, cheated and at last left in
a hopeless and humiliating position. The
final scenes, after they learned that
their idolized leader had deserted them in
the great emergency, were really pathetic.
They were dazed, stunned, despairingly
indignant. . . . It must now be clear to
all that the progressive debacle at Chicago
was inevitable. The life had gone out of
the party. . . . 'We followed Teddy in
1912, and he cannot desert us now' was the
progressive cry at Chicago. But his telegram of refusal put an end to that illusion.
And events had previously put an end to the
Progressive party as anything more than a
name . . . As an influence it may abide, but
as an organization its day is done.[76]

With Hughes' nomination, the Nation predicted,
all plans and hopes for a national progressive
party were ended:

Their fate is another evidence of the
fact that third parties do not create good
leaders. This is one of the reasons they
soon die. In this respect the record of
the progressives is much that of older
third parties.[77]

Hearst quietly and somewhat reluctantly
supported Wilson because he had directed the
passage of some progressive measures and promised to secure additional reform legislation,
and because he had pledged to keep America out
of the war.[78] The progressives' cause was not
lost, Hearst wrote, for they constituted a
majority of the nation's voters.[79] Wilson's
record in office coupled with his party's pro-

321

gressive platform attracted voters from the
defunct Bull Moose party.[80] During the campaign
Hughes became increasingly bellicose and, on the
stump, contended that America should be taking
a stronger stand in the European struggle.[81]
Roosevelt came to Hughes' assistance, but the
former president's declarations were so strongly
in favor of intervention that he reinforced the
Democratic strategy of presenting Wilson as the
candidate who could keep the nation out of the
war.[82] It was because of Roosevelt's support of
Hughes, the _Times_ observed after the election,
that the German-Americans had not come over to
Hughes' camp as had been expected.[83]

By and large Wilson attracted the vote of
rural America, labor, liberals, and intellectuals.[84] The election was so close that the
results hinged on the Minnesota and California
ballots. Hughes retired on election night
confident that he had been elected.[85] But the
southern and western vote swung the election
away from him. Wilson outpolled him 49.4 percent to 46.2 percent in the popular vote, and
in the Electoral College 277 to 254. It was
not a convincing mandate, but Wilson's appeal
for peace and progressivism had prevailed.[86] On
the election Hearst wrote:

> The citizens of radical thought,
> whether they call themselves Democrats or
> Republicans or Progressives, are in an over-
> whelming majority in the United States
> today. Two-thirds of Americans are radi-
> cals. I do not mean that a majority of the
> people are extremists, I do not mean that
> they are visionary theorists. . . . I
> simply mean that they stand radically for
> fundamental American principles, for Ameri-
> can ideals of impartial justice, liberty,
> and equality; for progressive steps to
> take the government out of the hands of the
> few and entrust it more and more to the in-
> creasingly capable hands of the people.

Wilson won because of the failure of the
Republican party to recognize the importance of the Progressive Movement and the
extent of progressive sentiment.[87]

Hearst believed that Wilson could be
trusted in his pledge to continue his domestic
and foreign policies. He wrote to a rival
New York City newspaper editor, urging him to
support Wilson:

> I think it is the solemn duty of all
> loyal American citizens to stand solidly
> back of the President in his efforts. . . .
> Notes are better than bullets; ink is
> cheaper than blood, and if there had been
> more writing in Europe there would have been
> less fighting.
> I firmly believe that our president
> will bring our beloved country through this
> crisis, as he has brought it through other
> crises, with peace and honor.[88]

To his editors he wrote, "Speak very highly of
Wilson, say he is a good president and undoubtedly
meant to use power for good purposes."[89]   In-
structing his editors to remain neutral in
editorials concerned with the war, he wrote
Lawrence:

> The _American_ speaks as a pacifist news-
> paper, if you please; at any rate, a news-
> paper which is not pro-ally, but so solely
> pro-American that it has been excluded by
> the allies from their territories: but
> the _American_ knows that even if some of our
> contemporaries are misguided in their atti-
> tudes, too partisan and too prejudicial in
> utterances, they are honestly misguided,
> honestly partisan, sincerely convinced that
> what they are doing is right.[90]

On April 6, 1917, America declared war on
the Central Powers and began the conversion to

full-fledged involvement in the hostilities. On
America's entry, Hearst wrote:

> Having once embarked on war, it was
> absolutely necessary that the war be won
> and that all dissension or division of
> opinion should be suppressed until after the
> war was over.[91]

Involvement caused the pre-war political Ameri-
canism and anti-hyphenism to become the intense
and intolerant patriotism of a nation at war.[92]
Once war was officially declared, Hearst and most
other progressive spokesmen supported involvement[93] and many popular schemes that Wilson
was advocating.[94]

During the spring of 1917 Hearst's name
was again circulated as a possible New York
City mayoralty candidate. Murphy appeared to
be flirting with him because of his strong ties
with the city's German and Irish voters.[95] But
Hearst was working to put together a Democrat-
Independent Fusion ticket.[96] When Tammany officials released their city platform on August
8, they still had not selected a mayoralty
candidate.[97] The platform, which had recapitu-
lated the principles of the Municipal Ownership League of 1905 and Roosevelt's New
Nationalism of 1912, declared for liberal social
policies.[98] Coming to support not only public
ownership and operation of public utilities,
but also the seizure by the city of any business
dealing in ice, milk, foodstuffs, or any other
necessity of life if it was becoming a monopoly,[99] Tammany was clearly indicating that it
had decided to support Hearst's liberal programs rather than oppose him again.[100] On
August 8 Tammany announced its ticket, which
included Al Smith for President of the Board
of Aldermen. Smith was an outspoken critic of
Hearst, charging that his flamboyance hurt the
party.[101] Hearst publicly challenged Smith's
qualifications and accused him of being con-

324

cerned more with political power than with progressive policies.[102] The publisher pledged that he would never run on a ticket that included Smith's name.[103] In early August a petition to place Hearst's name on the city ballot was filed with the Board of Elections. McClellan, to the surprise of most political observers, supported a Hearst draft, telling a _Times_ reporter that Hearst was "in a position to make a stronger fight against Mayor Mitchel than any other Democrat in the city."[104] But many Tammany leaders disagreed with McClellan's estimation of Hearst's strength and opposed his candidacy.[105]

Hearst had no intention of running and declared that the chief issue of the campaign was the defeat of the Mitchel administration.[106] Brisbane was pleased that Hearst had declined another political bid, writing in an editorial:

> It is better for Hearst to stay where
> he is able to wield much greater power and
> to do more for the people than he could as
> the mayor of only one city, even if that
> city is as large as New York. . . . Hearst
> with his newspapers all over the United
> States can regulate half a dozen mayors
> and make them attend to business.[107]

Hearst had broken his ties with Mitchel because of the mayor's public school program, his aid to the "privilege-seeking interests," and his position on American involvement in the World War. Mitchel's reorganization of the schools, the Gary plan, attempted to save the city money be better utilizing existing facities. Students would spend half the day in their home room studying traditional subjects. The remainder of the day would be spent in going from class to class, taking subjects such as art, music, home economics, manual training, and physical education. When school was not in session, the buildings would be used by community

325

organizations. Hearst opposed the plan because
he considered it not so much an educational plan
as a device for saving money. Students were
crowded together and received less individual
instruction.[108] Hearst charged that throughout
his term Mitchel had acquired socially prominent
friends, such as the Rockefellers, Vanderbilts,
and Reynolds, and was responding to their interests.[109] In response to the charge, Mitchel
answered, "Is that an issue? . . . I tell them
if they don't like my friends they can go to
Hell."[110] The Mayor's zealous advocacy of preparedness further alienated the publisher.
Mitchel was one of the very few Democrats to
give his unqualified support for American intervention. He once pleaded the cause so vigorously
to Wilson that the Chief Executive reminded him
that he was talking to the President of the
United States, whereupon Mitchel reminded the
President that he was talking to the Mayor of
New York City.[111]

Throughout the campaign Hearst made few
public appearances, but remained active in his
newspapers' efforts. The Hearst press supported the candidacy of Kings County Judge
John F. Hylan. No strong ties bound Hylan to
Tammany. He had been a Republican until 1915,
when he ran for judge on the Democratic ticket.
Because no Democrat conducted an active campaign for the nomination, Hearst's publicity
swung the Executive Committee of the Democratic
Fusion Committee to Hylan.[112]

The anti-Tammany press ridiculed Hylan's
obscurity. "Nobody knows better than Mr.
Murphy's advisers that the naming of a candidate
like Judge Hylan would be a confession that the
fight for the mayoralty was to be perfunctory,
the hope of victory being confined to those minor
offices which are the real aim of the politician," reflected the Evening Post.[113] A
Sun editorial confessed that the editors had to
look up in Who's Who? in order to learn something about Hylan.[114] The New Republic described Hylan as a Hearst loyalist.[115]

326

Mitchel tried to re-establish his coalition between Republicans and Independents. He was supported by the _Times_, _Sun_, _World_, _Tribune_, _Globe_, and _Evening Post_.[116] In the first direct primary of the city's history, Mitchel was challenged by William M. Bennett of Manhattan, a former State Senator and Assemblyman and a former progressive. He entered the primary with the support of no organized group or portion of a group.[117] In the first three weeks of September, he campaigned in every borough. Mitchel ignored Bennett's candidacy.

The voters went to the polls on September 19 and the next day the newspapers reported that Mitchel had escaped with an 1100 vote victory. Bennett demanded a recount. Numerous cases of fraud were uncovered and eventually sixty election officials went to jail. The Supreme Court declared Bennett the Republican nominee.[118] On October 2 Mitchel, flanked by Roosevelt and Hughes, was named head of the Fusion ticket. The mayor promised to make the fight against "Hearst, Hylan, and the Hohenzollerns . . . against men who raise their heads to spit venom at those who have taken a strong, active stand with America against Germany."[119]

The Socialists completed the field and nominated Morris Hillquit. The Socialists opposed the war as vigorously as Mitchel defended it. In his acceptance speech, Hillquit said that every Socialist vote would be "a loud and emphatic voice of protest against the war and militarism and their hideous social and political by-products."[120]

Patriotism became the main theme of Mitchel's campaign. The mayor told a group of women supporters:

> If I were to discuss with you the
> issues of the campaign I should begin with

327

the most important of them all, the maintenance of a stable, a secure, a strong and
an aggressive pro-American government in
New York, a government that can be relied
upon to support the hand of President
Wilson and the government of the United
States in the prosecution of this war, in
every phase.[121]

The mayor's use of the patriotic issue wasted
money and publicity that could have been better
employed describing the positive accomplishments
of his administration, the horrors of a return
of Tammany to City Hall, and the mediocrity of
Hylan.[122]

In the election Hylan carried every
borough and tallied 297,000 votes to Mitchel's
147,000, Hillquit's 132,000, and Bennett's
53,000.[123] Hylan carried forty election districts, Mitchel carried fourteen, and Hillquit
carried eight. Upper income areas voted solidly
for Mitchel, while Jewish, German, and Irish
areas voted for Hillquit.[124]

Throughout the war Wilson expanded his
broad federal powers. On August 10, 1917, he
signed into law the Lever Act, authorizing
federal control over the domestic economy. On
May 20, 1918, he signed the Overman Act, giving
himself almost unlimited power to reorganize
federal agencies directing the nation's resources
in time of war. The most drastic abrogations of
civil liberties were the Espionage Act of 1917
and the Sedition Act of 1918, which threatened
the freedom of both speech and the press. Wilson
and Congress had overstepped their bounds, Hearst
wrote, the obligation of the American newspaper
was to voice the sentiments of the American
people and to battle for their rights.[125] He had
instructed his editorial writers to oppose the
measures:

There should be a vigorous attack on
the espionage bill. Note that Senator

328

Cummins says 'the measure is the most
stringent and drastic ever proposed to
curb a free people in time of peace or
war.' The government would have absolute
power in war-time to suppress newspapers and
to prevent debate in Congress. . . .

The Democratic party seems to forget
that this is a republic in which the people
govern, and in which full information is
essential to intelligent government.

In fact this Democratic Congress seems
to be about the most undemocratic institution in the United States. It has passed the
literacy test immigration bill and is doing
its best to suppress free speech and free
press. It would be a remarkable thing if
the only hope of Democracy in this country
should lie in the Republican party.[126]

The signing of the armistice took place on
November 11, 1918. The war had lasted four
years, three months, and fourteen days, and resulted in more than 37,000,000 casualties. The
remainder of Wilson's term was dominated by the
debate over the League of Nations. Hearst had
been a pioneer in the concept of a league of
nations. On July 1, 1917, in an American editorial, he had written:

Our government is one government able
to suggest and form a 'League of All
Nations,' an arbitration tribunal composed
of representatives of these neutral nations
to which our trials with Germany and Great
Britain too, might be submitted, as well as
any and all matters affecting any and all
other neutrals . . . We think that our
government . . . should take immediate
steps toward the formation of this League
of Neutral Nations, and this international
board of arbitration.[127]

Yet he attacked Wilson's proposal. It was one of
his most intensive campaigns. Over one hundred
anti-League editorials appeared in the American
and the Evening Journal.[128] "Without the cam-

329

paign made by Hearst, Senator Hiram Johnson later said, "the United States would probably have been in the League of Nations."[129]

There were many differences between Hearst's proposal and Wilson's that explained the newspaperman's objections. He opposed giving votes to nations in the empires of Great Britain and other European countries; these votes, he argued, would be in the control of the Colonial powers.[130] Former Secretary of State Root agreed with him on this point.[131] Hearst also opposed the element of coercion in Wilson's league which contrasted to the principle of voluntarily accepted arbitration that his proposal contained.[132] The organizers of Wilson's league he viewed as a group of international financiers and greedy European nations aiming to guarantee for themselves the spoils of war.[133]

The Hearst press warned American voters that Wilson was directing the country toward autocracy.[134] "This matter profoundly affects the people of the United States," Hearst wrote, "and in any genuine democracy, the people should have the right to determine by their votes what policy the nation should pursue."[135] United States Senator John Sharp Williams was one of many prominent figures to tell Wilson the same thing.[136]

To rekindle enthusiasm for the League, which a majority of voters had initially favored,[137] Wilson set out on a nationwide speaking tour in September 1919. On October 2 he became victim of a cerebral thrombosis, a blood clot in his brain. It left him paralyzed on his left side, and totally disabled him for two months. On November 18 he gave Democratic Senators stringent orders to reject any compromise treaty. The following day the Senate rejected all attempts at ratification.[138] On March 19, 1920, the Senate voted the treaty down for the final time. There was never a popular referendum on it.

Wilson believed that the American press had deceived the people and insured the League's defeat.[139] Hearst argued that the League had discredited Wilson and destroyed his party. The party's presidential nominee in 1920, James Cox, reluctantly and half-heartedly supported the League while the Republicans were deliberately vague on the question. Considering the Republican victory a repudiation of the League, Hearst wrote:

> This historic election is purely and simply a repudiation by sterling American citizens of the Wilson party and that party's pro-British un-American policies. . . . Mr. Wilson wanted a referendum on the League of Nations, and he has had it.[140]

The war effort and the League debate had a significant impact on New York elections. In 1918 the Socialists were still formidable threats to both major parties. They had made notable gains the previous two years. Their strength was such that the National Security League persuaded the major parties to fuse against Socialist Congressional candidates to send "only one hundred percent Americans to Congress."[141] Wilson supported the proposal and by the end of July details of Fusion were worked out.[142]

Hearst's name was circulated as a possible candidate in the 1918 New York gubernatorial election. Brisbane now urged him to run,[143] and attempted to arouse pre-convention support for his nomination.[144] But a meeting of the Committee of Forty-Two, representing upstate Democrats, at Syracuse on July 9, gave him not a single vote, nor did his name come up at this gathering of state party leaders.[145] The _Times_ predicted that he would still be a candidate whether the Democrats nominated him or not.[146] At the Saratoga Convention, however, Hearst people nominated District Attorny Edward Swann for governor.[147] Al Smith secured the nomination the following day.[148]

In the election Smith united the Democratic party and was easily elected. He carried Manhattan by 105,000 votes. Tammany candidates were victorious in State Senate elections and all but three Assembly elections. Republican candidates lost every major election except for two Congressional candidates running on the Fusion ticket.[149]

On October 25 Wilson issued a blanket endorsement of all Democratic Congressional candidates,[150] and declared that the elections would be mandates of his administration.[151] In the election, control of the House of Representatives slipped to the Republicans. The Republican gain, David Burner argues, was the outcome of a campaign waged in a spirit of sectionalism over particular ephemeral issues; it was not a repudiation of Wilson's plea for a vote of confidence.[152]

The Republicans had come to control Congress, Hearst believed, more as a result of a popular repudiation of Wilson's foreign policy than because of party principles.[153] This was proof, he wrote in an _American_ editorial, that the nation demanded the formation of a new political party based on progressive principles:

> The producing classes of this country are advocating the formation of a new party--a new party which will be in favor of true democratic ideals, or real republican institutions, a party whose first consideration will be for America and for the interests of the vast majority of Americans. . . .
> Old parties are divided too much on issues that are dead and gone and controlled too much by the predatory wealth which contributed to campaign funds. The old parties are run too much for the interests of one-tenth of the public. A new party which should be conducted in the interests of the

great nine-tenths . . . should be formed.
. . .[154]

Hearst took an active interest in the operations of the Reconstruction Committee of the
American Federation of Labor, the American Labor
Party of New York, and the Farmer's National
Conference of Reconstruction. He encouraged his
editors to support the proposals for economic
reconstruction that these organizations were
making, which were in essence the progressive
programs that he had been advocating for the
past two decades.[155] These demands were revolutionary in spirit, he wrote, but moderate in
practice.[156] An *American* editorial charged the
old parties with being indifferent to the demands of the farmers and industrial workers:

> Believers in these reforms who oppose
> a new party argue that the old parties can
> be coaxed into granting them by appeals
> from within.
> But, as Mr. Hearst points out, the
> old parties are divided too much on issues
> that are dead and gone and are too much
> controlled by interests which do not want
> these reforms to come.
> A party that should bring together
> like thinking men and women of progressive
> outlook among the farmers, the organized
> workers and liberals in other callings
> would have to coax the old parties or
> worry over their barnacles. It could win
> directly or compel the old parties to
> outspeed it. . . .
> It would tremendously hasten the pro-
> gress of the common welfare in the United
> States if the great progressive groups among
> the farmers, among the organized toilers of
> the village and cities, among the business-
> men who are not extortionists or would be
> profiteers and among the honorable pro-
> fessions should, as Mr. Hearst suggests,
> unite to put through the popular measures

333

which are possible of more or less immediate
accomplishment.

The time was never more right.[157]

As the 1920 presidential election ap-
proached, Hearst urged the nation's progressives
to unite behind LaFollette.[158] He publicly stated
that if the Republicans failed to nominate
LaFollette, progressives should establish a third
party and nominate either LaFollette, Senator
Hiram Johnson, Democratic Senator James Reed of
Missouri, Republican William Borah of Idaho, or
Democratic Mayor William Hale Thompson of
Chicago.[159]

The Red Scare had drained the zeal of the
Republican progressives. Confident party
leaders and delegates, sensing the nation's
fatigue and selfishness, met in Chicago to
select a presidential nominee. One possible
choice was General Leonard Wood, who stood for
nationalism, militarism, and hellfire for the
radicals; Johnson, LaFollette, and Herbert
Hoover were others. But party leaders met in
the Blackstone Hotel suite of George Harvey, a
New York editor, and arranged for the nomination
of Warren Harding, conservative United States
Senator from Ohio. Harding secured the nomination on the tenth ballot and proceeded to
campaign on a platform that promised lower taxes,
higher tariffs, restrictions on immigration, and
aid to the farmers. It also damned the League
of Nations.

Hearst expressed disapproval of the Harding
nomination, and urged the formation of a progressive third party. But, he added, if a third
party movement failed to materialize, his papers
would support Harding because it was most important to defeat Wilson's party. He told a
Standard Union reporter:

I certainly shall not support Senator
Harding on the Republican ticket if the
third party gives us the opportunity to

support Senator Johnson, Senator Reed,
Senator Borah, Mayor Thompson, or any
other . . . man who represents the citizen-
ship and not autocracy in the Wilson party
or plutocracy in the Republican party.
. . . It must, therefore, while planning
to make its own success assured, plan to
make double certain the defeat of the
Wilson party which advocates this un-
American League of Nations and repudiates
the teachings of all great Americans . . . [160]

Democratic party delegates were at odds
with themselves as they convened to nominate
a successor to Wilson. Attorney General A.
Mitchell Palmer and Wilson's son-in-law William
G. McAdoo, Secretary of the Treasury between
1913 and 1919 and United States Director General
of Railways between 1917 and 1919, were the
frontrunning candidates, but party leaders
wanted no candidate associated with the Wilson
administration.[161] It took forty-four ballots
to swing the election to Governor James M.
Cox of Ohio. As a compromise, the delegates
chose as a running mate a young Wilsonian,
Assistant Secretary of the Navy Franklin D.
Roosevelt. The party's platform supported the
League of Nations, tax reduction, and Philippine
independence, and was otherwise undistinguished.

Wilson's presidency was put on trial in the
1920 election. Many progressives had come to
distrust him and to resent high taxes and labor
strife. Midwestern farmers were troubled by
falling food prices, urban Democrats were sus-
picious of Southern "drys," and Irish Americans
were hostile to Wilson's policy toward Britain.
Wartime regulations, along with the social and
emotional disturbance of war itself, had irritated
voters and had worked against Democratic fortunes.[162] Harding, polling 61 percent of the
popular vote, carried every state out of the
South and led Cox in the Electoral College vote
404 to 127.[163] The Republicans enjoyed a major-

335

ity of twenty-two in the Senate and one hundred and sixty-seven in the House of Representatives. Harding's call for a "return to normalcy" had resulted in a convincing repudiation of Wilson and his internationalism. It was not, Hearst[164] wrote, a repudiation of either progressivism or the Democratic party: "This historic election is purely and simply a repudiation . . . of the Wilson party."[165]

Harding's administration was highlighted by vulgarity and scandal. Normalcy produced a government that sought all the advantages of power but none of the responsibilities. Organized self interest produced favors in bonuses, bounties, lower taxes, and higher tariffs. Harding's "best minds," as his advisers were termed, created a spirit that contradicted the best hopes cultivated through the war efforts and in the progressive movement. The period was made almost unique by an extraordinary reaction against idealism and reform.[166] It also marked a noticeable abatement in Hearst's efforts to speak for progressivism and contribute to its leadership.

Footnotes

[1] Hearst to Brisbane, January 2, 1913, J.A.M.

[2] U. S., Congress, House, *Inaugural Addresses of the Presidents of the United States*, H. Doc. 93-208, 93rd Congress, 1974, pp. 200-210.

[3] *Ibid.*, pp. 201-202.

[4] New York *American*, September 2, 1913.

[5] New York *American*, December 13, 1913.

[6] New York *American*, April 14, 1913.

[7] Older, *op. cit.*, p. 356.

[8] New York *American*, December 31, 1912.

[9] New York *American*, May 6, 1913.

[10] Wilson to Brisbane, May 2, 1913, J.A.M.

[11] Hearst to Brisbane, October 12, 1913, J.A.M.; New York *American*, December 8, 1913.

[12] Hearst to Brisbane, September 13, 1913, J.A.M.

[13] Hearst to Bryan, August 25, 1913, J.A.M.

[14] San Francisco *Examiner*, October 9, 1913, J.A.M.

[15] New York *American*, October 22, 1913.

[16] Hearst speeches for Cooper Union (Manhattan) and Prospect Hall (Brooklyn) Rallies, October 21, 1913, J.A.M.

[17] New York *Times*, July 20, 1925.

[18] Edwin R. Lewinson, _John Purroy Mitchel: Boy Mayor of New York_ (New York: Astra Books, 1965), p. 87.

[19] New York _American_, October 22, 1913.

[20] Lewinson, _op. cit._, p. 82.

[21] _Ibid._, p. 87.

[22] New York _American_, November 3, 1913.

[23] Henderson, _op. cit._, p. 121.

[24] New York _Times_, July 31, 1913.

[25] Lewinson, _loc. cit._.

[26] New York _Tribune_, August 2, 1913.

[27] New York _Herald_, June 8, 1913.

[28] New York _Times_, August 22, 1913.

[29] New York _Times_, October 26, 1913.

[30] New York _Tribune_, August 24, 1913.

[31] New York _World_, August 22, 1913.

[32] New York _American_, September 5, 1913.

[33] Gaynor's death resulted from the bullet a would-be assassin had fired into his throat in 1910 which had not been removed. New York _Times_, October 13, 1913.

[34] Lewinson, _op. cit._, p. 93.

[35] New York _World_, September 27, 1913.

[36] New York _Times_, September 30, 1913.

[37] New York _Tribune_, October 17, 1913.

[38] "Governor Sulzer Impeached," _Outlook_, August 23, 1913, p. 875, J.A.M.

[39] New York _Tribune_, October 17, 1913.

[40] New York _American_, November 5, 1913.

[41] New York _World_, November 5, 1913.

[42] New York _Times_, November 5, 1913.

[43] New York _Tribune_, November 5, 1913.

[44] New York _World_, November 5, 1913.

[45] New York _American_, November 7, 1913.

[46] New York _American_, December 13, 1913.

[47] New York _American_, May 11, 1914.

[48] New York _American_, May 6, 1914.

[49] New York _American_, October 2, 1914.

[50] New York _American_, July 14, 1914.

[51] New York _American_, May 6, 1914.

[52] Raymond S. Baker, _Woodrow Wilson: Life and Letters_, vol. 4 (Garden City, New York: Doubleday, Doran and Company, Inc., 1931), p.155.

[53] Hearst to Brisbane, April 26, 1914, J.A.M.

[54] Hearst to Northcliffe; Hearst to Burnham, September 10, 1914, J.A.M.

[55] New York _American_, April 14, 1913.

[56] Hearst to Brisbane, August 5, 1914, J.A.M.

[57] Older, _op. cit._, p. 405. (See New York _American_, July 16, 1917; New York _American_, June 3, 1918).

[58] New York _American_, July 1, 1917.

[59] New York _American_, October 27, 1915.

[60] Brisbane to Francis, December 15, 1915, J.A.M.

[61] _Ibid_.

[62] Older, _op. cit_., p. 407.

[63] New York _American_, May 9, 1915.

[64] _Ibid_.

[65] Including the Federal Farm Loan Act, the Child Labor Act, and the Adamson Act, establishing the eight-hour work day.

[66] New York _American_, November 13, 1916.

[67] New York _American_, June 6, 7, 8, 9, 1916.

[68] Roosevelt to Hearst, April 15, 1916; Hearst to Roosevelt, April 17, 1916; Hearst to Roosevelt, May 26, 1916; Roosevelt Papers, Library of Congress.

[69] Roosevelt to Lodge, July 6, 1916, Roosevelt Papers, Library of Congress.

[70] Older, _op. cit_., p. 313.

[71] Hearst to Roosevelt, June 8, 1916, J.A.M.

[72] Roosevelt to The Conferees of the Progressive Party, June 10, 1916, Roosevelt Papers, Library of Congress.

[73] _Nation_, June 15, 1916, p. 1. Kilroe Papers, Columbia University.

[74] _Ibid_., p. 635.

[75] _Nation_, May 25, 1916, p. 556, Kilroe Papers, Columbia University.

[76] *Nation*, June 15, 1916, p. 636, Kilroe Papers, Columbia University.

[77] *Nation*, July 13, 1916, p. 27, Kilroe Papers, Columbia University.

[78] New York *American*, November 13, 1916.

[79] San Francisco *Examiner*, November 13, 1916, J.A.M.

[80] New York *American*, November 7, 1916.

[81] New York *American*, June 12, 1916.

[82] New York *Times*, September 22, 1916.

[83] For Analysis of the German Vote see New York *Times*, November 9, 1916.

[84] New York *Times*, November 9, 1916.

[85] New York *American*, November 9, 1916.

[86] *Ibid.*

[87] New York *American*, November 13, 1916.

[88] Hearst to "The Editor of The New York *World*," February 1, 1917, J.A.M.

[89] Hearst to Carvalito, March 4, 1917, J.A.M.

[90] Hearst to Lawrence, February 21, 1917, J.A.M.

[91] New York *American*, December 18, 1918.

[92] On November 13, 1917, the New York *Tribune* published an article which stated that since America entered the European conflict, the Hearst newspapers had been pro-German. The *Tribune* charged that the *American* had published 74 articles attacking the Allies, 17 articles defending

341

Germany, 63 articles conveying anti-war propaganda, and one article attacking a presidential proclamation--an average of 3 articles a week undermining the nation's activities. The _Tribune_'s charges triggered a nationwide attack on the Hearst press by rival editors. The Department of Justice conducted an official investigation of Hearst's activities, but concluded that there was "absolutely no substance to the charges," that the charges had "resulted purely and simply from a newspaper rivalry," and "that the Hearst newspapers were pro-American." Department of Justice file #9-12-4491244, National Archives.

[93] Hearst ran an extensive recruitment campaign in his newspapers and he established recruitment stations nationwide. Older, _op. cit._, p. 397.

[94] In a letter to one of his editors, Hearst praised Wilson for appointing Gompers to the Council of National Defense, pushing the eight-hour work day proposal, creating the War Labor Board and War Labor Policies Board to enhance labor's position and to minimize the exploitation of women and children, appointing Lawrence Veiller supervisor of dozens of housing projects for war workers, appointing Lee Frankel and Julia Thorp to draft the Military and Naval Insurance Act, appointing Newton Baker and Raymond Fosdick to establish a commission on Training Camp Activities, and nationalizing the railroads. Hearst to Dayton, May 11, 1918, J.A.M.

[95] New York _Times_, May 20, 1917.

[96] _Ibid._

[97] New York _Times_, August 9, 1917.

[98] New York _Evening Journal_, August 9, 1917.

[99] New York _Times_, June 30, 1917.

[100] Henderson, _op. cit._, p. 196.

[101] New York _Times_, August 8, 1917.

[102] New York _American_, September 1, 1917.

[103] New York _Sun_, August 14, 1917, Kilroe Papers, Columbia University.

[104] New York _Times_, August 29, 1917.

[105] Kilroe note to the New York Democratic Club, no date, Kilroe Papers, Columbia University.

[106] New York _World_, September 1, 1917.

[107] New York _Evening Journal_, August 15, 1917.

[108] New York _Evening Journal_, October 18, 1917.

[109] _Ibid._

[110] New York _World_, October 14, 1917.

[111] Lewinson, _op. cit._, p. 212.

[112] _Ibid._, p. 222.

[113] New York _Evening Post_, August 15, 1917.

[114] New York _Sun_, August 16, 1917.

[115] _New Republic_, October 6, 1917, p. 272, Kilroe Papers, Columbia University.

[116] _Ibid._

[117] New York _Sun_, August 14, 1917

[118] Lewinson, _op. cit._, p. 229.

[119] New York _Times_, October 2, 1917.

[120] New York _Call_, July 8, 1917, J.A.M.

343

[121] New York _Tribune_, September 21, 1917.

[122] Henderson, _op. cit._, p. 206.

[123] New York _Times_, November 7, 1917.

[124] Lewinson, _op. cit._, p. 245.

[125] Hearst to the Editor of the Washington _Post_, March 6, 1917, J.A.M.

[126] Hearst to Francis, February 21, 1917, J.A.M.

[127] New York _American_, July 1, 1917.

[128] Matthew Epstein, "A Study of the Editorial Opinions of the New York Papers Toward the League of Nations and the United States During the First Year of Life, 1919-1920, 1945-1946" (Ph.D Dissertation, New York University, 1954), p. 81.

[129] Older, _op. cit._, p. 415.

[130] Interview with William Randolph Hearst, Jr., September 25, 1978; Hearst argued that the British Empire, including four Dominions and India, would get six votes. Jean-Baptiste Duroselle, _From Wilson to Roosevelt_ (New York: Harper and Row, Publishing, 1968), p. 116.

[131] Root to W. H. Hays, March 29, 1917, Root Papers, Library of Congress.

[132] New York _American_, January 10, 1920.

[133] New York _American_, July 13, 1919.

[134] U. S., Congress, Senate, "Doctor to Carvalho," _Report on the Senate Judiciary Committee on the Brewing and Liquor Interests and German and Bolshevik Propaganda_, S. Doc. 62, 60th Congress, 1st session, 1919, p. 1612.

344

[135] Hearst to Francis, December 18, 1918, J.A.M.

[136] Williams to Wilson, January 13, 1919, Williams Papers, Library of Congress.

[137] Wilson to Williams, January 13, 1919, Williams Papers, Library of Congress.

[138] New York *Times*, November 20, 1919.

[139] L. W. Allibone to Wilson, November 4, 1920, Wilson Papers, Library of Congress; W. A. Brown to Wilson, November 7, 1920, Wilson Papers, Library of Congress; Wilson to Williams, November 15, 1920, Wilson Papers, Library of Congress.

[140] New York *American*, November 3, 1920.

[141] New York *Sun*, July 14, 1918, Kilroe Papers, Columbia University.

[142] New York *Times*, July 31, 1918.

[143] Washington *Post*, July 1, 1918.

[144] New York *Times*, July 2, 1918.

[145] New York *Times*, July 10, 1918.

[146] New York *Times*, July 23, 1918.

[147] New York *Times*, July 24, 1918.

[148] New York *Times*, July 25, 1918.

[149] Henderson, *op. cit.*, p. 237.

[150] New York *Times*, October 26, 1918.

[151] New York *American*, October 26, 1918.

[152] Only the countryside abandoned the Demo-

cratic party. In eight agricultural states of the interior--Indiana, Ohio, Illinois, Kentucky, Missouri, Kansas, Nebraska, and Colorado--the Republican party carried twenty-three districts that in 1916 had gone Democratic. Much of this resentment was directed at the Lever Act of August 1917, which allowed the Food Administration to fix the cost of wheat as low as $2.00 a bushel. The farmers were dissatisfied; wheat had sold for $3.40 a bushel in 1917. Despite an agricultural shortage due to bad weather, on June 7, 1918 Wilson vetoed a bill to raise the ceiling of wheat to $2.40 a bushel. David Burner, _The Politics of Provincialism_ (New York: W. W. Norton and Company, Inc., 1967), pp. 34-40.

[153] The New York _Times_ disagreed, contending that Wilson's plea for support had won votes for his party. Outside of the wheat districts, the House returns showed persisting Democratic strength. New York _Times_, November 4, 1918.

[154] New York _American_, January 21, 1919.

[155] Hearst to Lawrence, January 21, 1919, J.A.M.

[156] New York _American_, January 21, 1919.

[157] _Ibid_.

[158] Hearst to the Editor of the Chicago _American_, July 11, 1920, J.A.M.

[159] Hearst interview with Joseph J. Early of the Brooklyn _Standard Union_, July 7, 1920, New York _American_, July 8, 1920.

[160] _Ibid_.

[161] New York _American_, June 9, 1920.

[162] Burner, _op. cit._, p. 41.

346

[163] Hearst's influence was evident in New York City, where Cox polled only 19.9 percent of the immigrant vote and 27.3 percent of the city vote, and Chicago, where Cox tallied 36.2 percent of the immigrant vote and 26.3 percent of the total vote. *Ibid*., p. 71

[164] New York *American*, November 4, 1920.

[165] New York *American*, November 3, 1920.

[166] Arthur S. Link, "What Happened to the Progressive Movement in the 1920s?" Barton Bernstein and Allen J. Matusow, editors, *Twentieth* *Century* *America* (New York: Harcourt, Brace, Jovanovich, Inc., 1972), p. 118.

XII

Hearst and Hearstism in Perspective

At the turn of the century William Randolph
Hearst was indistinguishable from his newspapers
and the issues they propounded.[1] His was the
driving personality common to all Hearst publications.[2] "I cannot conduct any publication
with people who do not follow instructions,"
he wrote to Joseph Arthur Moore, editor of his
Good Housekeeping magazine: "I do not like
people to know so much more than I do that they
don't do what they are told."[3] A thorough
businessman, he carefully watched expenditures
and income.[4] "The two things that I desire,"
he wrote Moore, "are first that these papers
shall be conducted properly, of course along our
established lines; and second, that they shall
make money. I want to make money and I insist
that every paper shall make money."[5] The
American sold for a penny a copy until January
26, 1918, when its price was raised to two cents.
Hearst made money because he recognized the
appeal and potential of large scale media advertising. His empire grew; he insisted to his
editors that it "must be first."[6] By 1922 he
employed 38,000 people and was the sole owner
of nine morning daily newspapers, fifteen daily
evening papers, and fourteen Sunday papers. It
took thirty-two tons of paper and cost over
$90,000,000 yearly to produce his publications.[7]

Hearst was a spectacular and controversial
figure. More than any other publisher, he expanded the press's range of interests and added
to its devices. He believed in sensationalism,
writing to Moore that it had "put the American
at the head of journalism in this metropolis,
not only in point of circulation, but in reputation, in prestige and importance, and you have
the whole institution recognized as the most
dignified and important, as well as the most
popular institution in the country."[8] He urged
his editors to believe thoroughly in his insitu-
tion.[9] Much of the sensationalist technique he

349

employed has become the norm in twentieth century
newspapers. His first effort, the San Francisco
Examiner, would be considered dull by present-
day standards.

The Hearst newspapers were edited to appeal
to the masses because, he wrote, the people had
the intelligence and the votes necessary to enact into law the theories of reform that he was
advocating.[10] At a time when the nation was
becoming functionally literate, he aimed at
leading multitudes from looking at pictures to
reading captions, and from reading captions to
reading texts.[11] The newspaper was a national
educator, he believed, which could condense
every subject to an attractive and constructive
form.[12] He exploited his discovery that the
minority of the upper class to whom newspapers
had been previously directed could be disregarded in a time and country of mass production and popular government. Hearst's newspapers and their methods gave him the capacity
to reach more Americans daily than anyone else
in the country possessed except, perhaps, the
president. He was a folk leader, especially
among the new immigrants from Southern and
Eastern Europe who early in the century were
coming into a numerical plurality in Northeastern cities.[13] Many popular issues had become so because his newspapers had reported that
they were popular.[14]

Hearst's newspapers formulated their own
domestic, foreign, and political platform.[15]
Hearst served as a public watchdog on such
subjects as public school systems and slum and
working conditions.[16] He was instrumental in
securing factory regulations and inspections, in
the drafting of child, female, and convict labor
laws[17] and in establishing the eight-hour work
day.[17] He championed legislation that anti-
cipated the Sixteenth, Seventeenth, and Nineteenth Amendments to the Constitution. Despite
the disgust that his methods evoked, there were
few reformers of note in his day whose ideas did

350

not at one time or another parallel his; and
many wrote for a Hearst publication.[18] The list
would include William Allen White, William
Jennings Bryan, Samuel Seabury, Nathan Straus,
Ida Tarbell, Henry George, Lincoln Steffens,
Jack London, Upton Sinclair, Gustavus Meyers,
Tom Johnson, Susan Anthony, Gertrude Atherton,
Helen Keller, Belva Lockwood, Florence Woods,
Charles Edward Russell, John Altgeld, Clarence
Darrow, Adlai Stevenson, Winston Churchill,
Franklin D. Roosevelt, and even Theodore
Roosevelt. Hearst was labelled a demagogue, an
incitor of class conflict, an enemy of the established order. But the sum of his battles
against the railroad, gas, water, transit, and
beef trusts make it evident that he was working
to purify the existing order. He did not confine
himself to sensation-mongering attacks. Rarely
did he abandon his editorial and news coverage
of an issue until corrective measures had been
enacted.[19]

What of Hearst and the Cuban war? The
Spanish rule was reactionary and the Spanish
government was incapable of doing anything with
Cuba. The question of whether it was right for
the United States to intervene in another nation's
colonial affairs will be debated for generations.
If this country was right, if Cuban independence
was a step in the direction of progress, as
Hearst and most reform spokesmen had believed,[20]
then he deserves a great deal of credit. If
the nation was wrong, he must bear his share of
the guilt. Following Hearst's death, over a
half century after the rebellion, Cuban President
Carlos Prio Socarras cabled Randolph Apperson
Hearst that his father had been a "great and
good friend of Cuba":

Cuba will never forget his generous and
decisive contribution during the war for
independence and shall always reverence his
memory as a champion of liberty.[21]

In 1902 Hearst entered politics, appealing

351

to the unrepresented lower classes in an attempt
to build a broad coalition.[22]   His goals were
to abolish special privilege and insure equal
opportunity, to purify government, and to secure
the enactment of laws embodying principles of
social justice.[23]   His object, in effect, was to
revive American democracy within an industrialized
nation for which the old concepts of individual
self-reliance and limited government were inadequate.[24]   Later he would write:

> . . . The Hearst papers realized at that
> time that the economic or social movements
> could only go a certain distance and to
> secure full recognition and consideration
> the producing classes would have to organize
> politically as well as economically.
>   . . . The great producing elements of
> this country . . . must all organize
> POLITICALLY before they will receive any
> political consideration or any social and
> economic justice.
>   . . . No matter what the political
> opinion of any American might be, he must
> acknowledge the right of the progressive
> element of the citizenship to the political
> expression of their liberal opinion.   Con-
> sequently, the attempt of great financial
> interests to control all avenues of poli-
> tical expression and entirely to suppress
> the views of the liberal masses must be de-
> feated for the sake of the American free-
> dom--and can be defeated . . . [25]

As a representative in the Fifty-eighth and
Fifty-ninth Congress, he rarely appeared on the
floor and failed to work effectively with Congressional leaders.   His opponents claimed that
he did nothing as a Congressman that he could not
have done as an outsider working through a
mouthpiece on the floor.[26]   He mounted campaigns
on all levels and voters lined up as pro-Hearst
or anti-Hearst rather than by party affiliation.[27]   But as a candidate he lost more elections

than he won. His political influence was of a larger sort.[28] He did have much to do with the forging of an alliance between the American Federation of Labor and the Democratic party. And in his expanded use of political cartoons as well as other journalist methods and his emphasis on social issues, he pioneered in the modern media campaign.

In the progressive period there were many movements on many levels; Hearst's coalition was only one. Hearstism did for a time attract the reformers, the radical wing of the intellectuals, the conscience-ridden elements of society. But Hearstism was not progressivism; the progressive movement was never a united one. Progressivism meant too many things to too many people.

Because Hearst had almost unlimited resources, many distrusted him. Opponents charged him with having been self-serving.[29] But every newspaper publisher and politician is in some way self-serving. Charles Edward Russell, noted Socialist and former Hearst editor,[30] wrote:

> . . . I suppose, further, that only those of us who for years have been closely associated with Mr. Hearst, who have from intimate observation of him under all conditions have learned what he really believes and aims at and tries to do, can understand how much the men who do not believe in his sincerity have missed the dominant keynote in his character. Not freer than others from errors of judgement, no doubt, is Mr. Hearst. But none of the men who have known him intimately ever questions the honesty of his convictions, nor the essential excellence; and it seems unfair in one of these not to make a protest against what he knows very well is a radical injustice.
> . . . it was perfectly clear to me that

this man believed that he had work to do in bettering conditions, believed in his own ability to do it, and would follow his convictions to the end without the slightest concern about the opposition he might arouse. . . .

. . . I have no doubt about his sincerity in waging war on the men he believes are opposing the masses of people . . . [31]

In 1911 the Washington _Post_, reflecting on Hearst as a spokesman for progressivism, said:

He /Hearst/ has repeatedly shown that the success of the principles he believed in and in the measures he proposed was above and beyond personal ambition or selfish aims.
Brilliant in thought, energetic in action, his ability is recognized by the leaders in finance, in public affairs, and in intellectual circles throughout the world. Sincerity of profession and his faithfulness to declare purpose give him enduring and impregnable strength with the people at large. [32]

By 1910 the kind of progressivism that a short while before only Hearst and a few other reformers had articulated was a major component of American politics. Policies lodged a few years earlier in legislation sponsored by Hearst and pigeonholed in Congressional subcommittees had been incorporated in the Democratic party platform of 1908. But the growth of progressivism brought a diminishing in the political stature of Hearst himself. He was now one among many spokesmen for ideas that were in general circulation.

In 1906 Lincoln Steffens came closer to grasping Hearst's character than any other observer. He had been instructed to "expose" Hearst in a _McClure's Magazine_ article. But Steffens perceived in Hearst's public and private writings a dedicated, successful, and influential reformer. Twenty-five years after writing the article, he alloted five pages of his auto-biography to Hearst, whom he believed to be the most misunderstood public figure in the country. He wrote:

> . . . In my article I quoted the interview and made some comment, but I did not say what I really thought. I thought that Hearst was a great man, able, self-dependent, self-educated (though he had been to Harvard), and clear-headed; he had no moral illusions; he saw straight as far as he saw, and he saw pretty far, further than I did; and, studious of the methods which he adopted after experimentation, he was driving toward his unannounced purpose: to establish some measure of democracy, with patient but ruthless force. He had ambition, not to sit in the offices he ran for, but to do something in them, to do things which his candidates never did satisfactorily. . . . I was just getting over my own righteousness, but I had not yet arrived where Hearst was born, apparently, at the point of view whence one sees that it is economic rather than moral forces that count . . . The only criticism I think now, since I have watched his career worth writing is that Hearst, with his patience, his superb tolerance, does not require his own editors to under-stand his policies. He is so far ahead of his staffs that they can hardly see him, and so, of course, they cannot make either this remarkable man or his perfectly rational ideas comprehensible to his readers, the people Hearst would like to see served.[33]

Hearst downplayed his successes because he was not consistently victorious at the polls and never controlled 1600 Pennsylvania Avenue. Few progressives, however, could boast of

achievements remotely as impressive as his.
He is entitled to more credit than historians
have been willing to award him. He did something toward educating the lower classes and
involving them in politics. He exposed social
and economic inequities and forced politicians
to work to alleviate them. He challenged
trusts publicly and in the courts. He did
publicize and direct progressive legislation.
And he was a force that business and political
leaders had to reckon with. Hearst best summarized his role in American progressivism
when, in addressing a political rally, he told
supporters, ". . . and like Aeneas, I can tell
of a progressive fight, 'part of which I saw
and part of which I was.'"[34]

Footnotes

[1] Filler, op. cit., p. 132.

[2] William Randolph Hearst, Jr. to author, December 2, 1976.

[3] Hearst to Moore, July 10, 1917, Moore Papers, Library of Congress.

[4] Hearst to Moore, May 5, 1917, Moore Papers, Library of Congress.

[5] Hearst to Moore, April 23, 1919, Moore Papers, Library of Congress.

[6] Ibid.

[7] Villard, op. cit., pp. 17-19.

[8] Hearst to Moore, October 10, 1919, Moore Papers, Library of Congress.

[9] Hearst to Publishers and Editors, December 21, 1919, Moore Papers, Library of Congress.

[10] Hearst to H. L. Mencken, June 17, 1918, J.A.M.

[11] New York Times, August 15, 1951.

[12] Brisbane speech, Editor and Publisher, December 9, 1911, J.A.M.

[13] New York Times, August 15, 1951.

[14] Emery and Ford, op. cit., p. 309.

[15] New York American, May 29, 1908.

[16] London Times, August 15, 1951.

[17] Creelman, op. cit., p. 263.

[18] New York *Journal*, November 1, 1902.

[19] New York *Journal-American*, August 16, 1951.

[20] Filler, *op*. *cit*., p. 134.

[21] New York *Journal-American*, August 15, 1951.

[22] New York *American*, November 10, 1910.

[23] Hearst to Mencken, June 17, 1918, J.A.M.

[24] Hearst to Independent League Watchers, November 6, 1906, J.A.M.

[25] Hearst to Brisbane, August 18, 1924, J.A.M.

[26] Palmer, October 13, 1906, *op*. *cit*., p. 20.

[27] Palmer, September 22, 1906, *op*. *cit*., p. 19.

[28] Filler, *op*. *cit*., p. 134; Myatt, *op*. *cit*., p. 214.

[29] Interview with Dr. Maury Bromson, September 21, 1978.

[30] Russell, a recognized Socialist who had worked for Pulitzer, joined Hearst's staff in 1896. He served as managing editor of both the Chicago *American* and the New York *Journal*. He wrote several books and was Socialist candidate for Governor of New York in 1910 and 1912, for Mayor of New York City in 1913, and for United States Senator from New York in 1914. In 1916 he was nominated the presidential candidate of the Socialist party, but declined.

[31] Charles Edward Russell, "Mr. Hearst As I Knew Him," *Ridgeway's*, October 27, 1906, pp. 9-10.

[32] Washington *Post*, October 21, 1911.

[33] Steffens, The Autobiography of Lincoln Steffens, op. cit., pp. 541-543.

[34] New York American, June 27, 1912.

Bibliography

I was fortunate to have complete use of the
New York _Journal-American_ morgue, located in the
Balcones Research Center, University of Texas,
Austin. The Hearst family and the University of
Texas graciously opened up the files to me and
aided me in the research; the family put no restrictions on my use of the material or on my conclusions. Mr. William Randolph Hearst, Jr. was
most cooperative and helpful, spending hours in
discussion of his father's life. Mr. Hearst is
a serious student of history and had questioned
his father confidentially and in great detail
about the publisher's career.

The _Journal-American_ morgue consists of
thirty-nine file cabinets containing photo neg-
atives; one hundred seventy-one file cabinets
of prints; one hundred two file cabinets containing engravings; one hundred forty-six file
cabinets and four hundred thirty-seven trans-
files containing newspaper clippings, magazine
clippings, letters, telegrams and notes; several
mail carts containing letter books, photos, and
cartoon posters, which were seemingly assembled
for a display; and many unopened crates. The
scattered memos and telegrams were of great value
in my research. The Harry Ransom Center at the
University of Texas possesses the _Journal-_
American annotated microfilm. In many instances
it indicates who wrote the newspaper articles
and it shows editors' handwritten notes and comments. To move the collection, valued in 1966
at over two million dollars, from New York to
Austin took eight moving vans two years.

The materials in the morgue dating back to
Hearst's early years in New York are in very
poor condition. They have never been subject
to any type of treatment or protection and do
crumble when handled. The collection is not cat-
alogued and there is no separate letter collection.

Few Hearst letter collections exist. Phoebe
Hearst's personal papers are stored at the
Bancroft Library at the University of California,
Berkeley. The collection includes numerous
letters from her son, but few written after he
purchased the New York Journal. The best collection of Hearst letters and telegrams, other
than the memos and telegrams in the Journal-
American morgue, is a five-volume bound set in
the Joseph Arthur Moore collection at the Library
of Congress. These letters and telegrams were
all written between 1915 and 1923. A third
collection of Hearst letters appears in the
three-volume Report of the Senate Judiciary
Committee on the Brewing and Liquor Interests
and German and Bolshevik Propaganda, published
by the Sixty-sixth Congress in 1919. These letters are concerned exclusively with American
involvement in World War I. Hearst wrote and
received thousands of letters. There exists no
comprehensive Hearst letter collection.

Manuscript Collections

American Federation of Labor, Library of Congress.
Merle Armitage, University of Texas.
Albert Beveridge, Library of Congress.
William Jennings Bryan, Library of Congress.
Grover Cleveland, Library of Congress.
Howard Francis Cline, Library of Congress.
Department of Justice Files on William Randolph
     Hearst, National Archives.
J. L. Garvin, University of Texas.
Warren Harding, Library of Congress.
Robert Roberts Hitt, Library of Congress.
Charles Evans Hughes, Library of Congress.
Robert LaFollette, Library of Congress.
Richard LeGalliene, University of Texas.
Edwin Patrick Kilroe Collection of Tammania,
     Columbia University.
George McClellan, Library of Congress.
William McKinley, Library of Congress.
Joseph Arthur Moore, Library of Congress.
George Norris, Library of Congress.
Alton Parker, Library of Congress.

Gifford Pinchot, Library of Congress.
Joseph Pulitzer, Columbia University, Library
    of Congress.
Gilbert Roe, Library of Congress.
Alfred Rogers, Library of Congress.
Theodore Roosevelt, Library of Congress.
Elihu Root, Library of Congress.
George Bernard Shaw, University of Texas.
John Spooner, Library of Congress.
Oscar Solomon Straus, Library of Congress.
William Howard Taft, Library of Congress.
United States House of Representatives Labor
    Committee, Minutes, 1903-1907, National
    Archives.
William Allen White, Library of Congress.
John Sharp Williams, Library of Congress.
Woodrow Wilson, Library of Congress.

Newspapers

Baltimore Sun.
Chicago American.
London Times.
New York Commercial Advertiser.
New York Evening Post.
New York Evening Journal.
New York Herald.
New York Journal (American and Journal).
New York Journal of Commerce.
New York Mail and Express.
New York Sun.
New York Times.
New York Tribune.
New York Wall Street Journal.
New York World.
San Francisco Examiner.
Washington Post.
Washington Star.

Periodicals

American Federationist.
American Review of Reviews.
Arena.
Commoner.

363

Cosmopolitan.
Harper's Weekly.
The Independent.
Journalism Quarterly.
Labor Legislative News.
Literary Digest.
London Review of Reviews.
McClure's Magazine.
Nation.
Newsweek.
New York History.
Outlook.
Pearson's Magazine.
Public Opinion.
Ridgeway's.
Saturday Evening Post.
Tammany Times.
Time.
The Voter.

Official Documents Concerning
the Spanish American War

American Naval Policy as Outlined in Messages of
    the Presidents of the United States from
    1790. Washington: Government Printing
    Office, 1922.
Carlisle, Calderon. Report to E. Dupuy deLome,
    Spanish Minister: The Laws of Neutrality of
    the United States, with Reference to the
    Cuban Insurrection. Washington: Government
    Printing Office, 1896.
Cervera, Pascual. "The Spanish American War."
    Office of Naval Intelligence, comp. The
    Spanish American War. Washington: Govern-
    ment Printing Office, 1900.
Committee on Foreign Relations. "Report Relative
    to Affairs in Cuba." Fifty-fifth Congress,
    second Session, Senate Report 885, Serial no.
    3624. Washington: Government Printing
    Office, 1898.
Congressional Record. Washington: Government
    Printing Office, 1879–1899.

"Cuban American Commerce, 1887-1897." Bureau of
    Market Statistics, Circular no. 16. Washing-
    ton: Government Printing Office, 1897.
Department of State. Papers Relating to the
    Foreign Relations of the United States,
    1895-1898. Washington: Government Printing
    Office, 1896-1901.
Malloy, William M. Treaties, Conventions,
    International Acts, Protocals, and Agreements
    Between the United States of America and
    Other Powers, 1776-1909. Washington:
    Government Printing Office, 1910.
Naval Court of Inquiry. "Report Upon the
    Destruction of the United States Battleship
    Maine in Havanna Harbor, February 15, 1898,
    Together with the Testimony Taken Before
    the Court." Senate Document 207, Serial
    no. 3610, Washington: Government Printing
    Office, 1898.
President of the United States. "Message in
    Response to the Resolution of the Senate,
    Dated February 14, 1898, Calling for
    Information in Respect to the Condition of
    the Reconcentrados in Cuba, the State of the
    War and the Country, and the Prospects of
    Projected Autonomy in that Island." Senate
    Document no. 230, Serial no. 3610.
    Washington: Government Printing Office,
    1898.
Pulsifier, Pitman. Official Congressional
    Directory, Fifty-fifth Congress Extra-
    ordinary Session. Washington: Government
    Printing Office, 1897.
"Report on the Wreck of the Maine." Sixty-second
    Congress, second Session, House Document
    310, Serial no. 6321. Washington: Govern-
    ment Printing Office, 1911.
Secretary of the Navy. Annual Reports of the
    Navy Department for the Year 1898.
    Washington: Government Printing Office,
    1898.
Secretary of the State. "Annual Report of 1896."
    Papers Relating to the Foreign Relations of
    the United States, 1896. Washington:
    Government Printing Office, 1897.

Secretary of the State. "Report in Response to
    Senate Resolution, February 23, 1897,
    Relative to the Arrest, Imprisonment, and
    Death of Dr. Ricardo Ruiz in the Jail of
    Guanabacoa, on the Island of Cuba." Fifty-
    fourth Congress, second Session, Senate
    Document 179, Serial no. 3471. Washington:
    Government Printing Office, 1897.
Secretary of the Treasury. "A Reply to the
    Resolution of the House of Representatives
    on February 23, 1898, in Regard to the
    Conveyance to the Cubans of Articles
    Produced in the United States, Etc." Fifty-
    fifth Congress, second Session, House
    Document 326, Serial no. 3679. Washington:
    Government Printing Office, 1898.
Secretary of the Treasury. Statistical Abstract
    of the United States, 1898. Washington:
    Government Printing Office, 1899.
Senate Committee on Foreign Relations. "Report
    on the Annexation of Hawaii." Fifth-fifth
    Congress, second Session, Senate Report
    681, Serial no. 3622. Washington: Govern-
    ment Printing Office, 1898.
Spanish Diplomatic Correspondence and Documents,
    1896-1900: Presented to the Cortes by the
    Minister of State. Washington: Government
    Printing Office, 1905.
Walker, John G.; Hains, Peter C.; and Haupt,
    Lewis M. Reports on the Nicaragua Canal
    Commission, 1897-1899. Baltimore: Lord
    Baltimore Press, 1899.
War Department, Office of the Director of the
    Census of Cuba. Report of the Census of
    Cuba, 1899. Washington: Government Printing
    Office, 1900.

Government Reports

Congressional Directory. Washington: Govern-
    ment Printing Office, 1907.
Congressional Record. Washington: Government
    Printing Office, 1879-1920.

Inaugural Addresses of the Presidents of the
    United States. Ninety-third Congress, House
    Document 93-208. Washington: Government
    Printing Office, 1974.
Report of the Senate Judiciary Committee on the
    Brewing and Liquor Interests and German and
    Bolshevik Propaganda. Sixty-sixth Congress,
    first Session, Senate Document 62. Washing-
    ton: Government Printing Office, 1919.
United States Bureau of the Census. Historical
    Statistics of the United States: Colonial
    Times to 1957. Washington: Government
    Printing Office, 1960.
United States Industrial Commission. Reports.
    Volume XV. Report on Immigration. 19
    volumes. Washington: Government Printing
    Office, 1901-1902.

Court Cases

City of New York v. Hearst, 126 N.Y. Supp.
    (App. Div.) 917 (1911).
Hearst v. New Yorker Staats Zeitung, 71 N.Y.
    Misc. Rep. 7 (1911).
Hearst v. Ridder, 71 N.Y. Misc. Rep. 8 (1911).
In re Hearst, 96 N.Y. Supp. (App. Div.) 47 (1907).
In re Hearst et al., 48 N.Y. Misc. Rep. 441
    (1905).
In re Hearst et al., 48 N.Y. Misc. Rep. 453
    (1905).
In re Hearst et al., 96 N.Y. Supp. (App. Div)
    341 (1905).
International News Service v. The Associated
    Press, 248 U.S. 215 (1918).

Unpublished Dissertations

Beyer, Brother Anthony. "Woodrow Wilson and the
    San Francisco Press, 1912-1917." M.A.
    Thesis. The Catholic University of America,
    1956.

Browne, Henry J. "The Catholic Church and the
    Knights of Labor." Ph.D. Dissertation. The
    Catholic University of America, 1949.

Carlisle, Rodney Parker. "The Political Ideas
and Influence of William Randolph Hearst,
1928-1936." Ph.D. Dissertation. University
of California at Berkeley, 1965.
Cunningham, Miriam Ann. "A Thomistic Appraisal
of the Philosophy of Henry George." M.A.
Thesis. The Catholic University of America,
1950.
Epstein, Matthew. "A Study of the Editorial
Opinions of the New York Papers Toward the
League of Nations and the United States
During the First Year of Life, 1919-1920,
1945-1946." Ph.D. Dissertation. New York
University, 1954.
Glad, Paul W. "William Jennings Bryan and His
Democracy: The Opposition Years, 1896-
1912." Ph.D. Dissertation. Indiana
University, 1957.
Harris, Alice Kessler. "The Lower Class as a
Factor in Reform: New York, The Jews, and
the 1890's." Ph.D. Dissertation. Rutgers
University, 1968.
Jones, Thomas. "The Sociology of a New York
City Block." Ph.D. Dissertation. Columbia
University, 1904.
Kerr, Thomas Jefferson. "New York Factory
Investigating Commission and the Progres-
sives." D.S.S. Dissertation. Syracuse
University, 1965.
Kilroe, Frank E. "The Governorship of Charles
Evans Hughes: A Study in Reform, 1906-
1910." M.A. Thesis. Columbia University,
1934.
LuBove, Roy. "The Progressive and the Slums:
Tenement House Reforms in New York City,
1890-1917." Ph.D. Dissertation. Cornell
University, 1960.
Merrick, Mary Annunciata. "A Case in Practical
Democracy: Settlement of the Anthracite Coal
Strike of 1902." Ph.D. Dissertation.
University of Notre Dame, 1942.
Myatt, James Allen. "William Randolph Hearst and
the Progressive Era." Ph.D. Dissertation.
University of Florida, 1960.

Offner, John Layser. "President McKinley and the Origins of the Spanish American War." Ph.D. Dissertation. Pennsylvania State University, 1957.

Peterson, Eric Falk. "Prelude to Progressivism, California Election Reform, 1870-1909." Ph.D. Dissertation. University of California at Los Angeles, 1969.

Piller, Eleanor M. "The Hearst-Hughes Gubernatorial Campaign of 1906." M.A. Thesis. Columbia University, 1937.

Thompson, Richard. "The Yellow Peril, 1890-1924." Ph.D. Dissertation. University of Wisconsin, 1957.

Varcados, Peter R. "Labor and Politics in San Francisco, 1880-1892." Ph.D. Dissertation. University of California at Berkeley, 1968.

Private Printings

Addresses at the Jamestown Exposition, Labor Day, September 2, 1907. New York: McConnell Printing Company, 1912.

Congressman Hearst's Views on Democracy. Republished from the Chicago Tribune, January 9, 1904. New York: New York American Press, 1904.

Editorials From the Hearst Newspapers. New York: Albertson Publishing Company, 1906.

Hearst, William Randolph. Truth About Trusts. New York: New York American Press, 1916.

_____. Truth About Trusts. San Francisco: San Francisco Examiner Press, 1948.

Jefferson Day, April 13, 1907, Addresses by William Randolph Hearst. New York: New York American Press, 1907.

Selections From the Writings and Speeches of William Randolph Hearst. San Francisco: San Francisco Examiner Press, 1948.

Speech of William Randolph Hearst at a Congressional Rally, October 27, 1902. New York: New York American Press, 1902.

Articles

Brisbane, Arthur. "The American Newspaper and Yellow Journalism." Bookman. (June 1904), pp. 400-404.

Commander, Lydia Kingsmill. "The Significance of Yellow Journalism." Arena. (August 1905), pp. 150-155.

Creelman, James. "The Real Mr. Hearst." Pearson's. (September 1906), pp. 252-265.

Davis, Forres. "Mr. Hearst Steps Down." Saturday Evening Post. (August 27, 1938), pp. 66-67.

Davis, R. G. "Down on the Middle Classes." London Review of Reviews. (October 1910), p. 367.

"Does Nasty Fighting Pay in Politics?" Ridgeway's. (October 27, 1906), p. 11.

"The Failure of Fusion." Nation. (October 5, 1905), pp. 274-275.

Grenier, Judson A. "Muckraking and the Muckrakers: An Historical Definition." Journalism Quarterly. (Autumn 1960), pp. 552-558.

"Hearst, Tammany, Mitchel, and America." Literary Digest. (October 13, 1917), pp 11-13.

Huthmacher, J. Joseph. "Charles Evans Hughes and Charles Francis Murphy: The Metamorphosis of Progressivism." New York History (January 1965), pp. 25-40.

_____. "Urban Liberalism and the Age of Reform." Mississippi Valley Historical Review. (September 1962), pp. 231-241.

Lee, Fitzugh. "Cuba Under Spanish Rule." McClure's Magazine. (November 1898), pp. 99-114.

Lindsay, Dennison. "The Strange Hearst Campaign." Ridgeway's. (October 27, 1906), pp. 23-24.

Little, Arthur W. "Who's for Hearst--And Why." Pearson's. (March 1912), pp. 10-14.

Martin, Lawrence. "W. R. Hearst--Epitome of Capitalist Civilization." Social Frontier. (February 1935), pp. 10-14.

Merwin, Bannister. "The Real Mr. Hearst."
    Public Opinion. (December 30, 1905),
    pp. 835-837.
"The New York Campaign: The Outcome." Outlook.
    (November 13, 1909), pp. 572-573.
"The New York City Vote Analyzed." Nation.
    (November 16, 1905), p. 395.
"New York's Contested Election." Outlook.
    (December 23, 1905), pp. 945-947.
"The New York Election." Living Age. (December
    4, 1909), pp. 632-634.
"New York's Municipal Campaign." Independent.
    (October 19, 1905), pp. 936-937.
Palmer, Frederick. "Hearst and Hearstism."
    Collier's. (September 22, 1906),
    pp. 19-20.
_____. Ibid. (September 29, 1906), pp. 20-
    22.
_____. Ibid. (October 6, 1906), pp.
    16-18.
_____. Ibid. (October 13, 1906), pp.
    18-20.
Pomeroy, Eltweed. "A Political Forecast."
    Arena. (June 1904), pp. 569-582.
"Reformed New York Politics." American Review
    of Reviews. (August 1910), pp. 138-143.
Russell, Charles Edward. "Mr. Hearst as I Knew
    Him." Ridgeway's. (October 27, 1906),
    pp. 9-11.
Speed, John Gilmer. "Purchase of Votes: How
    Votes Are Bought in New York City."
    Harper's Weekly. (March 18, 1905), pp.
    886-888.
Steffens, Lincoln. "Hearst, The Man of Mystery."
    The American Magazine. (November 1906),
    pp. 2-22.
"Tammany's Confidence Game." Outlook. (October
    7, 1905), pp. 296-297.
Tarbell, Ida. "How About Hughes?" The American
    Magazine. (October 1908), pp. 462-464.
_____. "President McKinley in War Times."
    McClure's Magazine. (November 1898),
    pp. 208-224.

Secondary Sources

Aaron, Daniel. Men of Good Hope: A Story of
    American Progressives. New York: Oxford
    University Press, 1951.
Abbot, Willis. Watching the World Go By.
    Boston: Little, Brown and Company, 1933.
Adams, Thomas Sewall, and Sumner, Helen. Labor
    Problems. New York: Macmillan Company, 1915.
Alger, Russell A. The Spanish American War.
    New York: Harper and Brothers, 1901.
Anderson, Margaret. My Thirty Years War. New
    York: Covici, Friede Publishers, 1930.
Ashby, Leroy, and Stave, Bruce, editors. The
    Discontented Society. Chicago: Rand
    McNally and Company, 1973.
Atkins, Edwin F. Sixty Years in Cuba:
    Reminiscences. New York: Houghton Mifflin
    Company, 1926.
Baker, Raymond S. Woodrow Wilson: Life and
    Letters. Volume III. Garden City, New
    York: Doubleday, Doran and Company, Inc.,
    1931.
Banner, James et al. Understanding the American
    Experience. Volume III. New York: Harcourt,
    Brace, Jovanovich, Inc., 1973.
Barker, Charles Albro. Henry George. New York:
    Oxford University Press, 1955.
Barrett, James W. Joseph Pulitzer and His World.
    New York: The Vanguard Press, 1941.
Bates, Charles Austin. American Journalism.
    New York: Holmes Publishing Company, 1897.
Beard, Charles, and Beard, Mary. The Rise of
    American Civilization. New York: Macmillan
    Company, 1937.
Belmont, Charles, ed. The Adventures and Letters
    of Richard Harding Davis, New York: Beckman
    Publishers, 1974 (c. 1917).
Bemis, Samuel F. The United States as a World
    Power. New York: Henry Holt and Company,
    1955.
Bent, Silas. Ballyhoo: The Voice of the Press.
    New York: Boni and Liveright, 1927.
_____. Newspaper Crusaders. New York:
    McGraw-Hill Book Company, 1939.

372

_____. _Strange Bedfellows_. New York: H.
     Liveright, 1928.
Bernstein, Irving. _The Lean Years_. Boston:
     Houghton Mifflin Company, 1960.
Bernstein, Barton, and Matusow, Allen, editors.
     Twentieth Century America. New York:
     Harcourt, Brace, Jovanovich, Inc. 1972.
Bierce, Ambrose. _The Collected Works of Ambrose
     Bierce_. 12 volumes. New York: The Reale
     Publishing Company, 1912.
Bishop, John B. _Theodore Roosevelt and His Time_.
     2 volumes. New York: Charles Scribner's
     Sons, 1920.
Bleyer, Willard G. _Main Currents in the History
     of American Journalism_. New York: Houghton
     Mifflin Company, 1927.
_____. _Newspaper Writing and Editing_. New
     York: Houghton Mifflin Company, 1913.
_____. _Types of News Writing_. New York:
     Houghton Mifflin Company, 1916.
Bloomfield, Maxwell. _Alarms and Diversions:
     The American Mind Through American Magazines_,
     _1900-1914_. The Hague, Paris: Mouton and
     Company, 1967.
Blum, John et al. _The National Experience_.
     Volume II. New York: Harcourt, Brace,
     Jovanovich, Inc., 1973.
Blumberg, Milton, ed. _Official Report of the
     Proceedings of the Democratic National
     Convention_. New York: Publisher's Printing
     Company, 1904.
Blummer, H., and Lee, A. M., editors. _New
     Outline of the Principles of Sociology_. New
     York: Barnes and Noble, Inc., 1946.
Bolles, Blair. _Tyrant From Illinois_. New York:
     W. W. Norton, 1951.
Bonfils, Winifred Black. _The Life and Person-
     ality of Phoebe Apperson Hearst_. San
     Francisco: John Henry Nash, 1928.
Brisbane, Arthur. _Today and a Future Day_. New
     York: Albertson Publishers, 1925.
Bryan, William Jennings, and Bryan, Mary. _The
     Memoirs of William Jennings Bryan_. Chicago:
     Winston Publishing Company, 1925.

Buenker, John D. Urban Liberalism and Progres-
    sive Reform. New York: Charles Scribner's
    Sons, 1973.
Burner, David. The Politics of Provincialism.
    New York: W. W. Norton and Company, Inc.
    1967.
Callow, Alexander, ed. American Urban History.
    New York: Oxford University Press, 1973.
Carlson, Oliver. Brisbane, A Candid Biography.
    New York: Stackpole Sons, 1937.
Carlson, Oliver, and Bates, Ernest. Hearst,
    Lord of San Simeon. New York: The Viking
    Press, 1937.
Chambers, Walter. Samuel Seabury: A Challenge.
    New York: The Century Company, 1932.
Cisneros, Evangelina, and Decker, Karl.
    Evangelina Cisneros. New York: Continental
    Publishing Company, 1897.
Clark, Champ. My Quarter Century of American
    Politics. 2 volumes. New York: Harper
    and Brothers, 1920.
Coblentz, Edmund, ed. William Randolph Hearst:
    A Potrait in His Own Words. New York: Simon
    and Schuster, 1952.
Coletta, Paola. William Jennings Bryan:
    Political Evangelist, 1860-1908. Lincoln:
    University of Nebraska Press, 1964.
Commanger, Henry Steele. The American Mind,
    An Interpretation of American Thought and
    Character Since the 1880's. New Haven,
    Connecticut: Yale University Press, 1950.
Couperie, Pierre et al. A History of the Comic
    Strip. New York: Crown Publishers, Inc.
    1968.
Creelman, James. On The Great Highway. Boston:
    Lathrop Publishing Company, 1901.
Daniels, Josephus. The Wilson Era--Years of
    Peace, 1910-1917. Chapel Hill: University
    of North Carolina Press, 1944.
Davies, Marion. The Times We Had. Edited by
    Pamela Pfau and Kenneth S. Marx. Indian-
    apolis, New York: Bobbs-Merrill Company,
    Inc., 1975.
Davis, Elmer Holmes. History of the New York
    Times, 1851-1921. New York: New York Times,
    1921.

374

Davis, Richard Harding. *Cuba in War Time*. New
    York: R. H. Russell, 1897.
_____. *Notes of a War Correspondent*. New
    York: Charles Scribner's Sons, 1910.
deMille, Anna George. *Henry George: Citizen of
    the World*. Chapel Hill: University of
    North Carolina Press, 1950.
DeWitt, Benjamin Parke. *The Progressive Move-
    ment*. New York: Macmillan Company, 1915.
Dubofsky, Melvyn. *We Shall Be All*. New York:
    New York Times Book Company, 1969.
Dulles, Foster R. *America's Rise to World Power*,
    1898-1954. New York: Harper Brothers, 1955.
DuRoselle, Jean-Babtiste. *From Wilson to
    Roosevelt*. New York: Harper and Row,
    Publishers, 1968.
Emery, Edward, and Ford, Edwin. *Highlights of
    the American Press*. Minneapolis: Univer-
    sity of Minnesota Press, 1954.
Essary, Jesse E. *Covering Washington: Govern-
    ment Reflected to the Public in the Press*,
    1822-1926. Boston: Houghton Mifflin
    Company, 1927.
Fairchild, Henry Pratt. *Immigration*. New York:
    Macmillan Company, 1913.
Filler, Louis. *Crusaders for American Liberal-
    ism*. New York: Harcourt, Brace and
    Company, 1939.
Finer, Herman. *The Theory and Practice of Modern
    Government*. New York: Henry Holt and
    Company, 1939.
Frederickson, George M. *The Inner Civil War*.
    New York: Harper and Row, 1965.
Gabriel, Ralph. *The Course of American
    Democratic Thought*. New York: Ronald
    Press, 1940.
Geiger, George Raymond. *The Philosophy of Henry
    George*. New York: Columbia University
    Press, 1931.
Glad, Betty. *Charles Evans Hughes and the
    Illusions of Innocence*. Urbana, Illinois:
    University of Illinois Press, 1966.
Gompers, Samuel. *Labor and the Common Welfare*.
    New York: E. P. Dutton and Company, 1919.

_____. _Seventy Years of Life and Labor_. 2
   volumes. New York: E. P. Dutton and
   Company, 1925.
Gordon, Milton. _Assimilation in American Life_.
   New York: Oxford University Press, 1964.
Gordon, W. M. Evans. _The Alien Immigrant_. New
   York: Charles Scribner's Sons, 1903.
Greenston, J. David. _Labor in American Politics_.
   New York: Alfred A. Knopf, Inc., 1969.
Grob, Gerald. _Workers and Utopia_. New York:
   New York Times Book Company, 1961.
Hall, Prescott F. _Immigration and its Effects
   on the United States_. New York: Henry
   Holt and Company, 1908.
Handlin, Oscar. _Al Smith and His America_.
   Boston: Little, Brown and Company, 1958.
Harvey, Roland Hill. _Samuel Gompers--Champion
   of the Toiling Masses_. Palo Alto, California:
   Stanford University Press, 1935.
Hays, Samuel P. _Conservation and The Gospel of
   Efficiency_. Cambridge: Harvard University
   Press, 1959.
Henderson, Thomas M. _Tammany Hall And The
   New Immigrants_. New York: Arno Press, 1976.
Hofstadter, Richard. _The Age of Reform From
   Bryan to F. D. R._ New York: Alfred A.
   Knopf, Inc., 1955.
Horwitz, Howard. _Theodore Roosevelt and Labor
   in New York State, 1880-1900_. New York:
   Columbia University Press, 1943.
Howe, Frederick. _Confessions of A Reformer_. New
   York: Charles Scribner's Sons, 1925.
Howe, Irving. _World of Our Fathers_. New York:
   Simon and Schuster, 1976.
Hutchinson, E. P. _Immigrants and Their Children_.
   New York: John Wiley and Sons, Inc., 1956.
Huthmacher, J. Joseph. _Twentieth Century
   America_. Boston: Allyn and Bacon, Inc.,
   1966.
Ickes, Harold. _America's House of Lords_. New
   York: Harcourt, Brace, and Company, 1939.
Irwin, Will. _Propoganda and The News_. New
   York: McGraw-Hill Book Company, Inc., 1936.

Jessup, Philip C. *Elihu Root*. 2 volumes. New York: Dodd, Mead, and Company, 1938.

Johnson, James Weldon. *Black Manhattan*. New York: Arno Press, 1968.

Jones, Robert W. *Journalism in The United States*. New York: E. P. Dutton and Company, 1947.

Juergens, George. *Joseph Pulitzer and The New York World*. Princeton, New Jersey: Princeton University Press, 1966.

Kael, Pauline. *The Citizen Kane Book*. Boston: Little, Brown and Company, 1971.

Karson, Marc. *American Labor Unions and Politics, 1900-1918*. Boston: Beacon Press, 1958.

Kennedy, Lawrence, ed. *Biographical Directory of The American Congress, 1774-1971*. Washington: Government Printing Office, 1971.

Kessner, Thomas D. *The Golden Door*. New York: Oxford University Press, 1977.

Kobre, Sidney. *The Yellow Press and the Guilded Age*. Tallahassee, Florida: Florida State University Press, 1964.

Koenig, Louis W. *Bryan*. New York: G. P. Putnam's Sons, 1975.

Lee, Alfred M. *The Daily Newspaper in America: The Evolution of A Social Instrument*. New York: Macmillan Company, 1937.

Leonard, John William. *History of The City of New York, 1606-1909*. New York: Journal of Commerce and Commercial Bulletin, 1910.

Leopold, Richard W. *Elihu Root and The Conservative Tradition*. Boston: Little, Brown and Company, 1954.

Lewison, Edwin R. *John Purroy Mitchel: Boy Mayor of New York*. New York: Astra Books, 1965.

Link, Arthur S. *American Epoch*. New York: Alfred A. Knopf, Inc., 1955.

_____. *Wilson Campaigns for Progressivism and Peace, 1916-1917*. Princeton, New Jersey: Princeton University Press, 1965.

_____. *Wilson: The Road to the White House*. Princeton, New Jersey: Princeton University Press, 1947.

_____. *Woodrow Wilson and the Progressive Era, 1910-1917*. New York: Harper Brothers, 1954.

Lodge, Henry Cabot. <u>Selections From the Corre-
    spondence of The odore Roosevelt and Henry
    Cabot Lodge, 1884-1918</u>. 2 volumes. New
    York: Charles Scribner's Sons, 1925.

_____. <u>The War With Spain</u>. New York: Harper
    Brothers, 1899.

Loveman, Samuel, ed. <u>Twenty-one Letters of
    Ambrose Bierce</u>. Cleveland: George Kirk,
    Inc., 1922.

Lundberg, Ferdinand. <u>Imperial Hearst: A
    Social Biography</u>. New York: Equinox
    Cooperative Press, 1936.

Luthin, Reinhard. <u>American Demagogues--
    Twentieth Century</u>. Boston: Beacon Press,
    1954.

MacDougall, Curtis D. <u>Interpretive Reporting</u>.
    New York: Macmillan Company, 1949.

Madison, Charles A. <u>Critics and Crusaders:
    A Century of American Protest</u>. New York:
    Henry Holt and Company, 1947.

Mason, Gregory. <u>Remember the Maine</u>. New York:
    Henry Holt and Company, 1939.

McClure, S. S. <u>My Autobiography</u>. New York:
    Frederick Stokes, 1914.

McGurrin, James. <u>Bourke Cockran: A Freelance
    in American Politics</u>. New York: Charles
    Scribner's Sons, 1948.

McKinley, William. <u>Speeches and Addresses of
    William McKinley, March 1, 1897 to May 30,
    1900</u>. New York: Doubleday and McClure
    Company, 1900.

Mitchell, John. <u>Organized Labor</u>. Philadelphia:
    American Book and Bible House, 1903.

Morison, Elting, ed. <u>The Letters of Theodore
    Roosevelt</u>. 8 volumes. Cambridge, Massachu-
    setts: The Harvard University Press, 1950-
    1954.

Morris, Lloyd. <u>Postscripts to Yesterday;
    America: The Last Fifty Years</u>. New York:
    Random House, 1947.

Morris, Richard. <u>The Encyclopedia of American
    History</u>. 2 volumes. New York: Harper
    Brothers, 1953.

Mott, Frank Luther. <u>American Journalism</u>. New
    York: Macmillan Company, 1962.

Mowry, George E. _Theodore Roosevelt and the Progressive Movement_. Madison, Wisconsin: University of Wisconsin Press, 1946.

Munro, William Bennett. _The Government of American Cities_. New York: Macmillan Company, 1920.

Myers, Gustavus. _The History of Tammany Hall_. New York: Boni and Liveright, Inc., 1917.

Nevins, Allan, ed. _Letters of Grover Cleveland, 1850-1908_. Boston: Houghton Mifflin Company, 1933.

Older, Cora B. _William Randolph Hearst: American_. New York: D. Appleton Century Company, 1936.

Older, Freemont. _George Hearst, California Pioneer_. Los Angeles: Westernlore, 1966 (c. 1933).

O'Neil, William. _The Progressive Years_. New York: Dodd, Mead, and Company, 1975.

Ovington, Mary White. _Half A Man_. New York: Longmans, Green, and Company, 1911.

Park, Robert E. _The Immigrant Press and Its Control_. New York: Harper Brothers, 1922.

Parkhurst, Charles. _My Forty Years in New York_. New York: Macmillan Company, 1923.

_____. _Our Fight With Tammany_. New York: Charles Scribner's Sons, 1895.

Perlman, S., and Taft, P. _History of Labor in the United States_. New York: Macmillan Company, 1922.

Pollack, Norman. _The Populist Response to Industrial America_. Cambridge, Massachusetts: Harvard University Press, 1962.

Pringle, Henry F. _Theodore Roosevelt: A Biography_. New York: Harcourt, Brace and Company, 1931.

Pusey, Merlo J. _Charles Evans Hughes_. 2 volumes. New York: Macmillan Company, 1951.

Regier, Cornelius. _The Era of the Muckrakers_. Chapel Hill, North Carolina: University of North Carolina Press, 1932.

The Republican Campaign Text Book for 1908. Philadelphia: Dunlap Company, 1908.

Rhodes, James F. _The McKinley and Roosevelt Administrations, 1897-1909_. New York: Macmillan Company, 1922.

379

Richardson, James F., ed. The American City. Waltham, Massachusetts: Xerox College Publishing, 1972.

Riis, Jacob. How the Other Half Lives. New York: Sagamore Press, 1957.

Rolle, Andrew F. The American Italians, Their History and Culture. Belmont, California: Wadsworth Publishing Company, 1972.

Roosevelt, Theodore. An Autobiography. New York: Charles Scribner's Sons, 1926.

_____. Presidential Addresses and State Papers. 2 volumes. New York: The Review of Reviews Company, 1904.

Ross, Isabel. Ladies of the Press. New York: Harper and Row Publishers, Inc., 1936.

Rowell's Newspaper Directory. Buffalo: The Mathews-Northup Works, The Complete Press, 1902.

Rubens, Horatio Seymour. Liberty, The Story of Cuba. New York: Ams Press, 1970 (c. 1932).

Salisbury, William. The Career of a Journalist. New York: B. W. Dodge and Company, 1908.

Salmon, Lucy Maynard. The Newspaper and the Historian. New York: Oxford University Press, 1923.

Sargent, S. Stansfeld, and Williamson, Robert. Social Psychology. New York: Ronald Press Company, 1958.

Schlesinger, A. M., ed. History of American Presidential Elections. Volume III. New York: Chelsea House Publishers in association with McGraw-Hill Book Company, 1971.

_____. Political and Social History of the United States. New York: Macmillan Company, 1925.

_____. ed. Writings and Speeches of Eugene V. Debs. New York: Hermitage Press, Inc., 1948.

Seabury, Samuel. Municipal Ownership and Operation of Public Utilities in New York. New York: Municipal Ownership Publishing Company, 1905.

Seitz, Donald C. Joseph Pulitzer, His Life and Letters. New York: Simon and Schuster, 1924.

Sigsbee, Charles D. *The Maine, An Account of Her Destruction in Havanna Harbor; Personal Narrative*. New York: Century Company, 1899.

Smith, Mortimer. *William Jay Gaynor, Mayor of New York*. Chicago: Henry Regnery Company, 1951.

Steffens, Joseph Lincoln. *The Autobiography of Lincoln Steffens*. New York: Harcourt, Brace and Company, 1931.

_____. *The Shame of the Cities*. New York: Sagamore Press, 1904.

Swanberg, W. A. *Citizen Hearst*. New York: Charles Scribner's Sons, 1961.

_____. *Pulitzer*. New York: Charles Scribner's Sons, 1967.

Syrett, Harold C., ed. *The Gentleman and the Tiger; The Autobiography of George B. McClellan, Jr.* Philadelphia: J. B. Lippincott Company, 1956.

Tebbel, John. *The Life and Good Times of William Randolph Hearst*. New York: E. P. Dutton and Company, 1952.

Thompson, Charles Willis. *Party Leaders of the Times*. New York: G. W. Dillingham Company, 1906.

Ullman, Doris. *A Portrait Gallery of American Editors*. New York: W. E. Rudge, 1925.

Villard, Oswald G. *Fighting Years*. New York: Harcourt, Brace and Company, 1939.

_____. *Some Newspapers and Newspaper Men*. Freeport, New York: Books for Libraries Press, 1923.

Warne, Frank Julian. *The Immigrant Invasion*. New York: Dodd, Mead, and Company, 1913.

Watson, Thomas E. *The Life and Times of Thomas Jefferson*. New York: D. Appleton and Company, 1903.

Weems, John Edward. *The Fate of the Maine*. New York: Henry Holt and Company, 1958.

Weiss, Nancy Joan. *Charles Francis Murphy, 1858-1924; Respectability and Responsibility in Tammany Politics*. Gluckstadt, Germany: J. J. Augustin, 1968.

Werner, M. R. *Bryan*. New York: Harcourt, Brace and Company, 1929.

_____. _Tammany Hall_. Garden City, New York: Doubleday, Doran and Company, 1919.

Wesser, Robert F. _Charles Evans Hughes, Politics and Reform in New York, 1905-1910_. Ithaca, New York: Cornell University Press, 1967.

Wiebe, Robert. _The Search For Order_. New York: Hill and Wang, 1967.

Wilkens, James. _Themes in United States History_. New York: Glencoe Press, 1973.

Wilkerson, Marcus M. _Public Opinion and the Spanish American War: A Study in War Propaganda_. Baton Rouge, Louisiana: Louisiana State University Press, 1932.

Winkler, John Kennedy. _William Randolph Hearst: A New Appraisal_. New York: Hastings House, 1955.

_____. _William Randolph Hearst: An American Phenomenon_. New York: Simon and Schuster, 1928.

Winter, Ella, and Hicks, Granville, editors. _The Letters of Lincoln Steffens_. New York: Harcourt, Brace and Company, 1938.

Wisan, Joseph E. _The Cuban Crisis as Reflected in the New York Press, 1895-1898_. New York: Columbia University Press, 1934.

Wolmon, Leo. _The Growth of American Trade Unions, 1880-1923_. Washington: National Bureau of Economic Research, Government Printing Office, 1924.

Woodward, C. Vann. _Tom Watson_. New York: Oxford University Press, 1963.

Yellowitz, Irwin. _Labor and the Progressive Movement in New York State, 1897-1916_. Ithaca, New York: Cornell University Press, 1965.

Zink, Harold. _City Bosses in the United States_. Durham, North Carolina: Duke University Press, 1930.

Index

383

385

Roy Littlefield was born in Milford, New Hampshire. He graduated from Dickinson College, where he majored in American History and Political Science; and he attained his M.A. and Ph.D. degrees from The Catholic University of America, majoring in Law, Recent American Political and Social History, Politics, and European Intellectual History. His dissertation was a study of Hearst's role in American progressivism. Following four years of service on Capitol Hill, Dr. Littlefield now serves as Director of Government Affairs for the National Tire Dealers and Retreaders Association in Washington, D.C. Author of numerous magazine articles, he also teaches courses in law and politics in Catholic University's adult education program.